The Child Abuse

The Child Abusers

Research and Controversy

Colin Pritchard

Open University Press

Open University Press
McGraw-Hill Education
McGraw-Hill House
Shoppenhangers Road
Maidenhead
Berkshire
England
SL6 2QL

email: enquiries@openup.co.uk
world wide web: www.openup.co.uk

and Two Penn Plaza, New York, NY 10121-2289, USA

First published 2004

A catalogue record of this book is available from the British Library

ISBN 0335 21032 5 (pb) 0335 21033 3 (hb)

Library of Congress Cataloging-in-Publication Data
CIP data applied for

Typeset by YHT Ltd, London
Printed in the UK by Bell & Bain Ltd., Glasgow

Contents

Preface

It has been claimed that there are only two certainties in life, 'death and taxes' (Benjamin Franklin). On reflection, most would agree that the third certainty is 'childhood', contained in every human being, in each of their seven ages. The triumphs, disasters, joys, pain and memories echo throughout one's adult life. Thus *'in our ends are our beginnings'* (T.S. Eliot: East Coker: The Four Quartets), which are shaped in childhood and adolescence. In part, this is why this book was written after some 40 years of practice and research, to complete a journey that everyone travels, and which all owe a debt to those yesteryears, and to seek to enhance the lives of other children, whose lives were damaged through no fault of their own.

The book's origins started in an unlikely way. My practice background, which has continued throughout my academic career, was mental health, and although over the years the issue of child abuse has sometimes emerged in my practice, I was in no way a specialist. But I have long been concerned about evidence-based practice, that is, empirically supported practice. As an empiricist, I was invited in 1996 to evaluate the work of an NSPCC unit specializing in the treatment of male child sex abusers. There were major problems in seeking to determine outcomes, which could be related to improved child protection. My first lesson was just how complex the field was, and how much psycho-babble was around, which often obscured rather than clarified. To obtain some hard facts, rather than rely upon conjecture or exoneration, I collaborated with the Dorset Police and Probation, to map out something of the nature of the problem based upon life-time convictions of male sex offenders (Pritchard and Cox 1997). Like all good research, there was new information to be discovered, as well as confirming earlier findings.

The initial studies, based upon detailed analysis of police records, were extended to Hampshire, which in effect provided a baseline population of 3.2 million people, equivalent to more than 5 per cent of the English population, enabled a study of the prevalence of child abuse and its extremes, known to the police. This included a study of a decade of child homicides in the two counties, which identified the actual assailants and the relative risk of the various categories of child killers (Pritchard and Bagley 2001). Both sets of material were often distressing to handle, despite being an experienced practitioner and researcher, nothing could prepare one for the extremes, where a minority of men, had laid aside their humanity.

Work with students in practice and clients, the impact of the rough end of the continuum of child protection, and the way the public and sometimes management responded to these situations, made me concerned with the plight of the exposed professional. Irrespective of the field of human service in which we work, unlike the tabloid media stereotype, we can never have perfect hindsight, especially when dealing with the multiple complexities of living child protection situations. There is little need to rehearse the vortex that surrounds child protection, with the perennial clash of interests and rights, the efforts to make judgements in ever changing situations, when invariably one has less than all the information one needs. Work in this and the mental health field, has legal responsibilities and obligations, which often leaves the harassed practitioner, be they social worker, police person, psychiatrist or nurse – with the feeling that they are flying by the seats of their pants. Extreme pressure can surround such cases – even without a critical, unsupportive management wrestling with the problems of under-funding.

Continued practice involvement in psychiatric social work has always served to remind me of the *living* problems of practice. This has made me acutely sympathetic to the needs of the harassed professional, especially as the field of child protection and mental health are often surrounded with assertions, anecdotes and often unsubstantiated theories, or worse – theories and techniques that have passed their sell-by date, which means that sometimes the practitioner does not always have sound basis for practice.

Researching in the child protection field as a none specialist, allowed one to ask those 'obvious' questions, which are often missed by those immersed in the field. The major original studies, which charted the extreme end of child neglect and abuse had, virtually by accident, focused not upon the child victim but rather upon the abuser (Pritchard and Cox 1997; Pritchard and Bagley 2000, 2001; Pritchard and King 2004). Since Kempe's seminal paper in 1962 which, at the time, truly shocked the Western world community, the vast array of research has looked at the perspective of the child – self-evidently vital. But, in seeking to improve child protection, we also need to try to understand the abuser – not to exonerate him or very rarely, her, but to provide information for the practitioner, manager and policy maker that would equip them to take effective action in specific circumstance.

'Neglect' and 'abuse' are big labels, which cover a multitude of sins, and unless or until we can understand neglecters and abusers, we are unable to effectively take the life-affecting decisions required on behalf of children. Moreover, we need to be particularly concerned to break the cycle of potential neglect and abuse, which means that the practitioner not only has to consider the here-and-now situation, but the possible medium- and long-term outcomes.

It should be acknowledged however, that evidence-based practice can also serve to protect the rights of vulnerable adults, as undifferentiated labelling and 'over-the-top' reactions can lead to miscarriages of justice, which accumulative, undermine public confidence in the child protection and criminal justice systems (Webster 1998). And at the outset, it must be admitted that this book may well offend, as it challenges some old nostrums and ideological positions, often sincerely and fiercely held, but which new research contradicts or asks for a re-evaluation, in the continued search for improved child protection.

Everything in this book aims to contribute to the improvement of the protection of children. Typically, as the book unfolded, I had to re-think earlier positions modified as exploring current research and practice, provided new lessons and new insights. Hopefully the trap of many textbooks has been avoided, of sounding as if the author knew all the answers – I did not and do not, as is illustrated from the many cases presented, all self-evidently made anonymously, but highlighting the fraught nature of the field.

Each case presents enormous complexity reflecting a unique combination of social and psychological circumstances, and this can make effective decision making difficult. The cases outlined reflect the day-to-day dilemmas found in every practice across the disciplines concerned with protecting children.

The book has nine chapters; which although schematically presenting the issues, always stress needs to reflect the individuality of each specific situation, and the limits of our knowledge. While seeking a degree of detachment, it is admitted that the powerful emotions the topic arouses cannot be avoided, hence the sub-title, 'research and controversy'. Indeed, a number of politically-correct cows are taken on, and if not slaughtered, are left limping, for as Francis Bacon says,

> Those who would start with certainties, end in doubt. But if they be content to begin with doubts, then they can find certainties,
> (Francis Bacon: *Advancement of Learning*)

which means we are on a journey which may require us to re-consider old certainties of a more simple world, to make better sense of the new knowledge and incorporate it into practice. Indeed, as a lifelong supporter of the civil rights movements, Amnesty and Liberty, this research demanded that I think the unthinkable, in the uncomfortable ethical obligation, of having to report what one finds, rather than what one believes.

The core question is why do people, predominately adults, most often parents, shatter all the taboos in either the feckless neglect of children, or their active abuse? The enormity, indeed, abnormality of such behaviour comes from a classic source, when Jesus of Nazareth asked the rhetorical question,

What man amongst you when a child ask for bread, gives him a stone? What man amongst you when a child asks for a fish, do you give him a serpent?

Jesus's humanity is there for all to see when he appears incredulous that anyone could behave in such a way as he was one of the earliest to 'discover childhood' at a time and culture where neither children nor women were considered when he said, 'suffer the little children to come unto me – for such is the kingdom of heaven'.

And though like all parents, I know the little dears can be little swines, like the vast majority of parents, some of the greatest moments in my life has been the privilege of being a parent. Hence we need to understand, why the minority do what they do.

The chapter on the most prevalent group of abusers concerns the 'within-family' abusers and the continuum of neglect and abuse is explored, with an effort to understand, in the hope of better, focused practice to break the cycle, and assist in some reparation. However, it has to be realized that many 'neglecters' and 'abusers' were themselves earlier child victims, and we have to confront therefore the limits of what can be achieved with these sometimes damaged and damaging adults, within the time frame necessary to meet the exposed child's needs.

The 'extra-family' abuser is explored, starting with the child and adolescent bully, emotional, physical or sexual, who can make another child's life hell, along the continuum to the adult sexual abuser. The latter pose a whole host of problems, not least the problem of how to determine how best to protect the child. There is some evidence to suggest that sometimes social and legal services quite rightly, judge that full criminal proceedings would further damage an already traumatized child, especially when a conviction may be far from certain. A real problem here is that abuse and its impact upon the child can be so very varied, and the practitioner has to consider whether we are dealing with a metaphoric 'headache' or 'meningitis'. On the one hand, the evidence points towards the need to reach out to potential abusers struggling to achieve self-control with a degree of compassion, and on the other to press the need for indeterminate custodial sentences for those men whom our research has identified as violent and dangerous. This demands that the dangerous offender prove that they are safe to live amongst us – admittedly a formidable task for, as yet, I know no research in which they could demonstrate this with certainty. And on reflection, this is a very questionable ethical position, as it flies in the face of what is considered in a liberal democracy, as equity before the law and due process.

The increasing complexity of child protection is seen in Chapter 5 on 'special problems'. This addresses the so-called 'Munchausen-By-Proxy Syndrome'. Here new data is explored for the very first time, and some very worrying results are produced, in what is fortunately a fairly rare phenom-enon, but one, which has particularly dangerous outcomes. In addition, the recent high profile problem of the 'shaken-baby syndrome' is explored, and unusually, may well be simplified. Fortunately the new research does help to clarify what may be happening, but it is another example of how high profile cases can impact upon services, sometimes distorting more appropriately focused efforts.

A brief review of the 'sudden-infant-death syndrome' is evidence, if evi-dence were needed, of just how complex child protection is, and how, with the best will in the world, we professionals may inadvertently compound grieving parents' distress. The practitioner must seek to be empathetic and engage newly bereaved parents, while also having a degree of detachment to consider the unthinkable. It is very easy to get the balance wrong.

In Chapter 6, the perennial issue of the cycle of socio-economic dis-advantage is explored and the question is raised: to what extent does poverty contribute to the neglect or abuse of children? Undoubtedly the evidence shows that it is more poverty of spirit for neglecter and abuser, than economic poverty per se: but poverty, which people frequently 'inherit' 'blights all who come within its purview' (George Bernard Shaw: *Major Barbara*), seriously compounding earlier vulnerability.

At the extreme, child neglect and abuse can lead to the death of a child. There has been, however, some very positive research, which indicates that in terms of numbers of murdered children, British child protection is far better in outcomes than its public reputation would suggest (Pritchard 1992a, 1996a, 2002; UNICEF 2001; Pritchard and Butler 2003). Nevertheless, the chapter on 'who kills children?' is tough and perhaps surprising reading. Evidence is provided to highlight what might be seen as a culminating theme of the book, not only to re-discover the poverty-child neglect interface, but perhaps even more important, the child protection-psychiatry interface. What should be helpful is that this chapter enables us to make relative judgements about the degree of risk, based upon hard data, rather than theory. Inevitably, it will be controversial, because some will find the results unpalatable.

Are the media always wrong? After all the Victoria Climbié inquiry ac-knowledged that there had been downright bad practice and management (Laming Report 2003). These issues are tackled in a chapter entitled, 'Profes-sional Iatrogenesis', a term borrowed from medicine, which concerns illnesses inadvertently caused by 'the helping hand'. This list of inadvertent 'abusers' includes politicians, the media, law, psychiatry, the churches, the child pro-tection systems, some children's charities and the fortunately rare, feckless front-line practitioners. As with all professional disasters, which are con-cerned with direct service to people, the over-riding problem has been various forms of failure of communication, in which either a lack of knowledge or an ignorance of recent research contributed to the tragedy.

The final chapter is in the form of a debate which reflects some key practice and policy, which confront staff of all the disciplines involved – social workers, police, health visitors, community nurses, community psychiatric nurses, GPs, paediatricians, psychiatrists and their managers.

Hopefully, this book shows that we can improve the protection of children, and that through an evidence-based practice, can begin to resolve some of the controversies, giving children a better chance to enjoy the childhood that is the right of every human being.

This has been a difficult book to research and write and I must express my sincerest thanks to a number of people who have made significant contributions. First to Criminal Justice System colleagues, Deputy Chief Constable George Pothercary, Chief Inspector Mike Myton, Constable Andy Scarritt of Dorset Police and to Desmond Thompson, Deputy Chief of CID and the late Sir John Hodinott of Hampshire Police; from Dorset Probation Drs Malcolm Cox, Malcolm Lacy and CPO Barry Crooke; from Dorset colleagues in Social Services, David Joannides, Alan Brown, Pam Hewitt, John Rhynne, Phil Hodge and Chris Gallon; from Education, Richard Ely former Director, Malcolm Bray and Richard Williams; from Housing Peter Yeoman and Deborah Clooney of Bournemouth Churches Housing; from Health, Ian Carruthers, Adrian Dawson and Brian MacKenzie; from the University sector, Dr Elizabeth King and Professor Ian Diamond, now Director ESRC – all in their different ways have made invaluable contributions through their collaboration and professionalism. My thanks must also go to colleagues in the Open University Press, to Shona Mullen for her patience and guidance with what has been a difficult project and to Nick Pepper for invaluable copy-editing skills, carried out with tact and good humour.

I have many academic debts, as we all build on the work of others and these are clearly reflected in the Bibliography.

Acknowledgments can be almost formulaic but I must express my devoted thanks to my wife, Beryl Pritchard, whose own professionalism has been the exemplar for my career. Her affection, sympathy, understanding, tolerance, good humour and above all, friendship, has sustained me in an endeavour, which she and my other mentioned colleagues, encouraged in the hope that this study of 'The Child Abusers' may help to make our children safer.

Professor Colin Pritchard
Bournemouth and Southampton Universities

1 The Child Protection Controversy

Give me the child until he is seven and I will give you the man.
(Ignatius Loyola 1491–1556)

I am happy being a child. I am 60 years old, but I am still the child I was ... there is a tension in my 60 years between the child I was, and the child I could be. As a child, I am still constantly learning and understanding.
(Gilberto Freire 1982)

Introduction

The practical thesis of this book is that the precious time of childhood is one which should be nurtured by adults but Ignatius Loyola dictum reminds us, that precious nurturing shapes us, for better or worse, the adult we are to become 'and echoes of dreamland [sic or nightmares] bears us along'. But frequently the conditions of optimum care and socialization are subverted by negative social forces, and by individual actions of adults whose own childhoods were often distorted by psycho-socio-economic disadvantages, including abuse and neglect. This is not to exonerate them, but recognize those features which lead to child neglect and abuse. This book shares the Freire thesis, that we can review our past childhood, recreating ourselves, discovering new purpose. It is argued therefore, that those who abuse children can change, and become individuals who care about others rather than about their own wretched selves. However, if they cannot take up their humanity, and continue to be a risk of serious damage to children, they must recognize the possible far-reaching consequence to themselves from a society which will not tolerate abuse.

Children are abused, physically, emotionally and sexually in every country of the world. In Britain today the best evidence (based on adults recalling events of their childhood) is that up to 7 per cent of children have in the recent past been subject to severe physical abuse, 6 per cent have been physically neglected, 6 per cent have been emotionally abused, and 8 per cent have been victims of contact sexual abuse. These figures are based on a random survey of 2869 young adults (aged 18 to 24) in the United Kingdom, and thus refer to fairly recent events of neglect and abuse (Cawson et al. 2000). Although this report does not go into details, it is likely that there is an overlap between children experiencing various kinds of abuse and neglect. Moreover, there is evidence that the impact of prolonged neglect and/or abuse, which leads to the child being 'in care' or 'looked-after' by the local authority, places them at serious risk of being socially excluded as adolescents and young adults. Such young people are more likely to become involved in crime, both as victims and perpetrators, and in particular, both young men and women who were 'in-care' as adolescents, are far more likely to continue to be victims of violence and sexual assault (Biehel et al. 1995; Lyon et al. 1996; Pritchard and Butler 2000a).

While former abused adults in the UK survey were recalling events which often occurred several years before, there is no reason to suppose that the amount of child abuse has diminished in recent years, even though the rate of child murder in Britain is itself declining (Pritchard 1992b, 1993, 1996a, 2002; Pritchard and Butler 2003). Research from Europe and North America indicates that a substantial proportion of unsupported victims of abuse and neglect have serious mental health and behavioural problems in adulthood (Lyon et al. 1996; Pritchard and Butler 2000b; Glowinski et al. 2001; Rossow and Lauritzen 2001; Nelson et al. 2002; Soloff et al. 2002). Particularly distress resulted when the victim was in a relationship with the perpetrator (Bagley and Mallick 2000; Tyler 2002), a finding found across ethnicities (Anderson et al. 2002, Bhugra et al. 2002). It has been estimated that up to a third of adult child abusers are repeating the events which they were subjected to in childhood. Thus there is a statistically significant link between having been a victim and going on to be an adult abuser or neglecter of one's own children. This is an important finding, but one which leaves us in a considerable dilemma as social work practitioners, clinicians and social policy analysts (Coxe and Holmes 2001). In no way does this excuse or justify in any way people who abuse children, whoever they are. What is sought, however, is to contribute to a better understanding of abusers so that we can both improve child protection, and contribute to an effective understanding and treatment of the abusers. This, it is asserted, will only be accomplished if we act on the best available evidence. It is imperative that our child protection is 'evidence-based', as is expected in modern medicine, not least in order to avoid child protection overreactions, which resulted, for example, in the Cleveland and Orkney child care debacles. If this means challenging some dearly held nostrums, or questioning organizational values, then so be it.

One major problem facing anyone trying to approach these problems from an examination of the 'abuser' is the sheer emotion that can be generated. For example 'We shall name and shame the paedophiles' declared the *News of the World* headline (23 July 2000) – despite the fact that the campaign had been condemned by police chiefs, the Home Office, and virtually all experts in British child protection, who argued that such an approach endangered children more than protecting them. This had followed the tragic and brutal murder of Sarah Payne, and the public outcry understandably reflected the dormant public fear of the marauding stranger who is a threat to children and at the extreme, kills. The 'protest' came through the media, and British TV screens showed vigilante parents from a disadvantaged estate, patrolling with their children often no more than 10 years old, carrying placards saying 'Paeds Out', 'Hang the Paeds', etc. In addition were shots of council flats covered in similar graffiti where the suspected paedophiles lived, surrounded by angry people.

Parents were interviewed on national prime-time TV, screaming their abhorrence and claiming to 'know who they were [the paedophiles]' and, that as the police and social services were not 'keeping our kids safe, we'll drive them out ourselves'. What gave the scenes added poignancy, was the fact that many of the pre-pubertal children had fashionable youth hair styles and pierced facial decorations worn more typically by 17–20-year-olds, associated with the sexual signals prevalent amongst young adults.

Such furores led to the torching of houses of suspected paedophiles, and in a bizarre twist, a paediatrician's home was attacked by people who did not know the difference between her title and a paedophile. In Hull a man acquitted of an alleged paedophile offence was beaten to death by a vigilante group.

Such media and public responses to child abuse, and its extreme consequences, a dead child, evoke passionate public concern throughout the Western world (Atmore 1999). However, as might be expected from an academic and practitioner, the plea is made for a more rational response, both public and political, as sadly I have direct experience of media misrepresentation and how irrational media images are reinforced, and rarely challenged. For example, I was interviewed by a national newspaper, the *Daily Mirror*, the week before the threatened *News of the World* exposure of paedophiles was published. The interview concerned new research (Pritchard and Bagley 2000) published in the USA's leading academic child protection journal, the *International Journal of Child Abuse and Neglect*. The research revealed important variations in child sex offenders' behaviour. Based upon detailed police records of a sexual abuser's activity I argued for the urgent need to differentiate between a majority of possibly 'treatable abusers', of whom a proportion had themselves been abused as children, and a small but dangerous minority. The research evidence had led me to reject a previous strongly held ethical opposition to indeterminate sentences, and I advocated permanent but reviewable sentences until these men were no longer a danger to society. This position gives support to a very 'tough' British Government response (Home Office 2000) which is also likely to be enshrined in the new Mental Health Act (Birmingham 2002). This apparently contradictory position – compassion and understanding for some, combined with tough-ness for others – was hard for the journalist to summarize and the 90 minute interview ended with his words, 'I can see why you can't simplify that easily'. However, the *Daily Mirror* apparently could not dare to be seen as 'soft' after the screaming *News of the World* position and ran the headline *Exclusive – The Victims of Child Sex Monsters: Toll 500,000* (24 July 2000). Yet a careful *Mirror* reader might have dimly perceived that the information supplied by the person interviewed was at odds with the headline. This led to hate mail and telephone calls from irate members of the public.

It is probably necessary to acknowledge and confront these powerful feelings head on, before dealing in subsequent chapters with the issues of 'the abuser' in an objective and dispassionate way. Nonetheless, the dangerously emotional diatribe of sections of the press, will be confronted with evidence to show that their often sensationalist approach actually impedes rather than assists effective protection of children.

One consequence of the frequently oversimplified media reporting of child abuse tragedies in Britain has been to make every area of the multi-disciplinary child protective service very defensive. More will be said later, but one thing is known – abuse with the worst long-term mental health outcome essentially stems from psychological abuse, which more than any other type of abuse corrupts the normal, healthy development of the child (Andrews et al. 1990; O'Hagan 1993; Bagley and Mallick 2000; Rutter 2000; Davidson 2001; Pears and Capaldi 2001). There are other psychosocial elements of course in this process, with poverty undermining a parent's ability to meet their children's needs (Corby 2000; P.A.T. 2000; Coxe and Holmes 2001; Anderson et al. 2002; Nelson et al. 2002; Tyler 2002), but the key element which undermines the mental health of future adolescents and adults, and propels the cycle of abuse into the next generation, is the breakdown and corruption of the emotional relationship (Fromuth 1986; Fromuth and Bur-khart 1989; Pritchard 1993, 1996a). Clearly adults (especially parents) who currently neglect and abuse have psychosocial needs of their own. If the authorities initiate a punitive and inquisitorial approach to such people, they are not likely to engage them and consequently will fail in the key objective, of making children safer and enhancing their bio-psychosocial development. I shall return to this theme of prevention and development later, but see it as a twin arm of any practical step to improve the parenting skills of adults caring for vulnerable children.

Overly defensive social service intervention and clinical practice leads to a lack of the development of a rapport with the key participants, and suspi-cion and lack of adequate communication between the agencies. Crucially too, the front-line worker may feel exposed and threatened by an agency which should essentially be supporting front-line staff. Recent scandals in-volving children who have been tortured to death by parents even after social service and medical intervention, underscore the fact that social service and clinical intervention can be chaotically organized, leaving both vulnerable children and front-line staff exposed and unsupported.

A striking example of this emerged from the prolonged abuse by a blood aunt that led to the death of Victoria Climbié. This 9-year-old girl, whose photo showed all the joy and élan of a delightful child at the beginning of life, was handed over to her aunt in Britain, by her parents, for the assumed better opportunities Britain gave. This was a very typical cultural arrangement of many African extended families. Instead of being the warm caring maternal aunt the parents had expected, she and her male partner cruelly abused and tortured the child to death. A series of tragic errors by all the child agencies followed, not least because of their inability to interview Victoria in French, her native language. No one noticed that the aunt probably had a severe personality disorder. Her borderline psychotic personality did not emerge fully until her attendance at the Laming inquiry in 2002. This powerful, in-depth inquiry (Laming Report 2003) brought a damning denouncement of all of the services – police, NSPCC, social services and health – directly involved, since there were clear signs of severe abuse long before Victoria died.

The consequence of the accumulative impact of negative media reporting on fatality enquiries such as these is that front-line child protection staff face four inter-related pressures.

First, their desperate concern for the interests of the child, as they are front-line witnesses to the distress and pain of the child. Then pressure comes from the family, as so often the neglecting or abusing parents were themselves previously neglected or abused children, and staff have to carry the parental ambivalence, including not infrequently, their jealousy of their own child receiving a consideration they never did.

The third pressure, sadly, is often experienced from the system in which the social worker operates, as management instead of being professionally supportive and offering necessary practice supervision, is experienced as invigilatory, accusatory, or at worst, scapegoating. Fourthly, the practitioner and the service experience pressures from an uncomprehending general public, who demand the contradiction of total child protection and total parental rights. The public, spurred on by sensationalist media seek to allay any sense of collective guilt, and 'It shouldn't happen' is the frequent cry of interviewees in TV or press. To this we would all add Amen. But we need to understand *why*.

The perennial problem in child abuse is that contradiction and paradox run throughout. As a parent and a mental health practitioner I can well understand the strong emotions the abuse of children evokes. Instinctively, historically, and psychosocially, there is little more powerful than a parent's feelings for their child. Therefore when an adult in a parental role, instead of protecting the child is itself the assailant, the behaviour is so abnormal, so extreme, and so bizarre, we are compelled to pause and try to understand such an aberration. Indeed Jesus's profound insight reflects this when he said, 'If a child asks for a fish, do you give him a serpent? If a child asks for bread, do you give him a stone?' And when the answer is yes, then we need all our knowledge and detachment to understand this tragic situation, in order to prevent further tragedies.

During research on child abusers I had to endure the horror of going through police records and on occasions seeing photographs of child victims, one of which was particularly haunting. This was of a burly man in his early 20s, who had anally and vaginally raped a 3-year-old and then had beaten her to death. In another case a man had sexually tortured his 7-year-old step-daughter with safety pins. I was left in tears of anger and outrage, and commented to my police collaborator, that I was impressed by the ability of his officers to be restrained at the point of contact. Yet without that restraint, we cannot be effective practitioners, although the understandable human response to people who had laid aside their humanity in their brutalizing behaviour of children, is always likely to be one of abhorrence.

Nonetheless, a restrained reaction is expected of the detached professional but it shows just how emotionally demanding these situations can be, and how difficult it is to make proper judgements. Furthermore it is a reminder that it takes a restrained reflection to control what are often fundamental but nevertheless atavistic responses to 'protect' children. We all need to be aware of the very powerful feelings these situations engender, and calm judgement rather than the cries of the media-inspired mob hunting for alleged paedophiles needed.

Another kind of iatrogensis?

There are, however, other perspectives, which are also drawn from a recent case experience, requiring careful consideration. At a confidential case conference the antecedents of an 'unnatural death' of a 42-year-old man, 'Alan', with previous convictions for 'indecency against children', were explored. He had killed himself following release on police bail, charged with yet another illegal act involving children. It was readily acknowledged that in the public at large there would probably be little sadness at such an outcome, since paedophiles are amongst the most hated individuals in society. But what unfolded highlights the need for differentiating the types of child abusers.

'Alan's' last direct offence against children was eight years previous to his present offence, which involved possession of pornographic material depicting children. Self-evidently such material is totally reprehensible and the manufacturers of such material have, in filming or photographing the sexual abuse of children, committed the most serious of sexual crimes. Moreover, it can be argued that the users of such material are directly colluding in this reprehensible behaviour: it is because of the potential market that paedophiles create, that abuse of this kind may be perpetuated.

On examination of 'Alan's' history, however, it transpired that the origins of his sexual offending were complex and it was possible to understand his motivations, and why he was so tempted in ways which meant that he became enmeshed as a user of pornography. This became for him a drug as addictive as heroin.

When 'Alan' was 8, his father died and a new cohabitee almost from the outset, began to sexually exploit the vulnerable boy, which also included frequent beatings. 'Alan' spent some time in care where he was subjected to sexual abuse from older residents, but intermittently he was returned home and again became a victim of the cohabitee, who with the collusion of 'Alan's' mother involved him in *de facto* child prostitution. Back in care, 'Alan' was again victimized but on return home, despite the stepfather now being in prison, a paedophile ring recruited him and desperate for kind attention, he became both a victim and recruiter for the ring.

His personality meant that 'Alan' was never guilty of physical violence against children. He served his first prison sentence for sex involving young boys at the age of 24. In prison he was beaten routinely for 'being a nonce'. He returned to the community after two years but was convicted of 'indecency' again six years later involving an 8-year-old boy in one of his typical 'casual' pick-ups. It should be pointed out that this did not involve any penetration, or any hint of violence whatsoever, which have particular aversive outcomes (Hogg 2003), otherwise the charge against 'Alan' would have been 'gross indecency: rather than the lesser charge of 'indecent assault' which involved his usual efforts of mutual masturbation and fondling.

The court was presented with a familiar dilemma: a grossly damaging childhood had led to a pattern of adult offending. The court chose a punitive rather than a compassionate reaction, deciding on another prison term.

'Alan' served four years in prison, where at last he received some treatment for both his sexual difficulties and the associated depression with the guilt he had long felt. He declared he would never offend again by having direct sexual contact with a child, though one way of coping with his maladjusted orientation was to gain relief from child pornography.

In a police raid on the distributor his name was found and the police then raided his home and charged him with possession of the pornography. He asked to be kept in the cells for he was afraid that the police raid had alerted his neighbours, and also said that a return to prison 'would kill me'. The police response was hostile but he was discharged on bail and told how much paracetamol would 'solve his problem'. 'Alan' the victim and perpetrator returned home and hanged himself.

'Alan' had no other criminal convictions. His psychiatric notes revealed that he had sought help over the last six years for depression and his sexual orientation, indicating that he felt remorse. 'Alan' died a lonely and violent death, though perhaps few in the general public would mourn his passing. If his full story had been revealed in a different way, it might have given pause to people who carry placards that say 'Hang all pedos'.

The other side of the coin?

Perhaps an apology is required for presenting the opposite side of the coin, but in two subsequent forensic psychiatric case conferences I argued first for a 'hard line', and in the second, for a compassionate therapeutic approach. Not surprisingly perhaps, some colleagues suggested I was being inconsistent.

In the first case it was argued that an apparently well socialized professional male aged 30 with no previous convictions, should *not* be diagnosed as having a treatable personality disorder and given a psychiatric excuse for his criminal behaviour. His behaviour was a particularly heinous, corrupting and assaultative Internet offence. In brief, he had collected thousands of pornographic pictures showing the physical humiliation and torture of women and children. He deliberately 'befriended' a physically handicapped housebound 20-year-old women, taught her to use the computer and then had his co-fantasists send sadistic material, with her head superimposed on the victims' bodies. He admitted to his therapist that he gained great sexual excitement from the thought of her distress.

This was his first offence but we argued that the law on the mentally ill is a protection of all our human rights. This man's judgement was not detached from his cognition and he knew his actions were illegal, cruel and socially unacceptable. He was not mentally ill or disordered in a way which cut him off from conscious awareness. Therefore as he had exhibited both *actus rea* and *mens rea*, that is, guilty act and intent, the law should take its course, even though his background explained much of his behaviour. It was argued that our psychological insight could assist him take up his humanity, but could not exculpate him from the consequences of the impact he had upon his victim. He received a five-year sentence, combining different offences including stalking, since Internet crime at that time only carried a maximum of two years.

In the second case, a youth group leader, single, aged 49, with no previous convictions of any kind, was discussed at a psychiatric case conference. He was totally committed to his church and youth activities. There had never been a breath or hint that he had ever inappropriately touched any of his boys. Moreover, he had no convictions and was unknown to any of the agencies. Unbeknown to friends and colleagues he had always been attracted to early post-pubertal boys, which reflected the fact of his own sexual abuse at this age. But he had always known it was morally wrong and consciously was celibate.

He came to the attention of the psychiatric services following a visit to a concert to observe 'his love' from a distance (reminiscent of Thomas Mann's *Death in Venice*). Afterwards he found scrawled on his damp windscreen the words 'paeds out'. He feared that his distant longing for a young boy had been observed. He returned home immediately and made a very serious attempt to kill himself – indeed, he was saved quite by accident.

In therapy, his latent sexual orientation emerged. The question was raised: what risk did he pose to his charges in his youth group? A colleague had followed the letter of the law of the hospital policy and automatically referred the case to the police and social services, even though it was admitted there was no suggestion of an offence having taken place. Later police examination of his house and his computer revealed no evidence of any pornographic material. However, as he was involved in the investigation, this seriously increased his depression and suicide risk.

The issue was fiercely argued in the case conference, some believing that his feelings would always pose a risk, while others argued that since there was no evidence of prior offending, no particular restraints on his role in youth work should be imposed, not least because they were all post-puberty. It should be noted that the Home Office (2000) computerized risk scales assessed the risk of offending for this man as zero. The debates around this single case illustrate typical professional dilemmas, clash of interests, entrenched positions, panic reactions and the possibility of a humane and compassionate response for a deeply troubled individual, versus a safety-first approach, although the question of whose safety was being preserved might be debatable.

Conclusions

It is taken as axiomatic that children are innocent, and certainly do not cause or deserve the events of abuse and neglect which are imposed upon them. I base my approach solely upon the desire to improve the life chances of children, by breaking into the wretched cycle of neglect and abuse. To do this, we need to have better understanding of the perpetrators – including those who have been abused and neglected, emotionally, physically and sexually, and then go on to be abusers themselves. This is in no way an attempt to exonerate, but to assist practitioners be better equipped in order to prevent children being deprived of the joy and innocence of their childhood.

I will attempt to set emotion aside, and seek to focus upon the best evidence available in pursuing the policy goal of improved social and psychological justice for children. To this end the child abuser, in many of his or her guises, will be studied as well as key psycho-socio-economic interactive factors that lead some to behave unacceptably. On the way it is hoped to introduce and highlight an often missing dimension in the field, the importance of the psychiatric-child protection interface, which is as important as the socio-economic child protection interface.

2 Types of Abuse: Incidence, Overlap, Psychiatric Effects and Prevention

In their little worlds in which children have their existence, there is nothing so finely perceived and so finely felt, as injustice.

(Dickens 1849/1995)

Introduction

Although this book is primarily about child abusers, it is important to consider child abuse for three reasons. First of all, abuse and abusers are two sides of the same equation: for every act of abuse there is an abuser, and we cannot describe and evaluate the actions of abusers properly without knowing the range, type and impact of child maltreatment – acts of abuse and neglect which may cause physical and psychological harm to a child or young person. Secondly, the *impact* of child maltreatment must be considered in detail – those types and combinations of abuse and neglect which cause greater harm are worth the most study and policy innovation, in order to minimize their impact, and to prevent maltreatment itself (Pritchard 2001). Thirdly, in order to understand the problematic issue of the victim-to-abuser cycle – the psychological process by which some abuse victims go on to be abusers – there is a need to consider the psychological impact of maltreatment on its victims. For this reason the processes of *disordered attachment* is crucial in understanding both why some maltreatment is so harmful, and why some victims go on to be adult abusers.

The abuse, neglect and exploitation of children and adolescents is complex and multifaceted, and often different types of child maltreatment (outlined in Figure 2.1) overlap, interact or occur in sequence for the individual child (McCabe and Donahue 2000). The lessons from research (Bagley and Thurston 1996; Bagley and Mallick 2000) are that while some resilient children escape the most horrendous types of abuse unscathed (Rutter 1985), for the majority abuse of various kinds, can cause short- and long-term harm to the developing child's adjustment, and to his or her adult adaptation (Quinton and Rutter 1988; Oliver 1988; Bagley and Thurston 1996; Bagley and Mallick 2000).

	Abuse	**Neglect**
Physical	Frequent/severe hitting, slapping, beating, shaking, punching, kicking.	Failure to provide regular and adequate food, warmth, clothing, medical care.
Emotional	Threats to injure or kill; constant sneering/sarcasm or belittling; throwing away or destroying toys; forbidden to speak or play; scapegoating; favouritism to siblings; locked in room or confined space.	Ignoring emotional needs; failing to give affection or respond to child's cries of distress; failure to comfort or support when sad, hurt or worried.
Sexual	Interference with and needless touching of child's genitalia; forcing child to view/touch/sexually manipulate adult; penetration attempted or achieved of genital/anal area; sexual innuendo or threats; showing/making pornography.	'Sex is dirty/sinful/shameful' messages; no sex education for child; severe punishment if child is caught in sexual play or masturbation.

Figure 2.1 Types of Abuse and Neglect

Physical abuse

Physical abuse is the most commonly recorded type of abuse, and it is easiest to define, observe and take action against this kind of maltreatment. Severe bruising and fractures caused by blows, head injuries, shaking, eye damage, suffocation, poisoning, marks made by sticks, whips and cords, marks of burning, biting and scalding are the most extreme examples (Kempe et al. 1985; Meadow 1993). While these extreme forms of physical abuse may not effect more than 2 per cent of the population, 'ordinary' physical discipline in the form of frequent smacking and hitting is much more frequent, and can also cause long-term harm, even though such actions would not normally lead to social service intervention. While physical abuse and punishment is often imposed by isolated parents as an expression of psychological frustration, despair and illness, extreme forms of continuing punishment can extend over many years of a child's life even in a 'normative', two-parent family

(Rutter and Smith 1998). Corporal punishment in schools, although outlawed in British state schools, is still widely practised in many independent schools which often have a fundamentalist religious foundation (and, unfortunately in many so-called Christian households), and constitutes an institutionalized form of physical abuse (Wiehe 1990; Greven 1991; Straus 1991).

Important American research by Straus et al. (1990) has looked retrospectively at the childhoods of random samples of adults and shown clear, causal links between excessive but not illegal physical chastisement of children, and the later underachievement, depression and violence amongst these chastized children grown to adults. Children who learn that they deserve frequent physical punishment develop poorer self-esteem, which in the face of later stressors, makes them more vulnerable to severe depression (Lyon et al. 1996). Ironically, as Straus and Gelles show, physically beaten children who act with rebellion and anger are often subject to further, more severe physical punishment. At the extreme they enter a phase self-defeating behaviour and attribution, in which apparently deviant children are subjected to further punishment and rejection (Pritchard and Butler 2003).

These children learn too that violent chastisement is an acceptable form of interaction and control of others. There is a statistically significant link between having been a victim of frequent physical punishment as a child, and becoming a harsh, authoritarian parent. Such parenting diminishes a child's self-esteem, and leads to increased vulnerability to emotional abuse (Rutter and Smith 1998). Further American research by Straus and Kantor (1994) showed that 90 per cent of parents spanked their preschool children, or used additional forms of physical pain to obtain compliance. Almost half of young teenagers were hit, struck, beaten or slapped by a parent. Controlling for the effects of social class, the research showed that those who experienced persistent and frequent spanking, hitting and violence 'had an increased risk in later life of depressive symptoms, suicidal thoughts, alcohol abuse, physical abuse of children, and wife beating' (Straus and Kantor 1994: 543). Recent research by Straus and Mourandian (1998) indicates the persistence of 'normative' violence in the American family, confirming Knutson and Selner's (1994) annual surveys of American undergraduates over a ten-year period.

Legislation in 2003, which prohibited British childminders smacking their charges, irrespective of whether they have written permission from parents, brought the inevitable tabloid complaints of 'nanny state'. The right to be physically cruel to one's child in the privacy of one's home seems to be as sacred as the Englishman's right to rule his suburban castle.

Canadian researchers have recently begun to fill the gap in research on the amount, degree and sequels of physical abuse, and I perceive an urgent need for detailed studies in Britain beyond the survey by Cawson et al. (2000).

In the Canadian research (MacMillan et al. 1999) a random sample of 9953 Ontario adults was interviewed about their childhood experiences: some 5000 reported childhood and adolescent histories of physical harm or punishment. Those who reported being slapped or spanked 'often' or 'sometimes' (about a quarter of the total sample) had significantly higher lifetime rates of anxiety, alcoholism and aggression towards others.[1] Males were more likely to be physically abused (in 31.2 per cent of cases) compared with females (21.1 per cent of whom recalled such abuse up to age 14). Sexual abuse was more commonly reported by females (12.8 per cent of all of those interviewed) compared to males (sexual abuse rate of 4.3 per cent). One third of boys recalled either physical or sexual abuse, compared to 27 per cent of females. There are no reasons for supposing that figures for Britain are different. Go into our prisons and speak to men convicted of interpersonal violence, and you will find that virtually all were subjected to the severest form of physical punishment as children.

There is an overlap in incidence between 'abusive and neglectful parenting' and 'chaotic parenting'. Estimates of prevalence based on 'adult recall' surveys in Britain, Canada and the USA by Williams (1996), Straus and Mowandian (1998), MacMillan et al. (1999) and Cawson et al. (2000).

Emotional abuse

This is the hardest of actions in the abuse spectrum to define and measure, and difficult for social workers and other professionals to observe or assess (Hobbs and Wynne 2002). Nevertheless there is a growing literature attempting to define emotional abuse and to evaluate interventions to prevent and treat such abuse (Garbarino et al. 1986; O'Hagan 1993; Iwaniec 1995; Hobbs and Wynne 2002; Tyler 2002). The overlap of physical and emotional abuse, and various forms of neglect are outlined in Figure 2.2.

Garbarino et al. (1986) identify five different aspects of 'psychological battering': rejecting, terrorizing, ignoring, isolating and corrupting of a child. While many of these facets of emotional abuse occur together, the presence of one of these types of emotional abuse is sufficient to cause long-term psychological harm if it is profound and repeated in nature. Often (as is the case in physical and sexual abuse) only one child amongst several in a family will be singled out for emotional interactions which can be described as abusive. Though occasionally one finds 'serial' emotional abuse when the next child is targeted as the other becomes too old. Indeed, the contrast of the rewards and emotional support for other children, compared with the emotional rejection of one particular child can heighten a child's sense of isolation, despair and negative self-regard. However, a whole generation of children in a family may be corrupted by conditions of criminality and a general climate of squalor

Abusive and neglectful parenting – frequent, arbitrary physical abuse and/or chronic disregard for child's emotional and/or physical needs – some 5 per cent of all families	**Chaotic, neglectful parenting** with child's emotional and physical needs frequently ignored; random acts of violence – some 3 per cent of all families
Authoritarian, overly strict parenting – all physical needs cared for, but often emotionally cold, with frequent, non-arbitrary physical punishment for scheduled misdeeds – some 5 per cent of all families	**'Normal' parenting** which usually meets child's physical and emotional needs, without the application of persistent physical punishment (i.e. only occasional spankings) – some 90 per cent of families

Figure 2.2   Types and Estimated Prevalence of Physical and Emotional Abuse and Neglect

which constitutes a psychologically corrupting environment. This picture has emerged in the case studies by Oliver and Buchanan (1979) and Oliver (1983, 1988) who studied a number of British 'multi-problem families' in which all kinds of neglect and abuse were simultaneously present over several generations. Similar kinds of families in which children are both sexually and physically abused have been described in other English studies (Hobbs and Wynne 1990, 2002; Munro 1998).

O'Hagan (1993) defines psychological abuse as:

> The sustained, repetitive, inappropriate behaviour which damages, or substantially reduces, the creative and developmental potential of crucially important mental faculties and mental processes of a child; these include intelligence, memory, recognition, perception, attention and moral development.
>
> (O'Hagan 1993: 75)

Emotional abuse in O'Hagan's scheme can include instability of parenting figures, their sudden departure and the arrival of new parents or partners for a mother, as well as inconsistency in parental disciplinary activity, kindness and indulgence for short periods, followed by periods of harshness and emotional and physical cruelty. Sometimes a child's favourite or beloved toys (including the symbolic comfort figure of a favourite doll or stuffed animal) will be removed from the child, and destroyed. The child may be told frequently: 'I wish you'd never been born ... I hate you ... You'll never amount to anything ... Can't you do anything right?' The child is subjected to a persistent stream of criticism and belittlement, and his/her positive achievements or efforts go unrewarded or are sneered at. Often the emotionally abusing parent has been emotionally abused as a child themselves,

Cultural factors	Cultural values support physical punishment and chastisement of children. Poor quality institutions for care of 'unwanted' children. Exploitation of children for labour, warfare and sexual purposes tolerated. Ethnic groups and their children stigmatized and exploited. Prejudice and stigma regarding single parents, and/or children with disability.
Social system factors	Chronic poverty and reduced life chances in lower blue collar and 'underclass'. Underfunding and/or chaotic delivery of child support and protection services.
Personal factors in abusers	Parent figure(s) abused and neglected in own childhood. Parent figure(s) have chronically poor mental health and/or low self-esteem. Parent figure(s) have substance abuse problem. A current caretaker not child's biological parent. Parent(s) single and/or teenaged.
Child vulnerability factors	Male. 'Difficult' temperament since birth. Child's congenital disability. Child developmentally delayed. Child separated for long periods from parent(s) including child 'in care'.

Figure 2.3 Antecedents and Vulnerability Factors in Physical Child Abuse and Neglect

and is currently under considerable stress. This combination of psychological and social factors may lead to the child being scapegoated as a convenient target who cannot answer back, or defend themselves. Often too frequent, arbitrary and cruel physical punishments are combined with emotional rejection and abuse.

Child sexual abuse within the family involves patterns of deceit and manipulation of the child victim which, over and above the physical and sexual assaults imposed on the child, are often a form of psychological abuse. The father or stepfather in particular, enlists the child is a secret liaison, and predominately she, but it can be he, is bribed, threatened or cajoled into keeping the secret. The artful seducer will have reduced the child's self-esteem and made her emotionally dependent upon him: her efforts at resistance may result in psychological threats. Worse may follow when the child is finally able to appeal to a family adult for help, and is then accused of being a seducer or a liar, and is subject to emotional exclusion. This can lead to running from home and homelessness, which sets in train a pattern of survival techniques which can lead to the most fundamental sexual exploitation, that imposed on the child or adolescent prostitute (Pritchard and Clooney 1994; Barker-Collo 2001; Nelson et al. 2002; Hogg 2003).

The US-based Office for the Study of the Rights of the Child has published the following schema summarizing types of psychological maltreatment of children (Figure 2.4).

Implied in this continuum of abuse from the interpersonal to the ecological is the possibility that whole cultures can, through oppressive practices, cause grave harm to the psychological development of children. The use of child soldiers in rebel armies is an extreme case in point; the widespread use of children for sexual purposes is another.[2] Further examples are the use of terror to oppress children, by killing or torturing their parents in the presence

DIRECT AND PERSONAL ATTACKS ON A CHILD	Publicly humiliating child; Terrorizing a child with threats of extreme violence; Repeatedly making a child scapegoat for personal difficulties.
INESCAPABLE NEGATIVE CONDITIONS IN THE CHILD'S IMMEDIATE ENVIRONMENT	Making the child a captive for violence or chaos in the lives of significant adults; Modelling of substance abuse/harmful health practices by significant adults; Teaching a child racial/sexual stereotypes which degrade others; Modelling of community violence by family members.
DESTRUCTIVE PERSPECTIVES AND PRACTICES ENCOURAGED BY CULTURE	Presentations of excessive violence and distortions of reality through public media; Institutionalized restrictions to making the most of educational talent; Cultural disrespect for the competencies of young people; Warfare, and exploitation of child labour and refugees.

Figure 2.4 Psychological Maltreatment: A Continuum of Direct to Indirect Forms
Adapted from Hart (1984).

of the child, and the threat or actuality of torturing the child to make parents confess or co-operate with government armies in Central America (Lykes 1994). Being trapped in theatres of war in which they experience the killing of others, and sometimes are wounded themselves can have profoundly negative impacts on the child's ability to adjust in post-war settings (Garbarino 1993; Ullman and Hilweg 1999; Hobbs and Wynne 2002).

Physical and emotional neglect

Like emotional abuse, these forms of neglect occupy a grey area in the application of social scientific knowledge in the protection and care of children. In part this is due to the frequent overlap of physical abuse and neglect, and emotional abuse and neglect (Ethier et al. 1995; Iwaniec 1995). In Britain, social workers have been guided in the definition of abuse and neglect, and related actions by the 'Orange Book', which offered a guide to assessment and action if a child was thought to be neglected, in terms set out by the 1989 Children Act (DoH 1991).

One way of assessing physical and emotional neglect is by asking adolescents and young adults to report, retrospectively, on the conditions of their childhood (Williams 1996). While this method may give some accurate accounts of prevalence, it will not offer a guide for current social service investigations to investigate risk or allegations of neglect. In the front line, teachers and health professionals (health visitors and GPs) may occupy the front line in making assessments and referrals – but here the 1989 Children Act in Britain may actually impede social work action because of its emphasis on 'good enough' parenting, and the emphasis of keeping a family together, even in conditions of emotional poverty and physical squalor. The new guidelines for assessing neglect, deriving from the Child Support Act of 1995 (DoH 2002) have the overt purpose of supporting family life, rather than protecting children from abuse and neglect. Unfortunately, as the study by Saunders (2001) of the implementation of these new policy guidelines in a unitary authority in England shows, there is considerable variation between workers and family service teams in how to interpret these guidelines, in terms of the evidence to be gathered and the actions to be taken. The Department of Health has been unhelpful in offering definitive guidance on how to interpret these new guidelines (Saunders 2001) and in the face of rapid turnover amongst highly stressed and poorly rewarded child protection workers, training models are often haphazard, and decisions about whether or not to 'protect' a child often have an intuitive or haphazard basis.

This picture of a local authority social services department in organizational flux, with unclear guidelines for action, and with the employment of unsupported and sometimes untrained social workers is paralleled by the picture which has emerged of child protection in Haringey, in which there was a profound failure of social, medical, police and voluntary services, none of whom acted to prevent the death of Victoria Climbié in 2000 – an official inquiry severely criticized all services involved, social workers, police and medical, in failing to prevent the torture and murder of a child by her aunt and step-uncle (Laming Report 2003). This murder, one of many scandals to beset the British child care system, was predicted in the criticism of the working of the Children Act by paediatricians Speight and Wynne (2000) who argued on the basis of their experience in dealing with severely abused children, that social workers often left children with known severely abusive families, only acting to remove the child to a place of safety (if at all), when repeated, life-threatening injuries or assaults were apparent.

Conclusions of repeated inquiries into the deaths from abuse of British children known to social services or actually in care appear to be ignored (Munro 1998) – for example, the persistent failures over a three-year period by Cambridgeshire social services (*The Times* 2002). The most recent Cambridgeshire case involved 'horrendous abuse' on a series of children lodged with one foster parent. Children in foster and residential care in Britain are particularly at risk from their carers. Hobbs et al. (1999) identified 158 children over a five-year period who had been abused in public care: in foster care 42 children were physically abused, 76 were sexually abused, and 15 experienced both forms of abuse. The rate of physical and sexual abuse of those in residential care was about twice that in the fostered children. Not all of the abusers were foster parents: 23 per cent of the abusers were natural parents during periods of contact, while children (including foster sibs) were responsible for 20 per cent of the abuse. The picture which emerges is one of a social services system faced by overwhelming odds, finding themselves placing children with ill-prepared or unsuitable foster parents without adequate preparation or supervision.

In the case of Victoria Climbié, there are numerous organizations and individuals in theory responsible but all of whom 'failed' (Laming Report 2003). To this list should be added ourselves, as citizens and taxpayers, who have failed to lobby strongly enough for better and more adequately funded social services.

Sexual abuse

Sexual abuse of children has been of major concern for researchers and practitioners in the past 15 years, and reports in this kind of abuse greatly outweigh those on other forms of abuse or neglect. Bagley (1969) was one of the first British researchers in what had, until then, been a no-go area – the sexual abuse of children. Indeed it was not until the late 1970s and 1980s that the problem had come to the awareness of the professional. His later work exploring subsequent reporting depression and suicidal behaviour was, at the time, ground-breaking (Bagley and Ramsay 1997). Today, however, there is a plethora of research demonstrating the insidious effects of sexual abuse into later adolescence and adulthood (Fergusson and Mullen 1999; Jones and Ramchandani 1999; Barker-Collo 2001; Glowinski et al. 2001; Rossow and Lauritzen 2001; Anderson et al. 2002; Nelson et al. 2002; Soloff et al. 2002; Tyler 2002).

Using a conservative definition of contact sexual abuse, it has been estimated that 13 per cent of females, and 6 per cent of males experience unwanted sexual contacts (Oaksford and Frude 2001). Some 50 per cent of victims of sexual abuse in childhood, compared with less than 20 per cent of matched controls who experience no forms of physical, emotional and sexual abuse or neglect will manifest clinically significant forms of maladaption, which may last an individual's lifetime. Clinical sequels following sexual abuse include impaired self-esteem, chronic depression and suicidality, anxiety phobias and post-traumatic stress, runaway and acting-out behaviour, sexual terror, sexual promiscuity, eating disorders and various psychosomatic problems (for example Rossow and Lauretizen 2001; Anderson et al. 2002): in effect, virtually every aspect of stress symptoms. However, before a causal sequence can be inferred between sexual abuse and later problems, the co-existence or prior and subsequent occurrence of emotional and physical abuse must also be considered, including negative effects of the actual investigation of sexual abuse (Bagley and Ramsay 1997; Tyler 2002). Some children react in terms of their particular vulnerability, in seemingly opposite ways – the outcomes of sexual terror and sexual promiscuity are opposite ends of a spectrum of sexual disorders which, apparently both result from prior sexual exploitation of the child. The danger, of course, is to attribute every stress symptom down to some form of child abuse, which can be very counter-productive, and at the worst, lead to the Cleveland or Shetland type fiascos, where families were falsely accused because of very dubious medical tests (the so-called 'anal reflex' test) or unsubstantiated hearsay.

A hierarchical model of assessment and intervention in child abuse and neglect

In defining 'abuse', it is recognized that along with the word 'risk', these are often imprecise and over-used concepts in the field of child protection. The concepts invariably contain something of the value system of the persons defining 'risk' and 'abuse'. Indeed it is singular that even the Department of Health's *Messages From Research* avoided a specific definition, rather leaving it to 'common sense' of when an 'event occurs' which is 'obviously detrimental to the child' (DoH 1995: 35).

Epidemiological evidence shows that in the large majority of cases, the neglecter/abuser is either a parent or a person occupying a parental role (Finkelhor 1994; Fischer and McDonald 1998; Leventhal 1998, 2001a). Obviously these are people who have considerable proximity to the child, involving the opportunity to abuse, as well as motivations which may be endemic in the parenting role and its frustrations and dysfunctions (Pritchard 1991; Utting 1997; Fischer and McDonald 1998; DoH 2002).

In order to provide a working definition it is necessary to begin with a normative concept of child development. The 'task' for the child is to grow into an independent adult. The task of the parent-figures is to facilitate this development by meeting these needs within a protected environment. Thus it is expected that the adult/parent/child carers will appropriately meet the child's needs in respect to their physical, psychosexual and social development, thereby establishing health attachment styles, which are the basis for long-term mental health (Iwaniec 1995). Anything that impairs this development is potentially damaging and potentially 'abusive' (Richardson and Bacon 2002). Partially linked to these ideas is the notion of 'good enough parenting' (that is, acceptance of even marginally acceptable parenting, provided that there is some positive emotional tie to a parent), which has been accepted by the British social work profession, working under the guidelines set out in the 1989 Children Act.

A number of well-researched British, American and Canadian studies have shown that children at high risk of abuse and neglect come, disproportionately, from the most disadvantaged socio-economic groups (Krugman et al. 1986; Oliver 1988; Quinton and Rutter 1988; Lyon et al. 1996; Zunzungegui et al. 1997; Gillham et al. 1998; Banyard 1999; Bagley and Mallick 2000; Pritchard and Butler 2000a; Rumm et al. 2000; Lipman et al. 2001; Pritchard 2001). It needs to be stressed, however, that the large majority (at least 90 per cent) of socio-economically poor parents never abuse or neglect their children. However, these children may experience a more pervasive kind of institutionalized abuse. In that they fail to maximize their socio-educational potential (P.A.T. 2000; Social Exclusion Unit 2000), these children are experiencing in their impaired life chances, victimization by deeply entrenched class systems, in which extreme disadvantage in parents can breed extreme disadvantage in children. It is argued that failing to tackle problems of chronic family and child poverty, and leaving such children without adequate compensatory education is a form of institutional discrimination by the ruling state, which aids and abets the neglect and abuse of children by individual parents.

Whilst negative socio-economic features are often crucial spurs in the direction of negative parenting, the seminal work of Kempe et al. (1962, 1985) first alerted us to the fact that children can be neglected and abused in every social and ethnic setting (Leventhal 1998). This observation places all parents on a continuum, which recognizes that being 'the perfect parent' is not always easy: along this continuum of committed, devoted parents, is a gradient of failure in meeting the child's needs, ranging from physical and emotional neglect to physical, emotional and sexual abuse, which may become discontenting, damaging, disturbing, dangerous and at the extreme, destructive.

Baird and colleagues (1988) created a behavioural inventory which purported to differentiate between 'neglect' and 'abuse' and contained only seven and nine items respectively. When applied to British populations, it appeared to have a degree of reasonable validity (Pritchard 1991). Baird's inventory was aimed at identifying future neglect and abuse but also provides a useful guide to firmer definition. Moreover, Baird recognizes that there is an overlap between neglect and abuse, though often the differences depend upon external stressors and/or the psychological state of the neglecter or abuser. This analysis leads us to formulate the hierarchical model outlined below.

Schematically, there are temporal, contextual factors so that people are not always neglecters or abusers. Rather the continuum is from those who succumb, at certain times, to pressures that lead them to fail their child in terms of milder forms of neglect or abuse, to those at the extreme end of the continuum, whose persistent response is severely and chronically neglecting and abusing the child, in emotional, physical and perhaps sexual ways.

This observation leads to a schematic model of assessment/definition of abuse, with the advantage of an implicit intervention model. It posits a Resources-Needs-Demands interaction, assuming that the parent has certain psycho-socio-economic resources to meet the child's needs. External stress may create a deficit for the parent, who either passively or actively fails to meet the child's needs. This results in a situation where the child is either mildly, moderately or severely neglected or abused.

Such pragmatic gradations are based upon the immediate and long-term impact of the neglect and the abuse. This in turn leads to another complexity, namely that individual children seem to respond very differently to seemingly similar experiences, implying the notion of 'resilience' of some children (Rutter 1987, 1999; Quinton and Rutter 1988). Thus some children exposed to what appears to be very severe physical discipline, emotional neglect or sexual abuse, emerge into adulthood relatively unscathed. Conversely, others may appear seriously psychosocially disabled (Robins and Rutter 1990).

Schematically, there are three broad situations associated with different levels of neglect and abuse.

First is the transient situation where the parents, usually have adequate parenting skills but whom poverty and other stressors overwhelm. There is often a transient, almost accidental neglect and abuse. Generally, this is associated with the milder forms of neglect and/or abuse, which has the least long-term impact, providing that the core parent-child relationship is sound and the child receives enough affectionate parenting to enable stable attachments to occur. The intervention needed is clear: immediate relief of the material stressors, with support for the re-establishment of the usually adequate parenting skills. Often care of a child by a relative such as a grandmother for long or short periods can enable adequate attachments (crucial for long-term mental health development) to form.

Secondly, there occur predisposing situations, which impact upon parents with poor parenting skills. This results in a predominately passive but long-term response, and the child is neglected to a moderate degree. Occasional worsening of the situation can lead to more active abuse. Here the child's development of health attachments may be threatened, leading to greater risks of long-term mental health problems (Hawton et al. 1985; Bagley and Thurston 1996; Tyler 2002).

Thirdly, is the persistent neglect and active abuse situation where parents appear to have few adequate parenting skills (often reflecting their own abusive childhoods) necessary to meet the child's physical, emotional and developmental needs, in a family situation in which the child is predominately exposed to neglect and/or abuse. This may involve severe neglect and abuse. Indeed, when such a situation appears persistent there is a case for considering long-term, alternative forms of parenting until the child's situation can be improved within the time scale that the child needs to develop. Older child adoption is an obvious intervention strategy here, and can achieve successful outcomes not possible by leaving the child in an unstable and abusive environment (Bagley 1993). Without adequate interventions such as stable, long-term foster care or adoption, such children are often found in the subsequent caseloads of adult services, be they social services, health, child protection or the criminal justice system, as the cycle of neglect and abuse moves into the next generation (Audit Commission 1996; Rutter et al. 1998; Pritchard and Butler 2000a, 2000b).

Figure 2.5 succinctly illustrates our arguments on the interaction between levels of neglect/abuse and the necessary interventions.

A resources-needs deficit model of neglect and abuse

Inadequate psychological and socio-economic resources create deficits in parenting capacity, leading to:

1   New, transient stress responses: child's needs temporarily not met, involving mild neglect or abuse. Despite stressors, parents able to create affectionate parent-child attachments.

2 Initially, more severe psycho-socio-economic stressors, leading to more marked forms of child neglect or abuse.

3 Persistent situation of parents seriously lacking adequate parenting skills leads to moderate and severe neglect and abuse.

Deficits	Interventions
(1) Temporary break-down of coping mechanisms	Immediate stress reduction, with new socio-economic resources Initial Protection Plan to avoid future breakdown
(2) Transient new deficit in predisposing socio-economic situation	Stress reduction and new resources Protection Plan
(3) Chronically stressed adults with poor parenting skills, tend to passively neglect/abuse	Stress reduction, Protection Plan and re-educative intervention
(4) Deficits in psycho-socio-economic situation, poor parenting skills and coping mechanisms	As above and rehabilitation, possible respite care
(5) Persistent personality problems, poor parenting and inappropriate adult responses to child	If rehabilitation and re-educative intervention is inadequate early adequate substitute care, foster care/adoption should be considered

Figure 2.5 Continuum of Neglect/Abuse and Associated Interventions

The interplay of physical, emotional and sexual abuse and their negative impact on the child's mental health

Different forms of child abuse and neglect often occur together; and they can also occur in sequence in the life of the individual child. Thus a child whose low self-esteem reflects several years of emotional abuse and neglect (often linked to excessive physical punishments) may be unable to prevent or report the later sexual assaults of an older person. While there is no evidence-based information from British studies on the degree of this overlap of abuse and neglect types, there is good Canadian evidence from a number of community mental health studies of young adults (Bagley and Mallick 2000). These Canadian estimates suggest that up to 10 per cent of *all* children (up to age 16) experience *more than* one type of serious abuse (physical, emotional or sexual), while another 7 per cent experience one type of abuse (physical, emotional or sexual) with the simultaneous or prior occurrence of any other type of abuse.

Pioneering research in this field, the psychiatrist Philip Ney (1987) found in a study of 154 children investigated following complaints of various kinds of abuse that it was verbal abuse 'which left the deepest scars'. Cruel words, repeated day after day, and the belittling and demeaning of the child's efforts to become a self-regarding young person were more demoralizing than cruel blows. It is likely then that the work of Straus and colleagues (1990) referred to above on the long-term negative sequelae of physical punishment and abuse are explained in large part by negative emotional messages, reinforced by verbal criticisms of the child, which surrounded the acts of beating and hitting the child. American research by Wind and Silver (1992) supports these findings: it is not physical abuse alone, not sexual abuse by itself which causes the greatest long-term harm, but the emotional abuse which underpins the physical contact abuse, which causes the most long-term psychological harm.

In further research Ney et al. (1994) identified 'the worst combinations of child abuse and neglect' in a follow-up of children referred because of known abuse by parent figures. There was a strong overlap between abuse and neglect: in 63 cases neglect preceded the onset of physical and/or sexual abuse. Multivariate analyses established a statistically significant hierarchy of combinations of abuse and neglect, in terms of long-term, negative psychological outcomes:

1 Physical abuse, physical neglect, emotional abuse, emotional neglect;
2 Physical abuse, sexual abuse, emotional neglect, physical neglect;
3 Physical abuse, sexual abuse, emotional neglect, verbal abuse;
4 Physical abuse, sexual abuse, physical neglect, verbal abuse.

Ney et al. (1994) conclude:

> Having been deprived of the necessary ingredients to their normal development, children never seem to accept the loss of the childhood that could have been. They keep searching as adolescents and adults, only to find that those they search among are usually deprived people who not only cannot provide them with what they needed as children, but also tend to abuse them, partly out of their own frustrations in encountering somebody who they thought would give them when they were so hungry.
>
> (Ney et al. 1994: 711)

In extreme cases, the child enters the cycle of adult psychopathy described by Steinhauer (1984) and described with graphic force in a study of socially excluded adolescents who move into a cycle of disordered and violent adult relationships (Lyon et al. 1996; Pritchard and Butler 2000a; Pritchard

2001). It is in these ways, as will be shown, that some abused and neglected children may become abused and neglecting adults.

Reviews of published studies (Pelletier and Handy 1999; Tyler 2002) also conclude that it is emotional abuse, which causes the worst harm to children, rather than physical or sexual abuse alone. When emotional maltreatment and other forms of abuse are combined, outcomes are significantly poorer than in the case of a single type of abuse, because this results in a psychological attack on the core self-esteem of the individual (Moeller et al. 1993; Muller et al. 1995; Nash et al. 1993; Esman 1994).

Deriving hypotheses from these studies, Pelletier and Handy (1999) designed an important controlled study, comparing psychological outcomes for three groups of children: those experiencing sexual abuse alone; those experiencing long-term family dysfunctions (often involving emotional abuse and neglect) but with no reported sexual abuse; and non-abused children of similar age and class backgrounds. Results were clear cut and significant – although sexual abuse causes harm, it is an environment of family dysfunction which causes the most negative psychological impact on children.

Thus it is *emotional* abuse (compared to physical or sexual abuse), disrupting adult-child attachment relationships which causes the greatest long-term psychological harm. Emotional abuse combined with physical or sexual abuse has a slightly greater impact on long-term mental health than emotional abuse alone, while the combination of all three types of abuse (emotional, physical and sexual) has the greatest long-term, negative impact on a young person's mental health. Paradoxically then, many children can survive what to child protection workers seem to be horrendous amounts of physical abuse or sexual exploitation, provided that the child has a strongly supportive, close emotional tie with an adult throughout the abusive experiences. Paradoxically too, breaking the child's emotional bonds with a caring adult through sudden removal into a care situation following what seems to be horrendous abuse can actually cause greater harm to the child, particularly when the child is placed in local authority residential home along with children and adolescents with a range of emotional and behavioural problems (Brogi and Bagley 1998). The continuous breaking of affectional bonds between children and adults by the malign combinations of ill-considered interventions and the actions of unstable adults in the child's family leads to the situation described by the child psychiatrist Paul Steinhauer (1984: 484) as ' ... how to succeed in the business of making psychopaths without really trying'. Overall, these findings have important implications for how child protection teams intervene on behalf of children and families, and how offenders are perceived and processed. It is nevertheless acknowledged that sexual abuse of a child, in and of itself, often has harmful long-term impacts, independently of the psychosocial context in which in takes place (Bagley and Mallick 2000; Kendler et al. 2000). Put another way, while sexual abuse itself is harmful, it is likely to be very much more harmful when it is combined with emotional abuse which results in disrupted or distorted attachment patterns, for in effect it is the corruption and exploitation of the child-adult relationship, which is so damaging to the developing child.

Disordered attachments: the common thread defining the harms caused by child abuse and neglect

A particular helpful research based approach is that of Pamela Alexander and colleagues (Alexander and Schaffer 1994; Alexander et al. 1998) who, using models derived from the work of John Bowlby on attachment and loss, has shown how neglectful and abusive parenting can in its various forms undermine the foundations of the child's mental health. Rutter (1995) a leading authority in child psychiatry has given a lucid exposition of the importance of the attachment concept in understanding the successful socialization and adaptation of children and young people. The work by Rutter and colleagues (2000) on children in Romanian orphanages illustrates this dramatically.

Attachment styles, socialized in childhood and enduring in adulthood, according to an established body of research evidence, fall into four types:

Secure, reflecting a secure childhood, leads to adults who have a coherent and pleasing memory of their parents and caretakers; they are able to reflect on and integrate past events into a secure identity which enables them to meet future challenges with confidence. These adults are comfortable with a range of emotional expression; they are trusting in relationships, and are capable of supporting others. At least three-quarters of adults have childhood experiences and memories leading to secure attachment styles in adulthood.

Avoidant (dismissing) attachment styles in adults often reflect emotional abuse in childhood in which a parent has avoided close emotional contact with the child, has used negative emotional manipulation as a means of control, and has also frequently used excessive physical punishment. As adults these individuals have little coherent memory of childhood; their childhood seems to them to have a grey sameness; they are uncomfortable with close relationships, and are often lonely and hostile to others. Their marriages often break down, and they often also emotionally abuse or neglect their own children.

Preoccupied (anxious/ambivalent) adults have an attachment style which often reflects a childhood marked by insecurity and loss, and the threat of further loss of attachment figures (Alexander et al. 1998). Sometimes emotional abuse has taken the form of threatening to abandon or reject the child. As adults these individuals have high levels of anxiety, and the loss of a partner can precipitate a serious depressive episode. They are clinging, dependent, jealous and over-demanding in partner relationships. Ironically, such demands may alienate the partner, and as a consequence strong emotional demands are made upon children.

Fearful (unresolved) adults are often products of disorganized 'multi-problem' families in which socialization has been chaotic, and various adults may have physically and sexually abused the child (Alexander et al. 1998). As adults these individuals have been described as socially inhibited, unassertive, passive and avoidant. These states are sometimes described as 'learned helplessness', and women who have experienced these multiple types of neglect and abuse may drift into abusive partner relationships; these male partners may abuse the woman's children from previous relationships, in ways which the woman feels unable to prevent. Men with this attachment style may become alcohol or drug dependent, with histories of petty crime, suicidal behaviours and marginal partner relationships.

A knowledge of how abuse and neglect can interfere with the developmental of health attachments which foster the development of good mental health throughout the lifespan is a crucial requirement for any practitioner in the child protection field, and those engaged in therapy with victims and offenders (Iwaniec 1995; Alexander et al. 1998; Davies 1999). This attachment literature also explains why it is the overlay of emotional abuse upon other types of abuse (physical and/or sexual) which is so strongly associated with long-term harm. The attachment literature is also crucial for an understanding of why some victims of child abuse go on to become abusers themselves, which is explored in the next chapter of 'abuse' from within the family.

Notes

[1] Canadian law is notoriously conservative on intervening in the punishments which a parent or teacher may wish to impose on a child. Attempts using section 43 of the Criminal Code to prosecute a parent who whipped a 6-year-old girl with a horse harness failed, as did an attempt to prosecute a teacher who punched three 'naughty' boys in the face, breaking a tooth of one of them. The Canadian Teachers' Association has defended the right of teachers to use force in the classroom. A national poll indicated that 84 per cent of Canadians supported the right of Canadians to be able to discipline their children by the use of pain (Gadd 1999).

[2] An investigation by the UNHCR and Save the Children Africa, has found that workers from 40 agencies in refugee camps in Liberia, Guinea and Sierra Leone regularly traded sex for relief supplies, medicine and entry to schools with children and adolescents (Gillan and Moszynski 2002).

3 Within-Family Abusers

Introduction

The evidence reviewed in the previous chapter shows that it is emotional abuse, which often accompanies physical and sexual abuse, that is the most damaging: emotional abuse represents a corruption of the child-adult relationship. It is not surprising therefore, that the majority of abused children are victims within their own family setting, tragically assailed by those from whom they might have expected the most protection. Child neglect and abuse within families is ubiquitous, and has been found in every social class, ethnic and cultural group (Kempe et al. 1962; Pritchard 1993; Finkelhor 1994; Utting 1997; Bagley 1999; Al-Lamki 2000; Denny et al. 2001).

Thus for example, one of my earliest practice experiences was with a very affluent family who presented their 9-year-old son as suffering a borderline learning disability: whereas it was found that the former public school, army officer, industrialist father was systemically torturing his son by dragging him from cold to hot baths in a bizarre effort to motivate the boy's educational effort. Another case was of a medical consultant, sexually and physically terrorized his three daughters. Despite such examples, there is considerable evidence that neglect and abuse are more likely to be found in families with a range of overlapping psycho-socio-economic problems (Kempe et al. 1962; Creighton 1992; Pritchard 1992a; Ethier et al. 1995; Lyon et al. 1996; Zunzungegui et al. 1997; Felitti et al. 1998; Gillham et al. 1998; Ryan et al. 2000; DoH 2001).

Psycho-socio-economic aspects of within-family abuse

The key are the psychological concomitants because although socio-economic poverty is one of the most prevalent features in their background, the persistent neglecter and abuser essentially has psychological difficulties which impair their ability to respond appropriately to the child's needs (Kempe et al. 1962; Oliver 1985; Quinton and Rutter 1988; Parton 1994; Fischer and McDonald 1998; Fernandez et al. 1999; DiLillo et al. 2000; Gara et al. 2000; Kendler et al. 2000; Kerker et al. 2000; Rumm et al. 2000; DoH 2001). Since parenting skills are essentially learned through one's own childhood, many neglecters' and abusers' own childhood reflect Oliver's appropriate phrase, 'inter-generational mishandling of children' (Oliver 1985, 1988), which results in what Quinton and Rutter (1988) describe as 'parenting breakdown'. For many, however, it was not so much break-down, as failure to achieve even basic parenting skills (Gara et al. 2000; Kendler et al. 2000). This is often associated with rather infantile emotional responses from the adult carer, in that the adult reacts impulsively and aggressively to the dependent child, seemingly unable to exercise the needed core parental response of 'altruism' (Whipple and Webster-Stratton 1991; Ethier et al. 1995; Waterhouse et al. 1995; DiLillo et al. 2000; Gara et al. 2000). Indeed, as will be seen later, this inability to empathize with a child's psychosocial needs (reflecting disordered attachment styles) may become distorted in mental disorder (Stanton et al. 2001; Stroud 2001, 2003), as apparently mature adults who have demonstrated an apparent ability to form appropriate relationship with others, but then in the face of external stressors, because of their fragile personality, behave in a neglecting or abusive way (Bourget and Labelle 1992; Falkov 1996; Stroud 2001).

There is a dynamic interaction between the themes of psychological, social and economic deficit. This is best understood by looking at the life histories of neglecters and abusers: if one explores their childhood or early adolescence, one finds they have often been over-represented in the caseloads of all the community services – health, education, criminal justice and social service departments (Quinton and Rutter 1988; Pritchard 1992a, 1992b; Lyon et al. 1996; Pritchard and Cox 1997; Rutter and Smith 1998; Policy Action Team 2000; Pritchard and Butler 2000a, 2000b; DoH 2001). Indeed, unlikely support for this concept of 'cycle of deprivation' comes from the Audit Commission (1998) who re-discovered the paradigm, when it recognized that between 8 and 10 per cent of families in the general population are responsible for 90 per cent of all severe social problems.

It is only atypically, however, that the services intervene effectively across generational abuse and neglect, stretching from neglected infant, unruly child, truant, delinquent, early drug misuser, homelessness, early pregnancy, custodial sentence, to neglecting or abusing parent (Lyon et al. 1996; Audit Commission 1998; Rutter and Smith 1998; Social Exclusion Unit 1998a, 1998b; Ryan et al. 2000), though it is possible, as seen in examples of 'Sure Start' and school-based social work, which are designed to be preventive initiatives (Pritchard 2001).

This was graphically seen in a longitudinal study of school-based social work, which when examining the case records of socially unpopular, disruptive, disturbing and disturbed older adolescents, found their school reports as 8-year-olds. Here were the cheery photographs of the fresh-faced boy or girl, often associated with the teacher's comments about 'speech and reading problems, not surprising with his family difficulties'. This reflected five years of wasted opportunity, which failed to engage the child or his or her family, with the result that the new adolescent began the all too familiar cycle of educational and social alienation, so often found in other family members. Fortunately, the school-based social work service, was able to make a measurable impact upon this cycle of educational alienation, delinquency and child neglect (Pritchard 2001; Pritchard and Williams 2001), but this is the exception rather than the rule, as usually the services only act after the breakdown and alienation has occurred.

The age of the abuser is very much a factor, for the younger the parent or carer (male or female), the more they are over-represented amongst cohorts of neglecters and abusers. Classically, the teenaged young single mother is at high risk for abusing or neglecting her child (Felitti et al. 1998; Gillham et al. 1998; Gara et al. 2000; Lipman et al. 2001), often compounded with other problems associated with alcohol and drug misuse, as well as significant economic poverty (Lyon et al. 1996; Policy Action Team 2000; Wall et al. 2000).

Another key variable linked to mishandling of children is within-family violence between adults. Children both model such violence, and are often victims to spin-offs in prolonged physical quarrels between adult partners. In such households the dividing line between physical punishment for purposes of discipline (when a kind word would have been far more effective than a cruel blow) coupled with harsh words of blame, amount to criminal assaults which are unseen and unreported.

The evidence on the negative effects of physical punishment – cruel words linked to cruel blows – is overwhelming: physical violence often begets physical violence, as we argued in the preceding chapter. However, this evidence also shows that the worst outcomes related to intra-family violence, is not the violence per se, but the emotional attitudes surrounding it. The vast majority of people in prison for crimes of personal violence have experienced childhood violence within punitive and emotionally barren, often chaotically structured households (Farrington 1995; Cox and Pritchard 1997; Heck and Walsh 2000).

Worrying new research also shows that persistent psycho-physical stress upon children before and soon after birth leaves its detrimental mark upon the child's neurological and intellectual development, which influences the whole of their development including the emergence of conduct disorders (Van der Kolk 1994; Berkowitz 1998; Chess and Thomas 1998; Glaser 2000). This is in addition to the anxiety, depression and low self-esteem which are often co-morbid with conduct disorder, in children who have experienced maltreatment and abuse (DoH 2001; Finzi et al. 2001).[1]

Research has frequently found that 'domestic violence' is often associated with child neglect and abuse, especially physical and sexual abuse (Waterhouse et al. 1995; Kerker et al. 2000; Rumm et al. 2000; Wall et al. 2000).

Indeed, Rumm et al. argue that 'spouse abuse' is a highly significant risk factor indicating the probability of child abuse.

Abusers within the family

This chapter focuses upon abusers within the child's family. Table 3.1 sets out the main actors in relation to child victims. In recent research it was found that nearly one in five deaths involved two carers, acting in apparent collusion with each other (Pritchard and Bagley 2001). Thus in many cases of child murder both mother and her partner (often biologically unrelated to the child) are charged, because it was not possible for either police or the courts to determine separate culpability (Wilczynski and Morris 1993; Waterhouse et al. 1995; Pritchard and Bagley 2001).

The table sets out, in a schematic form, those involved in within-family maltreatment (including milder forms of neglect and abuse), and the abuse of children.

Table 3.1 Schematic Presentation of Within-Family Abusers, and Frequency and Intensity of Maltreatment and Abuse

Type of abuse	Intra-family Females	Intra-family Males
Neglect	Other relatives	Other relatives
Emotional	Rarely	Rarely
Physical	Rarely	Rarely
Abuse		
Emotional	Rarely	Rarely
Physical	Rarely	+
Sexual	Rarely	++++
Neglect	Mothers	Fathers
Emotional	++++	++++
Physical	++++	+++
Abuse		
Emotional	++++	++++
Physical	++++	++++
Sexual	+	++++

- + = Sometimes ++ = Occasionally +++ = Very Often ++++ = Virtually Constant
- Female abusers are according to a variety of studies, including adult recall studies of young adults, sexual abusers in only some 3 per cent of all cases (Lewis and Stanley 2000) although some argue that there is a bias in under-reporting such cases (Lawson 1994).
- Other relatives: Uncles and Grandfathers, most common abuse is by siblings.

Only in the last decade has research taken seriously the fact that children and young adolescents can abuse other children, involving the trio of emotional, physical and/or sexual abuse (Bagley and Sewchuk-Dann 1991; Vizard et al. 1996; Galli et al. 1999; Rasmussen 1999; Hagan et al. 2001; Wolfe et al. 2001). Previously there was too sanguine an attitude towards 'sex play' between children, with an assumption that it was part of the normal sexual development. It is increasingly recognized that the earlier a young person becomes sexually active with a child younger than themselves (that is, a non-peer), the more likely this is to continue into later adolescence and adulthood as a core part of psychosexual identity, with a fixation on children as sexual objects (Hunter and Figuredo 2000; LeSure and Lester 2000; Hagan et al. 2001; Wolfe et al. 2001). Moreover, these groups of adolescents, who themselves were likely to be victims of a range of abuse, often demonstrate low self-esteem, viewing their own damaged psychosocial situation as a norm, undermining their potential empathy towards their victims (Galli et al. 1999; Hagan et al. 2001).

Sexual contact imposed by one child on another (including their younger sibling) may be a form of rape. Moreover, there is a consensus in the literature that where the 'child' assailant is more than five years older than the victim, this constitutes sexual abuse (Galli et al. 1999; Greenberg et al. 2000; Hagan et al. 2001).[2]

Within changing patterns of family life, increasing divorce, re-marriage and family mergers (CSO 2001; DoH 2001) the 'step-sibling' dimension of sexual abuse becomes a bigger problem, and is likely to bring together non-bonded children of a greater age range, children and adolescents who themselves are having to cope with major re-adjustments in their families. Consequently, the older sibling may well make the young 'in-comer' a target for their own anger and sense of rejection. This was illustrated by the case of a 9-year-old boy, whose deteriorating educational record was found to be linked by systematic physical and sexual bullying by a disturbed 14-year-old boy, who resented his mother's new partner, the young boy's father. An alert and sympathetic school teacher was able to make a referral which benefited both boys.

In the national British survey by Cawson et al. (2000) of those experiencing within-family abuse, 43 per cent had been sexually victimized (achieved or attempted oral and other penetration) by a brother or step-brother. In addition, 19 per cent suffered serious sexual assault by their stepfather. Since stepfathers are still in a minority in British families, in real terms this represents a rate of sexual assault by stepfathers which is at least twice that in biological fathers, confirming North American research (Bagley and Thurston 1996).

Sexual abuse by female siblings may occur but there is little research evidence on this form of assault. In the Cawson et al. (2000) survey of 2869 young adults, no one reported any kind of attempted or achieved intercourse or penetration by a sister or stepsister, although 6 per cent of those reporting sexual abuse between ages 5 and 16, said that they experienced sexual pleasure with a sister/stepsister. This is in contrast to the picture found with older male siblings who are capable of serious sexual abuse, and are over-represented amongst cohorts of convicted child sex offenders (Simon et al. 1992; Waterhouse et al. 1995; Pritchard and Bagley 2000; Hagan et al. 2001).

Consider, for example, the case of 'Adam' (a pseudonym) who was 14 years old. His mother's remarriage after a turbulent and violent relationship with Adam's father appeared to repeat this pattern, since the stepfather, was often physically very punitive to all in the family. The boy already had serious indicators of psychological distress and the many moves by his family had left him isolated, without friends of his own age. He began systematically to physically and sexually abuse his stepsisters aged 7 and 9, using bullying tactics to make the girls accept his unwanted sex play. Typically, 'Adam' did not have any age appropriate peer friendships, but sought out the company of younger children. Initially the sex was simple exploration, but quite quickly moved to full penetration, which went undiscovered for more than two years until 'Adam' was apprehended following sexual assault upon a 10-year-old neighbourhood girl.

'Barbara' was a 15-year-old who imposed herself sexually on her 6-year-old stepbrother. This took the form of unwanted physical exploration, not discovered for a year. The boy was then referred to a Child Guidance Clinic for 'late onset' enuresis. It was recognized that 'Barbara' had borderline learning difficulties, which had been overlooked during earlier marital conflicts, difficulties which led to the creation of a new family. Ironically, although sibling sexual abuse tends to be more direct and brutal than the seduction of a child by an adult (Bagley and Thurston 1996), the 'gentler' seduction of the child by an adult who insidiously corrupts the adult-child relationship by psychological enmeshment of the child, causes the more severe long-term harm. But, relative to other forms of incestuous abuse, sexual assault by brothers imposed upon sisters is an understudied field (Rudd and Herzberger 1999).

Sexual abuse by 'other' adult relatives

Apart from siblings, fathers, stepfathers and cohabiters, the next other most common type of abuser in the family setting are uncles and grandfathers. Because of the 'emotional' distance from most children, emotional or physical neglect and abuse is uncommon; the imposition of sexual assault, however, usually involves the psychological manipulation of an emotionally vulnerable child. The research shows that these men's abuse is predominantly sexual, using 'accessible' children within the family (Simon et al. 1992; Fischer and McDonald 1998; Pritchard and Bagley 2000). Consider the following case example. It was first thought that the accusations involving sexual abuse against a 69-year-old grandfather might have reflected family feuding rather than actual abuse. In the man's police interview, his indignation, apparent outrage and moral abhorrence of such an act seemed completely genuine. However, when the police records were checked, it was clear that he had been sexually abusing children in his care over three generations!

It has been found also that foster mothers can emotionally and physically neglect and abuse the child, though retrospectively it is often found that such women have mental health problems which should have debarred them from becoming foster parents (Falkov 1996; Stroud 2001). Foster fathers have been known to sexually exploit the new child in their family – this more often happens when the child has been sexually abused in his or her own family, and has been taught to trade emotional warmth for sex. These findings underscore need for careful pre-fostering checks, as well as supportive education for prospective foster parents. Although the overwhelming majority of approved foster parents bring enormous benefits to needy children, nonetheless in a cohort study of a decade of child homicides it was found that 4 per cent of assailants were foster mothers, which is disproportionately high (Pritchard and Bagley 2001). Hence the 'sound byte' assertions of some politicians to make adoption and fostering assessments easier, demonstrates both their arrogance and ignorance of the field.

Parent abusers

The most damaging neglect and abuse of children occurs when the abuser is the parent or parent figure – so often physical neglect and abuse is wrapped in emotional cruelty, or emotional indifference to the child's developmental needs – the corruption and exploitation of a close relationship, the effects of which can be so long lasting and destructive (Kempe and Kempe 1978; Dubowitz et al. 2000; Ryan et al. 2000; DoH 2001).

Neglecting mothers

Mothers in our culture are still the most frequent neglecters, a reflection of the fact that even modern social structures still impose on mothers (including unsupported mothers) the main duties of child care. The younger the mother, the higher the rate of child neglect (Oliver 1985; Creighton 1992; Gillham et al. 1998; Lipman et al. 2001). This neglect reflects the way in which society sexualizes adolescence but denies adequate access to birth control and free and early terminations, and the failure to provide adequate social and economic supports for teenagers whose years of happy development have been robbed through a pregnancy whose implications they often barely understand. Too often such mothers come from families in which there have been few good models of adequate child care, and often a cycle of neglect may be repeating itself. These mothers may damage the child by omission rather than active animosity. However, a number of researchers have shown the relationship between a mother's damaged self-esteem and her inability to parent adequately, including women with low educational achievement to mothers with depression (Hawton et al. 1985; Oliver 1985; Brown et al. 1990; Read 1998; Stanley and Penhale 1999; DoH 2001; Lipman et al. 2001).

The typical young, often single-parent neglecting mother is like 'Cony', aged 17 at the birth of her first child; by the time she was 22 she had her fourth child. Her family background was littered with separated and warring parents and turbulent siblings, and many of her relatives were well known to all the community-based agencies. Whilst of average intelligence, she left school with a reading age of barely 12 years. She appeared overwhelmed by her physical and social circumstances. She smoked and drank heavily in an effort to lift her mood, which compounded her inability to manage her sparse finances. A series of live-in men added to the disorganization; sometimes after drinking binges she would forget where or with whom she had left the children. The fourth pregnancy was the final straw and she clearly could not manage, and badly physically neglected the children, and although she obviously loved them, she simply could not manage. It is important to note too that the children in families such as this are often prey to predatory paedophiles, who offer financial and emotional support to single mothers in order to gain sexual access to their children, which was discovered in a recent preventive project (Pritchard and Williams 2001). Even when there is no intention to sexually abuse children in such families, this can happen when a child has been sexualized by a previous cohabitee. Such men, themselves frequently products of violent and abusive childhoods have not bonded to the children of the woman's previous relationship. These men physically abuse and even kill these children with a much higher frequency than would be expected by chance (Reder and Duncan 1999) and as will be seen constitute the third highest of five categories of 'child killers' (Pritchard and Bagley 2001).

Consider a further case example, with a positive outcome to maintain the balance. 'Doreen' had emerged from her family relatively successfully, even though she had been exposed to neglect by her mentally ill mother, and sexual abuse by her stepfather. She was intelligent, had done well at school and made a very good marriage with 'the boy next door'. Unfortunately 'Doreen's' self-esteem was very fragile and she had a number of episodes of depression, during which she neglected her two children. A health visitor referral to an understanding GP and psychiatrist improved the situation, as her depression was treated with anti-depressants and long-term counselling support which she received from a psychiatric social worker. But crucially, the marital relationship was sound and the husband assisted his wife through the worst of the crises. The family remained intact and effectively reversed the neglect linked to 'Doreen's' depressive symptoms, ensuring that her children received adequate care for their developmental needs.

Neglecting fathers and father figures

Fathers of course play a vital role in the care of their children, but it is the quality of the relationship rather than absence or presence that is either a positive or negative influence upon the child (Dubowitz et al. 2000). Fathers or father figures can sometimes compensate for a potentially neglecting mother, or equally, compound and worsen the effects of earlier neglect, especially if they are stepfathers or cohabitees (Daly and Wilson 1991, 1994; Pritchard 1991; Temrin et al. 2000).

The majority of the research of 'father figure' roles in child neglect and abuse has centred mainly upon physical and/or sexual abuse. Nonetheless, an emotionally rejecting paternal figure can result in serious neglect, as seen in the following example.

'Eric' was a highly intelligent but severely physically disabled man, the father of six children. He had never been gainfully employed. His repressed anger about the disabilities appeared to be projected upon his children, especially his sons. His constant caustic belittling of them undermined their self-esteem. Moreover, he resented any of his wife's attention being given to the children, and caused their neglect by his constant demands upon her. His behaviour crossed the boundaries from verbal abuse to maltreatment, into a particularly undermining and vicious form of emotional abuse. The situation broke down when at the extreme, two adolescent sons were involved in suicidal behaviour. Intervention by psychiatric services enable the boys to escape from the poisoned home life into a residential educational setting. One of the reasons for 'Eric's' prolonged emotional cruelty to his sons, was that all the professionals failed to recognize, that despite being physically disabled, he was far more damaging emotionally than many who simply beat their children. The above example highlights the difficulty of separating emotional neglect from emotional abuse.

Abusing mothers

Typically, it is easy to overlook the fact that mothers are equally at risk of physically abusing their children, as the most cruel and rejecting father figure. Maternal abuse seems to centre upon the mother's cold, hostile perception of her child/children, and her expression of anger against them, often as a projection against her own negative psychosocial history (Gara et al. 2000; Kendler et al. 2000). Many mothers can be physically punitive and display overt violence, including the so-called 'shaken-baby' syndrome (Fulton 2000b), especially when her often desperate social circumstances are compounded by drug and alcohol misuse (Pritchard 1991; Browne and O'Connor 2000; Currie 2000; Rumm et al. 2000; Wall et al. 2000).

It is this generalized psychosocial chaos that is so characteristic of the family situation of mothers who cross the boundary from passive neglect and abuse into active emotional and physical abuse. Typically, their own childhood was disturbed, disturbing and disruptive, and they and their parents were and are known to virtually all the services, reminding us of Oliver's (1985) seminal study of 'five generations of mishandling of children'.

Consider the following case examples: 'Frankie' was a depressed young woman with a history of a neglected childhood by her own depressed mother. Her father was a strict religious man, who tyrannized 'Frankie' in a misguided effort to provide 'discipline', which her frequently depressed mother could (according to his martinet principles) not consistently provide. She was intelligent but failed to achieve her potential and dropped out of university.

She married a man considerably older than herself, who was powerless to protect the two children from severe emotional abuse in the name of 'spare the rod and spoil the child'. Although severe physical punishments were rare, as these were against her 'Christian' principles, she verbally terrorized the children with her cold threats of hell, and often locked them up in a darkened room. Their resulting enuresis, night fears, panicky screaming attacks at home and social timidity of children outside, was further proof to the mother of the 'work of the devil' in her children. The oldest daughter at 13, took a severe overdose and left a letter for her father, who then exposed the litany of the emotional abuse. The arrival of social services precipitated a serious suicide attempt by the mother, who went into a severe clinical depression.

'Gay' had spells in care as a child, being victim of physical abuse from both mother and a series of father figures. Sexually assaulted by an older stepbrother, this led to a further time in care. Whilst of average intelligence, she was an educational underachiever and became virtually unemployable, in part because of her inability to concentrate, her lack of social skills as much as her lack of formal knowledge. She left care before the implementation of the Children Act of 1989, and therefore at 16 was unsupported, and entered a series of disastrous short-term relationships, interspersed with periods as a sex worker. During this time she was heavily into drugs and alcohol, and was often a victim and perpetrator of violence, sometimes against other female sex workers. Moreover, she often 'attacked' herself following particular stress by self-mutilation with needles, scratching and cutting herself. Despite efforts of social services that dealt well with the crises, there was little preventive work. Consequently her home was little more than a dirty hovel, and she neglected and mistreated her five children aged between 3 and 9 years, by various partners.

Her only way to assert herself with the older three was to beat them. She was always remorseful after the event but all the children were removed, when in one of her rages she sent the 9-year-old into intensive care with a fractured skull, after knocking him down the multi-storey flat stairs. 'Gay' was a good example of an abusing mother, who nonetheless loved her children, making it hard for the services to intervene, for she always denied to herself that the only consistent element in her parenting was its erratic and extreme behaviour towards the children. The social work dilemma was that of needing to break affectional bonds between mother and children which remained despite her severe abuse of them.

In another remarkable case, 'Iris' was physically and emotionally abused by her mother (a sex worker) with numerous beatings and cigarette burns. Her mother's partner, with mother participating, would strip her naked and gag and blindfold her, and tie her to a bed. She would be raped and pictures taken of her. Her head was forced into a toilet and she nearly drowned. Her mother cut her throat with a butcher knife, not fatally, but in threat rather than in a deliberate attempt to kill. 'Iris' became pregnant at 12 and her mother performed an abortion with a coat-hanger. 'Iris' recalled the extreme pain of this procedure, but her worst memory was of the killing of a small dog she had befriended. Her stepfather took the dog by its tail and bashed the animal's head against the wall until its brains were spattered everywhere. As an adult 'Iris' never married, and her abiding good memory from child-hood was of the time she had spent with her grandmother, who genuinely loved her. These events took place in the 1950s, and neither the social ser-vices nor the schools (because of the family's mobility) were involved. 'Iris' was, not surprisingly, also subject to the most severe emotional abuse. As an adult she made frequent suicide attempts, but eventually settled with the aid of her female partner. Because of the severity of her earlier abuse 'Iris' never wanted to enter a heterosexual relationship, or to have children of her own. Her family of origin has many similarities to those 'multi-problem families' in which severe forms of all kinds of abuse coincide. The extreme epitome of the dysfunctional, abusive family, was illustrated by the West family in which multiple incest coexisted, with multiple forms of violence and murder.

Mothers are infrequently active figures in the sexual abuse of their child. When such abuse happens however, they appear to be much more likely than abusive fathers to have serious psychotic or personality disorders, or act in a state of fugue (Bagley and Thurston 1996; Harris et al. 2002). However, mothers in families in which a father or stepfather perpetrates sexual abuse are, paradoxically, much more likely to have been sexually abused in their own childhood. Yet often in practice one finds that in families in which incest was revealed, the mother (who is often subjected to physical brutality by her partner) was frequently unaware that her daughter was being sexually abused.

An important sub-group of mothers, is that in which older men have married young teenagers (including a number of single mothers) apparently offering them the chance to escape from their abusive family lives. In many such cases these men, closet paedophiles, cynically exploited the trust the woman had placed in them (Green et al. 1995) with the result that revelation often precipitated a mental health crisis for the mother. This is an important time for mental health services to support the mother, for her role is crucial in the therapy which her sexually abused daughter will require (Bagley and LeChance 2000). If a good enduring attachment exists between mother and daughter, the long-term harm wrought by sexual abuse can be minimized (Alexander and Schaeffer 1994). Incest victims who have had effective treatment will, when they are mothers themselves, be able to protect their own children from sexual assault (Kreklewetz and Piotrowski 1998).

Mothers still carrying the scars of their own childhood sexual abuse, especially when that is reflected in unstable relationships and substance misuse, are particularly likely to have daughters who are at risk from trauma-inducing sexual assaults (Paredes et al. 2001). When a mother disbelieves her daughter or fails to support her on revelation of sexual abuse, psychological outcomes for the daughter can be impaired (Elliott and Carnes 2001). In disorganized families there may be sexual abuse of daughters over three generations, each new generation of mothers being unable to protect or support her own abused child (Leifer at al. 2001).

Physical and emotional abuse by fathers and father figures

Most earlier research on abusive fathers centred upon physical and emotional abuse (Dubowitz et al. 2000) but there are crucial differences between birth, stepfathers and men in paternal roles such as cohabitees, surrounding the age of the child when the men enter the family situation, and the quality of the relationship (Cannon et al. 1998; Daly and Wilson 2000). For example with regard to physical abuse and its extremes, stepfathers and cohabitees were much more likely to severely beat the child, whereas the genetic father might use a weapon but were often found to be mentally disordered (Falkov 1996; Daly and Wilson 2000).

Consider: 'Harry' was 23 years old, the fourth cohabitee in the last six years of a women eight years older than himself. He exploited her physically and economically and gloried in the power over her four children. The oldest, an 11-year-old, he sent into hospital after the boy tried to fight back and protect his mother. 'Harry's' own turbulent background and general social inadequacy made him a particularly difficult man to deal with and the discovery that he had previous convictions for assault led to a successful prosecution, and led to some long-term support and refuge for the mother and her children.

'Ian' severely physically abused his two sons from his second marriage, aged 7 and 9 years, often on the classic Friday night alcoholic binge. His assaults frequently included his wife, who in part for self-protection, colluded with his escapist drinking. This was the second family he had physically abused. Typically, he was often remorseful after a particularly severe violent episode, seeking forgiveness from wife and the boys, explaining that his father had beaten him because he wanted to 'make a man of me'. Whilst the main precipitating problem was the abuse of alcohol, he became especially dangerous when mixing alcohol with drugs misuse, and unusually for his age (42), he often glue-sniffed. 'Ian's' drinking problems finally made him unemployable, and being at home more, increased the boys' exposure to his mounting, frustrated aggression. His obvious ambivalence confused both boys, who experienced the pull-push situation of children desperate for affection from someone who should have been able to meet their needs. The youngest boy's acute admission to hospital following his stepfather's assault, motivated the mother to accept social services help to exclude 'Ian' from the home. A subsequent successful prosecution led to an injunction which prevented 'Ian' from harassing the family.

The above examples of paternal abuse are relatively easy to deal with in child protection terms, as the evidence of bruises still assists the courts in separating the abuser from his victims. In terms of paternal child sexual abuse, this is often far more problematic.

Child sexual abuse: further considerations

Of all the actors in the wretched drama of child abuse, men in parental roles who sexually impose themselves on children have been the least studied. Not surprisingly they are an elusive group because they utilize the child's vulnerability, dependency, incomprehension, and the corrosion and corruption of making the child 'guilty' if they betrayed 'Daddy's/Uncle John's special secret' (Finkelhor 1994; Bagley and Thurston 1996; Fischer and McDonald 1998; Pritchard and Bagley 2000).

Here the focus is entirely upon intra-family sexual abuse, which involves at least a third of all men charged with a sexual offence against a child (Simon et al. 1992; Waterhouse et al. 1994; Bagley and Mallick 1999; Pritchard and Bagley 2000). Because in most cases a parent figure has seduced a child and forced him or her into a relationship bringing 'years of terrified silence', there are frequent and long-term negative effects upon the victim, which stem not so much from the sexual abuse itself, but from the emotional abuse and manipulation which accompanies the activity (Moeller et al. 1993; Famularo et al. 1994; Oates et al. 1998; Gara et al. 2000; Lipman et al. 2001; Pears and Capaldi 2001). It is readily acknowledged that much within-family sexual abuse is not reported in criminal statistics because of the difficulty of securing a conviction or from an attempt to 'spare' child victims from cross-examination (Brewer et al. 1997; Leventhal 1998; Grubin 1999; Wyatt et al. 1999; Pritchard and Bagley 2000). Another reason why child sexual abuse is only atypically reported, is that victims, cowed into silence, may endure such abuse over many years of childhood and adolescence (Somer and Szwarcberg 2001; Paine and Hansen 2002).

Adult recall studies of sexual abuse indicate that many children were made to feel guilty and ashamed, blaming themselves for the abuse which they were unable to reveal or get help in ending. Some sexual abuse with the family is brief and not involving penetration – this form of abuse is less likely to cause long-term psychological harm, especially when the victim has a warm and stable attachment to another adult in the family (Alexander and Schaeffer 1994), or a family with few overt conflicts (Meyerson et al. 2002). This can explain the paradox of some studies of sexual abuse – that many victims show no long-term psychological damage, except where sexual abuse overlaps with emotional or physical abuse (Rind et al. 1998; Wyatt et al. 1999). It is the corruption and exploitation of the relationship, which is so crucial in terms of long-term outcome.

At this point two important studies should be mentioned, which appear to have explained why consummated incest by biological fathers is relatively rare (involving less than 1 per cent of all fathers). Parker and Parker (1986) found that men who sexually assaulted their biological children were, compared to non-assaultive fathers, significantly more likely to have been absent during the child's early years. The study proposed that engaging in the tasks of changing, feeding and bathing early in the child's life allowed a special kind of bonding or attachment to form which acted as a profound, natural deterrent to sexual interest. This factor could explain why mothers so rarely sexually abuse their children. Williams and Finkelhor (1995) replicated this study using naval personnel – men drafted overseas soon after the birth of their child were, as predicted, significantly more likely to sexually abuse their children later on. Early child care duties proved to be the powerful antidote to the development of later sexual interest, but with an important exception for a sub-group: men who had themselves been sexually assaulted in childhood sometimes used their trusted position to 'groom' their child for later sexual assault. Stepfathers and cohabitees are usually introduced past the crucial stage of infancy, and this could explain the much higher rate of sexual assault at the hands of these men. It is possible that predatory paedophiles actually seek out lone parents in order to gain sexual access to their children, paralleling those men who cruise areas where they are most likely to meet disadvantaged, emotionally needy children, desperate for some affection, which they ruthlessly exploit.

These findings mesh neatly with biosocial explanations for incest avoidance, which prevails in the vast majority of families, especially in those in which the father figure is present from the child's infancy (Erickson 1993). A likely hormonal basis for the early devotion of fathers has been identified by Storey et al. (2000) – following the birth of their child, levels of testosterone fall markedly in fathers, and this correlates significantly with the degree to which the father is solicitous of his infant's welfare. This 'dotage' is the basis of bonding and close attachment of father to child, which in turn profoundly inhibits sexual interest in one's child.

There are a disproportionate number of stepfathers or cohabitees and 'uncles' who sexually offend, compared to the proportions amongst biological fathers, and adoptive fathers who have been present since the child's infancy (Leventhal 1998; Daly and Wilson 2000). Non-biological father figures who sexually abuse often have a history of non-sexual criminal behaviour, and evidence of socially disorganized lives (Simon et al. 1992; Fischer and McDonald 1998; Pritchard and Bagley 2000). It is stressed, however, that some biological fathers do sexually abuse their children, and this violation of the incest taboo is likely to have particularly harmful outcomes for the child victim, especially when the abuse is prolonged and penetrative. In such cases the father should be required, through criminal sanctions, to leave the family he has abused.

Many paternal-role sex abusers also physically and emotionally maltreat their children. When this is not the case this can complicate the decision about permanently separating the abuser from his victim, and there are advocates of family therapy who argue that keeping the family together – a family which contains a penitent father who has received a suspended sentence following his temporary separation from the family, in return for this co-operation – is a viable option (Larson and Maddock 1986; Bagley and LeChance 2000). In the systemic and humanistic treatment models (Giarretto 1982; Trepper and Barrett 1989; Sheinberg and Fraenkel 2000) the father is included in the treatment matrix, though often at a distance when his criminal conduct requires that he should be separated, albeit temporarily, from his family. For the victim to be able to forgive her abusive father, and for the father to penitently accept such forgiveness is an important stage in survivor therapy (Freedman and Enright 1996).

Consider the following case, which would have been a good candidate for the humanistic, family therapy approach: 'John' was a middle-class professional man, with no record of any anti-social behaviour. He was an only child of elderly parents, a shy, nervous child and adolescent, described as a 'loner'. He married an equally shy woman, when they were in their early 30s. Their relationship was always courteous, considerate but not passionate and their behaviour to each other was more of polite friendship. 'John', however, doted on his only daughter and almost welcomed the mother's 'mild' depression, giving him the opportunity for extra time with his daughter. On one of the mother's absences 'recuperating', he sexually seduced his 9-year-old daughter. Later, she recalled her pain, confusion and unhappiness, as the abuse continued regularly and lasted for six years. When discovered by the mother, 'John' made a serious attempt at suicide. At both the wife's and daughter's insistence, they promised not to take the matter further, providing the sexual abuse stopped. John made no further assaults, and social services and police were not informed at the time. But nearly 40 years later, the now adult daughter had an abnormal grief reaction at the death of her father, as her ambivalence and confusion re-emerged. Such a case poses all sorts of dilemmas, as the victims, wife and daughter, went to great lengths to protect 'John', who appeared to be able to give up his abuse, and resume his role as a normal, caring father. Society maintains an abhorrence of the crime of incest and it is often not difficult to persuade some fathers that their behaviour is profoundly wrong. The problem of the detection and deterrence of non-biological offenders, however, presents society with problems of a different dimension.

'Ken' is more typical of cases which reach the authorities. Aged 32, he had had a series of live-in relationships, often with vulnerable women and their children. 'Ken' was of low average intelligence not very competent socially, and always one of the first to be made redundant at times of economic turndown. He had a series of petty offences and was a local nuisance as a peeping tom. Three previous liaisons had ended when his partner discovered 'Ken' was routinely sexually abusing the daughters of the house, all under the age of 7 – he never involved older children, apparently fearing their better understanding of the unacceptability of his behaviour. The last offence led to an angry mother involving the police and 'Ken' was convicted for indecent assault. The angry mother of his last victim described him as 'pathetic', which was actually very accurate.

Along the continuum of dangerous was 'Len', aged 41 years, who had previous convictions and prison sentences for child abuse, both physical and sexual, as well as multiple criminal convictions including sex offences against adults, and personal violence. 'Len' was an abused child himself and was in care in the early 1970s, when he was permanently excluded from school – he was a bully and was bullied. Any relationship he entered ended in disaster as his infantile demands, allied with an almost pathological jealousy, often culminated in a serious physical assault. He had sexually assaulted both his natural daughters and two sons, repeating the behaviour in three other 'live-in' relationships. He terrorized his victims, and it was not until ten years had elapsed since his last conviction for child sexual abuse, that his physical assault and rape of a 'stepson' led to the 10-year-old's emergency admission to hospital. This alerted social services, who were able to find a refuge for the partner and her three children, who then felt confident enough to give evidence which sent 'Len' to prison for a lengthy period. This was clearly a case in which family reunification would never be an option.

'John' and 'Len' could not be more different extremes. Yet both were guilty of serious maltreatment and abuse of children in their care. 'John' had real affection and good intentions towards his daughter, which paradoxically, made the abuse more insidiously corrupting and damaging: but would a successful prosecution have helped the wife and daughter? It has been argued that while sexually abusive men should always be prosecuted, in certain cases, the sentence could be suspended if the man agrees to take part in therapy for himself and co-operates in victim therapy as well. This has shown that, in comparison with untreated control families, the model can be highly effective in healing victims and preventing further abuse (Bagley and LeChance 2000).

In contrast, 'Len' with his long history as a victim and then as a victimizer was a potential menace to any children in his care, and one wonders whether even lengthy treatment would make him safe to live with an access to children. He perhaps is a suitable case for a 'reviewable' (indeterminate) sentence, a position that will be debated later.

These men in father roles highlight the complexity of the situation, which demands highly individualistic responses to ensure that the child's best interests are served. Whilst there is evidence that 'treatment' can reduce re-offending in some types of abuser (Becket et al. 1994; Greenberg et al. 2000; Timmerman and Emmelkamp 2001; Maletzky and Steinhauser 2002), self-evidently primary prevention is better than intervention after the act of abuse. Furthermore, we need to be aware of the challenges posed to child protection services by disorganized families in which stable attachments between adults and children are rarely achieved, in which multiple forms of abuse and neglect occur (Oliver and Buchanan 1979), including the 'poly-incestuous families' which Faller (1991a) describes as 'surprisingly frequent' in child protection caseloads. These children in disrupted families can be abused by multiple perpetrators within disorganized family systems (Long and Jackson 1992). In these families abused children (who often experience multiple emotional trauma) are particularly likely to go on to be abusing adults (Faller 1989).

A linked problem is that of sex rings, in which children from disorganized, incestuous and otherwise abusive families are recruited by paedophiles into pseudo-families in which warmth, drugs and material favours are traded for sex – often too these sex rings, involving in some cases dozens of children, form the basis for recruitment into commercial sex work (Potter et al. 1999; Willis and Levy 2002; Siegel and Williams 2003). Tragically, there are cases where parent figures have taken the role of pimp and pander and 'groomed' their children for such terrible abuse. Based upon the research available, fortunately such activities are rare in within-family abuse, not so in the next group we explore, the extra-family abuser.

Notes

[1] One of us has argued from date on children experiencing seizures (which are often correlated with conduct disorders) there are pseudo-genetic effects in that families marginalized by a combination of poverty and inter-generational patterns of deviance also carry an excessive number of genes disposing them to seizure disorder (Bagley 1972). Children marked by seizure disorder can be singled out for specially negative treatment within the family in a 'spiraling down' process in which excessively punitive treatment leads to self-confirmed patterns of conduct disorder. These ideals received some confirmation from the work of Ounsted (1981) who has also argued that feotal growth in marginalized multi-problem families may be impaired, and is an aetiological factor in seizure disorders and later psychiatric problems. Ounsted illustrates his work with the case history of 'Granny Smith' whose multiple progeny had by the mid-1970s cost the state some £2 million in health care, social service and prison costs.

[2] Canada has, in theory at least, probably achieved a good balance in legal definitions of sexual abuse and age of consent, which is set at 14; 14- to 17-year-olds can have sexual relations with an older person of any age *except* when the older person is in a position of authority (for example a teacher) or is close kin, or offers a reward or bribe to achieve the sexual relationship. Sexual relations between children aged 12 to 13 are not illegal, but no person is allowed to have sexual relations with a child under the age of 12 (Wells 1989). In theory this law protects adolescents from exploitation in the child sex trade; in practice it does not (Bagley 1999; McIntyre 1999).

4   Extra-Family Abusers

Introduction

Perhaps the most common extra-family abusers of children are other children and adolescents in the form of emotional and physical bullying. Despite the frequent distress that bullied youngsters in most cultures feel (Pritchard and Williams 2001; Womgyaramannava et al. 2001), some of these older children and adolescents move on to become serious and often serial physical abusers, way outside the 'normal' range (Galli et al. 1999; Hagan et al. 2001). They can start both as physical bullies and then move on to sexual exploitation. Conversely, the *adult* extra-family physical abuser appears to be a relative rarity, and there are few reports in the research literature. He does exist however, and has been described in psychiatric diagnosis as suffering from *Sadistic Personality Disorder*. In extreme cases the cruelty and rage of such men is directed against both adults and children, with the assaults sometimes murderous, sometimes sexual and sometimes both (Berger et al. 1999).

Extra-family sex abusers

The extra-family abuser who causes the greatest concern is the sexual abuser, and high profile cases lead to short-lived, but recurrent, intensive media interest, sometimes described as 'moral panics' (Pearson 1988; Atmore 1999). Irrespective of whether these intermittent moral panics are justified (Pritchard 2002), they do mean that both the front-line social work and health practitioners and their managers have to make judgements in specific cases, within this very pressurized context. Because of this the importance of an evidence-based practice approach is stressed, to aid the practitioner make judgements about risk and types of danger to the child and family.

Extra-family sex abusers are a very heterogeneous group (Camargo 1997; Ridenour at al. 1997), but with considerable overlap between a range of offenders, both sexual, non-sexual and violent, reflecting the often disrupted, chaotic socially incompetent lives of convicted offenders (Briggs and Hawkins 1996; Ward et al. 1996; Pritchard and Bagley 2000, 2001; Soothill et al. 2000; Craissati et al. 2002).

There is some general agreement that about a third of men convicted of sexual offences against children, were themselves, victims of child abuse

(Simon et al. 1992; Briggs and Hawkins 1996; Haywood et al. 1996; Ward et al. 1996; Galli et al. 1999; Hunter and Figuredo 2000; Hagan et al. 2001; Craissati et al. 2002). However, it would be easy to be cynical and suggest that offenders are seeking to exonerate or excuse their behaviour in terms of their past trauma. What is certain, is that the earlier the abuse commences and the longer it lasts, the more likely the older child and adolescent themselves will become a future abuser (Galli et al. 1999; Hagan et al. 2001). However, in Briggs and Hawkins's study (1996) of incarcerated child molesters, matched with equally socio-economically deprived non-offenders, they found a remarkable rate of abuse of all kinds in the childhoods of those who later offended against children. Both groups (later offenders and non-offending controls) found the 'one-off' sexual abuse by a stranger unremarkable and non-damaging, whereas the hurt and later distress and dysfunction was associated with long-term abuse carried out within the confines of a relationship (Briggs and Hawkins 1996).

This leads us to a consideration of the small number of women (relative to the number of men) who sexually abuse children. On the one hand, all known female offenders were involved with children they knew (Green and Kaplan 1994; Lewis and Stanley 2000); but often the boys and young adolescents involved did not feel victimized (Briggs and Hawkins 1996). In the few studies of women convicted of sex offences, all came from distressing backgrounds with multiple forms of abuse (Green and Kaplan 1994; Lewis and Stanley 2000). This seems to reflect the lifelong vulnerability that such young women experience, as Pritchard and Butler (2000b) found in five-year cohorts of adolescents who had been in care and who were far more frequently victims of crime in their adulthood – theft, physical violence and sexual assault – than were the general population. In part this may have been associated with their poorer socio-economic circumstances, as the less-well-off are far more often victims of crime from their neighbours, than their more affluent fellow-citizens (Cox 2001). But it was the rate of being victims of sex crimes in young adulthood that was so striking amongst this most socially excluded group of young people, namely former child-in-care and the permanently excluded-from-school adolescent (Pritchard and Butler 2000b). This high rate of victimization was equally true for the males in the five-year samples, reinforcing the notion, if it requires re-enforcing, that the cycle of deprivation does not end in childhood, but is perpetuated into adulthood and gives a further twist to the cycle of deprivation into the next generation (Farrington 1995; Graham and Bowling 1995; Lyon et al. 1996; Audit Commission 1998; Social Exclusion Unit 2000; Pritchard 2001). Not surprisingly, adolescents who have moved from being victims to perpetrators, are significantly more pessimistic and have poorer family support than their peers (Hunter and Figuredo 2000). But it is reiterated, the earlier a child or adolescent is involved with other children sexually, the more likely are they to remain in this mode and become abusers as older adolescents and young adults (Vizard et al. 1996; Galli et al. 1999; Hunter and Figuredo 2000; Hagan et al. 2001). This is exactly the same pattern for all crime (Farrington 1995; Rutter and Smith 1998). Indeed, the Home Office's recent prediction of re-offending test is crucially based upon the age of which the offender was first convicted (Home Office 2000).

Adult male child sex abusers

Focusing now upon adult male child sex abusers, what is known about their 'psychology'? Despite a proportion being a previous victim, male adult child abusers have comparatively poorer empathy with their victims than do non-sexual criminals (Haywood and Grossman 1994; Fisher et al. 1999). Indeed, they often have a marked denial about both the reality of their crimes and any possible damage to their victims, not infrequently claiming that the victim was in part responsible for what occurred (Fisher et al. 1999; Wright and Schneider 1999). This latter aspect can make direct work with such men very frustrating for the professionals who seek their rehabilitation.

With respect of those who use violence in furtherance of their sexual assaults, Smallbone and Milne's (2000) study suggested that this was not part of the gratification of the abuser, rather an instrument to achieve their aims. Yet studies which have compared child molesters with other criminals, in particular, rapists and violent but non-sexual offenders have not found it so clear-cut. Child sex offenders and rapists have been found to be more in-troverted than violent offenders (Gudjonsson and Sigurdsson 2000), but their use of alcohol is similar to that of rapists and violent offenders (Aromaki and Lindman 2001).

One other area of comparability with non-sexual offenders is the pattern of recidivism. Whilst non-sexual criminals may be re-convicted earlier than sex offenders, over a 15–30 year period, there is a convergence of rates. Within the first two years in one British study, re-convictions were less than 7 per cent for sex offenders and 40 per cent for non-sex criminals; but later it was in excess of 60 per cent and 80 per cent respectively (Hanson and Bussiere 1998). Moreover, the type of crimes committed remain broadly the same, so that adult petty criminals do not become violent criminals; and the adult patterns of sex offending remain the same, that is, either non-violent sex offences or violent sex offences occur, but predominately without overlap (Haywood et al. 1996; Hanson and Bussiere 1998; Pritchard and Bagley 2000, 2001; West 2000). Thus the non-violent sex offender is generally non-violent over time, whereas the violent offender, continues to be violent in his pursuit of his aims, well into his later years. This is an important finding when trying to make judgements about risk and danger.

Another finding with practical implication is the 'sexual orientation' of child abusers. Unlike the media stereotype of gay men being more likely to be abusers of children, for both within-family and extra-family abusers, 75 per cent of the men are exclusively involved with females. Around 14 per cent are involved with both boys and girls, and 11 per cent exclusively with boys (Simon et al. 1992; Cantor and Kirby 1995; Fisher and McDonald 1998; Pritchard and Bagley 2000). All that can be said with confidence is that child sex abuse is predominately, a heterosexual activity.

Crucially, there is evidence that can differentiate between broad types of child sex abuser, based upon their actual behaviour. Three distinct patterns were found, which held true for both within-family and extra-family abusers in a two-year cohort of all men charged with a sex offence against a child, screened from a population of known offenders within a general population of 1.2 million men 'at risk' (Pritchard and Bagley 2000).

Within the cohort, 374 men, half of the men were exclusively 'sex-only' offenders, that is, they had no other convictions except for sexual offences against children and young people, right across the age ranges. The remainder had other convictions for non-sex crimes, for example theft, burglary, criminal damage, and often many motoring offences. Indeed these 'Multi-Criminal' offenders had far more non-sexual convictions, than offences against children. However, this 'Multi-Criminal' group could be further categorized between the offenders who had no history of violence and those who in addition to their 'Multi-Criminal' convictions, added violence to their portfolio. These were designated the 'Violent-Multi-Criminal' child sex offender, and their activity ranged through theft, burglary, to robbery, possession of offensive weapons, and violence against the person. Of interest was that a number of men in this latter group had earlier contact with the police concerning cruelty against animals. These 'Multi-Criminal' violent child sex offenders are a group who merit later exploration.

Three other important researches, one British, two from the USA, showed that the cohorts studies could also be differentiated between sex-only offenders and multi-criminal offenders (Simon et al. 1992; Cantor and Kirby 1995; Fischer and McDonald 1998).

The importance of this division is that the best indicator of the types of crime a person will commit are those he/she has already committed, and this is true for sex offenders as it is for other types of offender (Cantor and Kirby 1995; Craissati et al. 1996; Hanson and Bussiere 1998; Greenberg et al. 2000). Thus past convictions are a key criteria in determining future risk and danger.

Finally, in view of the interest in 'attachment', an interesting study by Ward et al. (1996) measured attachment across a control group of non-offenders, child molesters, rapists, violent non-sex offenders and non-violent-non-sexual offenders. Whilst all the four offender groups had insecure attachment, there was a similarity between the rapists and the violent non-sex offenders; but the child molesters and the 'ordinary' criminals had somewhat more normal attachment styles than the other two groups.

But how is this research reflected in practice and the handling of actual cases? In an effort to show the continuum of physical danger, the following typical case examples are offered to illustrate the point. Paradoxically, the first are a group of people who probably never come to the attention of the child protection service, namely those men who whilst having a sexual attraction to children, have sufficient psychosocial and moral resilience never to offend, and consciously elect celibacy. Why is this relevant in a chapter on extra-family abusers? One problem for men who might well seek help to contain their attraction to children, is that they also live in the context of public outrage against sex abusers, and are reluctant or simply frightened to seek advice. This means that a group of men who are perhaps at the threshold of offending who could seek a most important element of treatment, namely accepting their problem and voluntarily wishing to change, are deterred from seeking the help which would ensure their 'celibacy', as far as children are concerned. So, within the continuum of extra-family abusers, the practical question is: what if anything, should we do about men when it is learned they fantasize about sex with children, but, as far as we know, do not act on these impulses?

Others are clearly unable to control their impulses of fantasies – some way along the continuum was 'Michael' aged 15. He was a frustrated neighbourhood rowdy, frequently excluded from school. He was a bully, and the list of his aggressive acts made very unpleasant reading, especially for his child victims and the householders whose property he damaged, and the teachers whom he tried to dominate. He came to police attention when a parent complained that he had sexually fondled their 9-year-old daughter. Social services argued against his exclusion from school, after it was discovered that he himself had a history of physical and sexual abuse by transient father figures, who took advantage of his mentally ill mother. It transpired that despite 'Michael's' disruptive behaviour, he was the only relatively stable person in a family of three. With the co-operation of the family of the girl and the police, charges were not pressed and 'Michael' started intensive treatment involving cognitive behaviour therapy. After a year his progress was such that he stayed on at school achieving decent GCSE results, the bullying ended and there was no more inappropriate and sexually exploitive behaviour.

The more typical extra-family sex abuser is like 45-year-old 'Oliver'. He had been sexually offending against little girls for years, either exposing himself, and/or genitally fondling them, at the 'extreme' getting them to masturbate him. He may have had as many as 50 to a 100 contacts a year, almost invariably with different children aged between 5 and 10 years old. 'Oliver' virtually never became emotionally involved with his victims, which meant that the incident might well be less traumatic than the whole panoply of the medico-forensic legal process, which was rarely invoked. Nothing is known about 'Oliver's' history other than often, if he was involved in an adult relationship sexually or emotionally, he was not very successful in maintaining that relationship. Moreover, on at least three occasions, adults had discovered his abuse in the park toilets and he bore the scars of his beating, but never reported them to the police.

The 'twin' of 'Oliver' in terms of behaviour and the continuum of dangerousness is 'Peter' who is another psychologically, sexually and socially incompetent man, who was also involved in petty crime. The 'Peters' and 'Olivers' make up the bulk of the *known* extra-family sexual offenders. In terms of assessing 'dangerous', the evidence on these men is that like general criminals, they maintain the pattern of their offences, and if there was no overt violence early on in their sad 'careers', it is highly unlikely, to occur as they grow older (Hanson and Bussiere 1998; Gudjonsson and Sigurdsson 2000; West 2000).

In no way is the behaviour of 'Oliver' and 'Peter' being minimized, rather trying to put this into a better comparative perspective. The real damage comes when an ongoing relationship with the victim is established, and there is emotional manipulation as well as sexual assault, but this is not the usual *modus vivendi* of such men. However, some men do prey on children who are emotionally vulnerable because of weak attachments to care figures in their own families. Unequivocally, all child sex abuse and exploitation is a crime and should be dealt with accordingly. Having said this, then in the classic equitable tradition of British justice, each case should be judged on its merits, crucially always taking the best interests of the child as paramount.

The continuum of dangerousness

'Ray's' case was brought to my attention, in the interim between him receiving assessment for alleged sexual abuse of 14- and 15-year-old boys, and going to trial. 'Ray' was in his mid-50s, a mild mannered, educated, professional man, who was active in his Church's youth programme. He denied any wrong-doing,

> How could I? I am a Christian. I have a calling, and if 'paedophile' means a lover of children, then I and Jesus stand condemned ... I understand these lads. In their distress and confusion, they misunderstood their feelings for me ... I was probably one of the few people to show them an affection ... if anything they fancied me ... when I showed them that I was not interested, they probably felt rejected ... but they're worldly wise ... I'm not blaming them,

they've had to learn the hard way ... they got into a temper, they made this all up and hoped to earn a few quid ... but there's no other word for this but this was a set-up, a 'shake-down' I think the Americans call it ... the whole thing is a pack of lies ... but I've already forgiven them ... I'll take them back into the club and will forget all about it.

'Ray' was very persuasive and nearly all were virtually convinced by him. However, in liaison with the police, it was discovered that this was 'Ray's' third charge, and he had been to prison for serious sexual assault against boys when he was 24 years old. In prison he 'found God' and on release moved cities, found a church and quickly moved into youth work. This pattern was repeated 12 years later, and after serving another sentence, he changed his name and moved to a new area, a new church and new youth group. The psychiatric assessment unit did not avail themselves of the police data since they did not wish to compromise their 'independence', and their 'client focussed' orientation. When evidence of prior conviction was revealed to 'Ray', his counsel advised the fullest co-operation with the police, which avoided the need for the new victims to have to give evidence in court.

There are serious ethical issues here, for without due process of law there is an increased likelihood of victims' complaints being ignored or downplayed (Marshall et al. 1997) and 'miscarriages' of justice, both against victims and alleged offenders can occur. Yet as will be discussed later, in practice this 'equitable' legal rights approach is not without its difficulties.

'Shadow Men'

Undoubtedly, the best child protection practice, is not only multi-disciplinary and collaborative (DoH 1991, 1995, 2001), but is also evidence-based. Even though empirical research does not have all the answers, it is still the safest way to proceed, both in the interests of the child and in terms of human rights and 'natural justice'. However, in the murky field of child sexual abuse, there are traces of other men who do not fit any the patterns so far described. I am a little anxious about highlighting them, but these predators do leave a trace of their existence.

These are apparently socially well-integrated men, who frequent and exploit child sex workers. The extent of such behaviours crosses national frontiers and cultures and recent research shows that trafficking in young women in particular, involves such shadowy people as the village head man or relatives of the girl victim who are in effect abducted from their Nepal villages and taken into India and Bangaldesh and sold into the de facto sex slave trade (Simkhanda 2003). Sadly this direct economic exploitation of children and adolescents as sex workers, appears to involve virtually every country in the world (Willis and Levy 2002). My first trace of these 'shadow men' came from research which examined detailed police records on sexual offenders (Cox and Pritchard 1997; Pritchard and Cox 1997). It was noted that not only did a significant minority of the offenders have contact with each other, either as 'known associates' or continued contacts after prison, but had also been observed as passengers in up-market cars, registered to some surprisingly eminent people. The suspicion, and it could not be more than that, was that people like 'Peter' and other men we have yet to meet, were acting as pimps for these economically successful men. These apparent 'contacts' were drawn to the attention of the police, and in one case this led to a successful prosecution against a businessman who was exploiting adolescent sex workers.

The other evidence on the 'shadow men' – the world of eminent men who sexually abuse young boys procured for them by the men who 'own' these boys – is more controversial, but what is in the public domain we can share. I gave evidence to the North Wales public inquiry [chaired by Sir Frank Waterhouse] into the sexual abuse of children in children's homes. For sound legal reasons Sir Frank did not lift 'reporting restrictions' on the inquiry, although *The Independent* newspaper said that some of the names mentioned were 'well known public supporters of Mrs Thatcher'. But these names remained under the protection of the law – on the solid grounds that an uncorroborated accusation is tantamount to defamation – hence no prosecutions have ever been mounted against these prominent individuals, to the chagrin of the investigative reporters.

What of the victims – the vulnerable boys shamelessly pimped, and then used by men who knew they came from children's homes? It was found that subsequently, the young men who had been in the four children's homes and who were known sexual abuse victims, had a suicide and violent death rate far in excess of the general population for their age group, 15–24-year-olds (Pritchard 1998). These were mainly an excess of suicides, and remarkably, two murders. It transpired that a number of the sexually abused boys in the homes had become sex workers, in a de facto brothel for upper-class clients. Some of these young men gave evidence to the Waterhouse inquiry, but in a number of instances their accounts appeared to lack credibility and crucially, corroboration. Some of these young men's lifestyles, which included drugs, sex working, crime and so on could easily be considered as compensation seeking, a reaction to extreme trauma. However, the former Assistant Chief Constable of East Sussex, speaking on regional television about two of the young men who had been murdered, confirmed their backgrounds but was frank that he had no idea as to the motive for the crimes. That these young men had been silenced because of what they knew remains an ominous possibility. Self-evidently, child sexual abuse by strangers, will almost always be practised in the shadows, which means that we will only be able to adumbrate those who emerge from the darkness, and become part of a data base which can be evaluated.

Because much child sexual abuse takes place in the shadows, panic and hysteria when some cases are revealed do sometimes feed excessive public concern (especially when the media feed public hysteria), with over defensive child protection practice including the unnecessary removal of children into care. Fortunately, at the extreme only rarely does sexual assault result in a dead child. Many more children are killed on our roads than are murdered by people outside the family (Pritchard 2002; WHO 2003). But consider the following case.

'Steve' was 32, from a turbulent background of family disruption, abuse, neglect and educational failure with disruptive behaviour from primary school onwards, turning to active petty crime in his early teens. His lack of most basic educational or social skills, made him virtually unemployable and with his local reputation from the first he was on the margins of society, and had no steady relationship. His offences were mainly property related and by his late teens he already had three spells in custody, similar to a number of his male relatives, his father and two previous 'stepfathers'. He preyed sexually upon young girls aged 11–14 years, and learned those children with in-adequate supervision, from disadvantaged and deprived backgrounds, were the most vulnerable. Classically he 'groomed' the girl, finding as much ex-citement in the 'chase' as in the indecent assaults which followed. This in-cluded giving them attention, which they found flattering from an apparent adult, with overt enticement with presents, moving to direct fondling, and then inducement to fellatio and to full sexual intercourse. He drank heavily and used alcohol as bait for impressionable girls, sexually abusing his in-toxicated victim. That this was his version of 'consensual' sex.

On two occasions he had introduced his 'girlfriends' to making porno-graphic videos, shared with other abusing associates, and also began pimping these young girls. His chaotic lifestyle and general social incompetence matched his inability to relate to women, and resulted in his exploitative use of young girls. He had intermittently attended a treatment unit for his sexual abuse but failed to complete the programme, and his third appearance at the Crown Court led to an eight-year sentence. A key element in the efforts to treat 'Steve' was that not only had he became aversive to adult women, but he also denied he was an offender because 'they liked it, they liked me ... I never hurt one of them'. He showed a total lack of understanding or empathy for his victims; the only positive factor was that on discovery he confessed to the assaults, which helped the victims avoid the often-associated stigma of people who live in relatively small communities in attending court.

In a remarkable but sickening documentary the BBC, in conjunction with the specialist paedophile unit at New Scotland Yard followed a long investigation of a paedophile ring and a Mr Levine in particular (BBC2 2002). He can be named as remarkably he actively collaborated in the programme. He personified the total denial of the paedophile. He had previous convictions and the police had reason to believe he was active in a ring focusing upon young girls. Levine's self-justification was breathtaking in that he asserted that he was being persecuted 'because he loved children', whereas the Law and the BBC were afraid to pursue physical abusers who damaged children, namely in respect to female circumcision, because they were 'afraid of the religious groups'. Whilst he certainly had a point about female circumcision, which is behaviour we should not accept in the name of multiculturalism, he totally denied that the girls with whom he was involved were damaged in anyway. Any viewer who could stomach his performance must have thought 'a brick wall', so closed was his inability to see his criminal behaviour from his victims' point of view. The police traced a niece whom he had persistently abused over a number of years and she could both demonstrate and testify to the damage he had done to her. Professionals are trained to avoid vindictive responses, but Levine's closed mind would make any viewer despair, and endorse the police's view that with his record he merited a life sentence. Against expectations, despite the harrowing evidence of his niece, he received a six-year sentence, certainly not a result that would markedly impact upon his complete self-justification of giving loveless children love. To the best of my knowledge, such intransigence means that he is unlikely to benefit, let alone, accept treatment whilst imprisoned.

Finally, let us turn to a case which whilst representative of a certain type of abuser is fortunately relatively quite rare, although the damage such men create can be enormous.

'Tom' was 24 years old, from a chaotic family background which included most forms of abuse, and considerable violence. In his later teens he involved young children in the pursuit of his sexual abuse and this led to him being permanently excluded from school.

It is established, that adolescents excluded from school are amongst the most socially outcast (Pritchard and Butler 2000a; Social Inclusion Unit 2000), and there are little or no preventive services available to them until they commit a significant crime. 'Tom' had become a dangerous, vicious bully to anyone who crossed him in his community, and he intimidated many people, including some of his fellow property offenders. By his mid-20s he had already had three spells in prison for offences including bodily harm, robbery and received an extension to his prison sentence for a severe and unprovoked attack on another inmate. His criminal record, at first sight, would appear typical of those dangerous 'personality disorder' offenders, whose disruptive and disrupted lives are associated with serious, long-term criminality. His three short-term, live-in relationships had ended with domestic violence. There were two rape charges concerning young women, but both were withdrawn because of possible intimidation, as well as two charges of gross indecency against a boy and a girl.

Following a violent argument with his last female adult contact, on a mixture of drugs and drink he waylaid a 13-year-old boy and because the lad refused to co-operate, raped and then beat him so severely he needed intensive care. Indeed, the boy might have died since 'Tom' left him unconscious. While few would doubt he merited the long sentence he received, in view of what is known about the sequels of educational alienation in young people (Farrington 1995; Pritchard and Butler 2000a, 2000b; Pritchard 2001; Pritchard and Williams 2001), to some extent the lack of an adequate preventive service to address such vulnerable people when they are children and adolescents, means that society in its inadequate provisions for delinquents in the early stage of their careers, inadvertently 'colludes' with such a 'sowing of dragon's' teeth.

'Tom' did not kill, but at the extremes of child abuse, children die, but those who do are analysed in the next chapter.

Conclusions

The world of the extra-family abuser involves a set of activities usually conducted in the shadows. Only the grossest forms of sexual assault, carried out in disorganized neighbourhoods by very aggressive and disturbed individuals come to the immediate notice of authorities. The most successful child sex abusers hide behind pimps or computer screens, leaving an obscure trail that is difficult for the authorities to follow.

Research on men convicted of sexual offences involving children identifies three distinct types of extra-familial abusers. First are the 'career paedophiles' whose lives are dedicated to the covert sexual pursuit of children and adolescents. Some men with these deviant sexual desires are able to control themselves, but many cannot.

The best predictor of an offence of the 'serial paedophile' type is a previous conviction. Either these men are very difficult to treat, or treatments available are largely ineffective. The second type of offender is a man with a history of many non-sexual offences, with sexual assaults upon a child of either sex carried out almost casually as part of a pattern of personality disorganization. The third type of offender who are considered in more detail in the next chapter, is a man with a history of non-sexual violence who also applies this violence in sexual assaults against both adults and children. However, before turning to the extremes, it is necessary to explore a number of those problematic issues associated with child protection and medicine.

5 Some Special Problems for Child Protection Teams

Introduction

One of the perennial problems confronting practitioners in the child protection field is that amongst its many complexities, child abuse is related to a number of other shadowy syndromes, which cross agencies' boundaries. In part they have become 'issues' by the coincident publicity of high profile cases, for example the 'shaken baby' syndrome, or the confusions that can surround the unexpected death of a child, the so-called 'sudden infant death syndrome'. The somewhat schematic brief outlines of eight such problems are offered based upon the current available research. First, however, is the problem of definition, for the definition of a problem determines the particular agency that will deal with the problem.

(1) What is a paedophile, and how many are there?

Although the term paedophile is widely used, there are some disagreements on its definition (Bagley and Thurston 1996). This is partly because the age of legal consent for sexual intercourse varies quite widely between different countries, and different states – 14 in Canada, 16 in Britain and 18 in some US States for example. In Canadian law a 14-year-old may freely have sexual relations with someone of any age provided that the other person does not use force or threat, reward of inducement (as in a prostitute-client relationship), or does not misuse a position of authority to achieve that relationship (for example a caretaker, teacher or biological relative) (Wells 1989). Prendergast (1993) along with other American writers uses the term *hebophile* to define those (almost always men) whose sexual focus is on adolescents who have achieved some level of sexual maturity – a paedophile in this definition is someone whose interest is on sexually immature individuals.

Some men have fixated interests, preferring children of a certain age and sex – which Prendergast (1993) thinks, may reflect the age at which they themselves were abused. But this is by no means universal, as some individuals have strong sexual orientation to children and young people of all ages and genders, as well as to adult sexual partners. Such men can present themselves as 'normal' to investigators in terms of phallometric (a measure of physiological arousal when presented with 'deviant' sexual images), and psychological profiling.

There is a traditional typological distinction between regressed and fixated offenders. The fixated offender is likely to be primarily interested in boys, will not (usually) have married, is not a homosexual in the sense of having an adult partner or adult sexual outlets, and often devotes himself with obsession, to finding boys (and sometimes girls) for sexual purposes. Such men have in the past infiltrated child care institutions, youth clubs and religious orders, and it is only in the recent past that vocal victims of institutional and institutionalized abuse have emerged, and the offenders prosecuted (Franks 1997).

The regressed offender is likely to be a man who tries, with marginal success to maintain adult heterosexual relationships, but finds sexual relations with children easier in terms of the interpersonal relationships involved. Stress factors, including marital stress, may precipitate the onset of sexual offending involving minors (both boys and girls). The regressed offender may become fixated in his deviant sexual preferences over the course of time.

The regressed-fixated dichotomy is by no means exclusive, and there is a third important category, that of sociopathic offenders whose sexual offending against children is part of a casual pattern of cruelty in a generally disorganized criminal life (Pritchard and Bagley 2000). A Home Office study (Home Office 2000) of some 9000 male offenders found that around 9 per cent of *all* criminals fall into this category of violent offender, attacking men and women (and occasionally children) in physically and sexually violent ways, in addition to a chronic pattern of offences involving drugs, property and robbery with violence. This, unfortunately, is by no means the end of categorizing offenders, and there are many who sexually assault children who defy categorization, except that they often offend against incest taboos and sexual assault biologically related children (DeMause 1991). But, as we argued earlier, biological fathers who have been present since the child's birth, and conform to the modern norm of being involved in childcare roles are particularly *unlikely* to be incest offenders.

How many men have a history of sexual offending against minors? Since most cases do not come to the notice of authorities (Waterhouse et al. 1995) this figure is impossible to determine with accuracy. An additional problem in counting individual offenders is that because a fixated offender may assault literally dozens of children over a lifetime, we cannot generalize accurately from the number of known offences to the number of estimated offenders. Because of the difficulty in knowing the actual number of offenders, studies estimating offending potential are important. In a study of 750 Canadian males aged 18 to 27, randomly sampled from the population of Calgary, information was gathered about their sexual interests. The men entered their responses, anonymously, on a laptop computer – a technique known to be successful at eliciting statements about 'deviant' sexual behaviours (Turner 1998).

Twenty men (2.7 per cent) said they were currently interested in sexual relations with a female pre-adolescent (aged less than 13), and 14 (1.9 per cent) declared a sexual interest in a pre-adolescent male. An overlapping 22 individuals (3.2 per cent) had sexual interest in a male aged 13 to 15. This was in contrast to the number of men (63 individuals, or 8.4 per cent) who were interested in having sexual contact with an adolescent female aged 13 to 15. Having elicited sexual abuse history and current psychological profiles, the motivation of this latter group was described as stemming *not* from any developmental factor or any overt psychological dysfunction, but rather from the general norms of sexism prevalent in western society. It appears that it is 'OK' for a young man aged between 18 and 27 to try and 'make it' or make sexual suggestions with any young, teenaged girls (Bagley et al. 2001). Perhaps this should not surprise people, when, on the one hand they see virtually every product advertised on television, can be sexualized, and on the other, increasingly children are dressed as miniature young adults, as boundaries are eroded in a world of moral relativism and the cult of 'whatever turns you on'.

It must be stressed that the above figures relate to sexual interest, and not to sexual contacts as such. Nonetheless in this survey five men (0.7 per cent) admitted to having sexual contacts (since their 18th birthday) with a female under 13, and a non-overlapping four individuals (0.5 per cent) admitted sexual contacts with males in this age range. Another 43 men (5.7 per cent) admitted at least sexual touching involving a female aged 13 to 15, while 14 men (1.9 per cent) acknowledged sexual contact (when they were young adults aged 18 or more) with adolescent males aged 13 to 15.

This survey asked in addition, why the men with a sexual interest in minors had not acted on these interests or impulses. An average of about one-third of those with various sexual interests in minors responded that 'I've had no opportunity'; about a half said that 'It's just fantasy, I would never do it'; an overlapping third said that they would feel guilty if they fulfilled these deviant sexual desires; another, overlapping group, about 50 per cent of those with such desires were inhibited by fear of being found out; but, ominously some 15 per cent responded affirmatively to the question 'I have someone in mind – I will have sex with them when I can.' Given the fact that the 750 respondents in this survey were relatively young (18 to 27) it is likely that the sexual offending career of a small but important minority is only just beginning. Given the size of this sample, it was estimated that up to 5 per cent of Canadian males will have contact sexual relations with someone aged under 13 at sometime in their lives. These figures are compatible with findings from parallel 'adult recall' studies which show that some 12 per cent of females, and 6 per cent of males experienced long-term, unwanted sexual contacts up to age 15 (Briere and Runtz 1989).

(2) Munchausen Syndrome by Proxy (MSBP)

A controversial, complicated and challenging category is that of 'Munchausen Syndrome By Proxy' (MSBP) first described by Dr Roy Meadow (1977). It concerns situations where carers (95 per cent of them mothers) present the child as having a seriously acute but apparently unusual medical condition (Meadow 1994; Guillaume et al. 1999; Hall et al. 2000; Meadow 2002b). Whilst it is relatively rare, only 18 reported cases per annum being reported in New Zealand (Denny et al. 2001) and about 50 a year in the UK (Meadow 1994) it has been reported from 24 different countries (Feldman and Brown 2002), is often baffling, and can often create inter-disciplinary tension (Neale et al. 1991; Meadow 2002b). Because it is clandestine and concealed abuse in which a carer produces symptoms of illness in a child, its prevalence could be much more widespread than the cases known to child abuse specialists. Moreover, it has particularly serious morbidity and can even be fatal (Bools et al. 1993, 1994; Meadow 1994; Denny et al. 2001; Griffiths 2001; Tessa et al. 2001).

From the outset, however, Meadow (1977, 1994) stressed the heterogeneity of the 'syndrome', which with hindsight might have been better named, since Meadow borrowed the category from adult psychiatry, namely 'Munchausen Syndrome' which is an established although not common adult psychiatric condition described throughout the Western world in which the patient imagines or simulates signs of physical illness (Oepen 2001; Philpot 2001; Weihrauch et al. 2001).

The original name was derived from an extravagant nineteenth-century storyteller, Baron Von Munchausen. The term was coined to describe people who made extraordinary claims about themselves, often involving a false medical condition, invariably with unusual, extreme albeit vague symptoms, which progressively became more dramatic, and which could also involve serious self-mutilation (Oepen 2001; Philpot 2001; Weihrauch et al. 2001). Currently it is categorized amongst the contentious 'personality disorders', though recently there is evidence suggesting neurological factors associated with the condition (Oepen 2001).

Munchausen's Syndrome, is defined in the International Classification of Diseases (ICD10) which comments that:

> The imitation of pain may be so convincing that repeated investigation and operations are performed at different hospitals, all invariably yielding negative findings ... The motivation ... is almost always obscure ... a condition best interpreted as a *disorder of illness*

behaviour and the sick role. Individuals ... usually show other marked abnormalities of personality and relationships.

(WHO 1992: 223)

Meadow (1977) used the concept to describe a series of parents who presented their children as seriously ill to the extent that the children had unnecessary medical investigations. Often it later emerged that the symptoms had been fabricated or caused by the parent themselves (Bools et al. 1994; Meadow 1994; Steele et al. 1999; Al-Lamki 2000; Fulton 2000a). Indeed, sometimes the parents go to greater and greater lengths to convince increasingly sceptical paediatricians that there is something wrong, by inflicting serious physical damage upon their child (Hall et al. 2000; Griffiths et al. 2001; Tessa et al. 2001).

In an effort to gain some idea of the epidemiology of MSBP, McClure et al. (1996) reviewed all cases in Ireland referred to a paediatric surveillance unit over a two-year period. There were 128 cases, of which 55 appeared to be MSBP. The children were mainly under 5s, the mean being 20 months, and 85 per cent of the perpetrators were mothers. Sixty-eight children suffered severe illness and eight died. If we extrapolate from McClure's, to compare with other categories of assailants known to physically damage children (Pritchard and Bagley 2001), and compare them to official estimates of the percentages of these groups in the general population, we can calculate the rate of child fatality for each assailant group.

It would appear that in terms of comparative dangerousness, whilst undoubtedly rare, MSBP parents have proportionately the *highest* child fatality rate amongst known categories of assailants. The extremes of child abuse resulting in child death, will be discussed more fully in a later chapter.

Table 5.1 shows that the most reliable estimates of the rates of the various categories of child homicide assailants, the possible MSBP parent is more than seven times more fatal to their child than is the next highest category of extra-familial male multi-criminal and violent child sex abuser.

Recently the Royal College of Paediatricians and Child Health (DoH 2002) recommended that the syndrome be re-categorized as 'Fabricated Illness Induced by Carers' (FIIC) as being more accurate, being specifically descriptive rather than suggesting a psychiatric syndrome per se. However, as this term is not as yet generally used in the literature, I will continue with the label MSBP. Nonetheless, ongoing research into mothers who have killed children, found that apart from the women who had obvious psychotic breakdowns at the time of the serious injury or killing of their child, a significant number fitted the MSBP or FIIC category (Stroud 2003).

Crucially for practitioners, MSBP parents often continue to deny their guilt, or later when accepting what they had done, manifest a severe depression, with suicidal ideation, or even a psychotic breakdown. Such a

Table 5.1   Estimated Child Fatality with MSBP Parents with Other Assailant Groups

Category of assailant	Estimated % in general population	Child fatality rates per 100,000 [pht]
Mentally ill mother *	2.9%	10 pht
Male with previous violent conviction *	0.9%	44 pht
Mother on 'At Risk of Abuse' register [with cohabitee] *	0.7%	83 pht
Male multi-criminal-violent child sex abuser *	0.05%	869 pht
MSBP parents #	0.008%	6,250 pht

Estimate based on age-related female/male population in Ireland (WHO 2003). Data from Pritchard and Bagley (2001)* and McClure et al. (1996)#.

scenario fitted a well-publicized British case, in which a mother was convicted of smothering two of her children at different times, within six months of their birth. Both the Judge and the investigating police officer, expressed concern that whilst the conviction for murder was correct, the mandatory life sentence was inappropriate for the woman. However, she had refused a psychiatric opinion, denying any wrongdoing. Similar controversy surrounds another case in which a woman was convicted of killing her two children, who were originally thought to have been 'cot deaths' (Meadow 2002a).

There is some suggestion then, that MSBP could be linked to 'Sudden Infant Death Syndrome' (SIDS), in a small minority of these tragic cases (Steele et al. 1999). But while there is no doubt the rate of SIDS has increased dramatically in the western world (Pritchard and Hayes 1993), it would be dangerous and indeed cruel to suggest that the overlap of SIDS and MSBP is large. The issue of SIDS is discussed below. Some have argued that MSBP evolves out of unrecognized and untreated post-partum depression (Gojer and Berman 2000), which would fit many of those cases identified in a cohort of mothers who have killed their children (Stroud 2003).

The following case illustrates the complexities of MSBP, and the challenges, which such a case can have for child protection services. 'Mrs G.' was childless, and she and her husband had an infant placed with them for adoption. Soon after the adoption was finalized, the child was admitted to hospital with acute diarrhoea, with an initial rapid recovery. On second admission hospital staff became suspicious and covert observation by a concealed camera showed the mother administering adult laxatives to the child. Confronted, the mother was hysterical and then acutely depressed, denying all memory of her actions. Social services sought to remove the child, but a Family Court held that since the mother had undergone therapy (she had been abused in her own childhood) and with her husband's support was now a caring mother, the child should stay with her.

This case illustrates the complexities and dilemmas which social and medical services face in cases such as this, as well as the fact that some parents harm their children in subtle but serious ways in a state of fugue, or dissociation – dissociation which can reflect their own abusive childhood. This appeared to be the case in a 22-year-old woman convicted in 1998 in Oxford of subjecting her infant daughter to severe burns. The defence that she was suffering from MSBP was entered, and the prosecution accepted that the personality-disordered woman had burned the child without any consciousness of what she was doing.

A study by Southall et al. (1997) illustrates the dilemmas in this field when he and colleagues covertly videotaped 39 children and their parents in hospital, following suspected MSBP. Not surprisingly, the use of 'covert surveillance' in hospital settings is very controversial (Tenney et al. 1994; Samuels and Southall 1999). Nonetheless in the Southall and Samuels study it was found that one or both parents were subsequently charged with assaulting the child in 33 of the 39 cases. More worryingly, and reflecting the McClure et al. (1996) study, a further eight children who were siblings of the 39 probands, were thought to have possibly been fatally suffocated by a parent. Similar to McClure, children in these families were also poisoned with disinfectants, or fed their parent's anti-convulsants: of the children's 41 siblings, 11 had died of apparent 'cot death' or SIDS, a diagnosis which was now in doubt. But, as the Foundation for the Study of Infant Cot Deaths said of these results, it would be grossly unfair to presume that many SIDS cases put a parent under suspicion (Ward 1997).

The complexity of investigating and drawing inferences in alleged cases of MSBP is illustrated by Adshead et al. (2000) who also used covert video surveillance (in a hospital situation) of 15 English women suspected of smothering their babies. Although a third of the mothers interacted in a hostile way, a third largely ignored their child, and a third displayed normal maternal behaviours. Not surprisingly, it is very difficult for the child protection services to act preventatively because so often there is only limited information available, and of course the last thing anyone wants is to add to innocent parents' anxieties about their sick child.

I was consulted about a case in a northern metropolitan city which highlights the legal, ethical and moral tightrope practitioners and their managers walk daily. Mrs ZZ was a member of an ethnic minority group. Her husband had died following a violent assault. The following year, her 10-year-old daughter apparently committed suicide. On reflection, it was realized that since the death of her husband, Mrs ZZ's behaviour had deteriorated, with some quite bizarre episodes. However, she fitted no clear diagnostic category, and in exploring the events surrounding her daughter's death there were elements of MSBP that caused anxiety. She had seen a psychiatrist who gave a mixed diagnosis of depression and personality disorder. Seeing a psychiatrist was a partial response to Mrs ZZ's conflict with the local housing department in which accusations were made about racial harassment. This obscured the fact that there was an almost invisible 12-year-old son; that Mrs ZZ had shown some fugue-like behaviour and had expressed transient suicidal ideas; that she was facing a double bereavement – for what greater nightmare is there than a child pre-deceasing its parent, apparently by its own hand? Moreover, Mrs ZZ had just given birth to a new baby. Her attitude to 'authority' was hostile and she was very resistant to any overtures from most services. At a case conference in which police, education, housing, community health, the GP, mental health and child protection services all expressed concerned interest, the problem was under which auspices could support be offered? The legal and ethical complexities were profound. Were either of the children, the son and the new baby, at risk, or was mother at risk because of her unclear mental health? Statistically, Mrs ZZ's situation, a murder and a suicide, was extremely rare, but if mishandled, any offer of support could be seen as intrusive and might make the situation worse. But the mother, and therefore her children, were clearly vulnerable, and if something amiss occurred and the multi-disciplinary services had not intervened, they would be hugely criticized.

(3) Sudden-Infant-Death-Syndrome (SIDS) and child abuse

Another problematic area is the issue of Sudden-Infant-Death-Syndrome, the so-called 'cot death' phenomena, which could in a small but crucial minority of cases (less than 5 per cent of SIDS deaths) reflect extreme neglect or abuse (Reece 1993). In brief, this occurs where a baby or infant, usually under 8 months old, though up to 18 months, suddenly dies without any apparent cause. The syndrome is now recognized in the International Classification of Disease, though not all Western countries report such deaths under this category, but continue to use the ICD8 categories of 'death from unknown or ill-defined causes', or 'undetermined deaths' (WHO 2003). However, deaths from this supposed syndrome have increased markedly between 1974 and 1990, in virtually every Western country (Pritchard and Hayes 1993), which is in direct contrast to the more than halving of baby and infant deaths from all other causes over the same period (WHO 1979–2001, 2003). While there has been some reduction over the past five or more years, in most Western countries there are more SIDS deaths than there are stillbirths (Sullivan and Barlow 2001).

From the mid-1980s some authors began to ask the question: was SIDS in a small minority of cases, a form of 'hidden child abuse'? Initial results found an over-representation of SIDS amongst families in poverty (Nam et al. 1990).

However, despite the continuing concern and speculation as to the possible 'social' cause of some SIDS deaths, one consistent finding remains, namely the association of SIDS with parents who smoke, which in turn is associated with people from the disadvantaged socio-economic groups (McGlashan 1989; Guildes et al. 2001; Kellen 2001; Wisborg et al. 2001). Undoubtedly accurate diagnosis of such deaths can be problematic, especially in the USA where there is an apparent under-assessment of child abuse as a cause of mortality (Herman-Giddens et al. 1999; Overpeck et al. 1999). The UK, however, probably has one of the most reliable systems for determining 'unexpected deaths' (WHO 2003), though there is a need for a specialist paediatric pathologist, who is not always available (Gould 2001). Confounding variables of socio-economic factors – particularly the association of SIDS with poverty-related variables – produce anxiety amongst professionals (Beggs 2001; Bennedsen et al. 2001; Guildes et al. 2001). For example it has been argued that 'SIDS doesn't exist' because on closer forensic examination there is usually a clear underlying cause for the death of the child, causes which include problems of nutrition, accidental poisoning, parental smoking, and co-sleeping with a parent as well as deliberate and malign actions by some very small minority of parents (Sawaguchi and Nishida 2001). This argument carries some weight because the association with smoking by parent(s) may account for more than 30 per cent of SIDS related deaths (Kallen 2001; Wisborg et al. 2001). Other supposed causes range from sleeping arrangements, under-lying genetic abnormalities, febrile seizures, pyloric and other infections, and congenital CNS, heart or lung malformations (Beggs 2001; Bennedsen et al. 2001; Flick et al. 2001; Franciosi 2001; Gessner et al. 2001; Kairys et al. 2001; Luft 2001; Ratclif-Schaub et al. 2001; Toomey 2001). SIDS may also reflect an infantile form of panic attacks, which creates acute stress to babies with inherent weakness (Sullivan and Barlow 2001).

At the other extreme, however, it has been found that some deaths initially assumed to be SIDS were in fact homicide (Stanton et al. 2001; Meadow 2002a) and there have been calls to determine whether some apparent SIDS are not the result of child abuse (Committee on Child Abuse and Neglect 1997; Maloney et al. 2000; Mehanni et al. 2000; Stroud 2001; Meadow 2002a). Interestingly, there is reassuring evidence that SIDS is not related to the UK immunization programme – indeed, immunized babies are marginally less likely to be part of an unexpected death cohort (Fleming et al. 2001).

There are some helpful signs distinguishing SIDS from child abuse fatalities (Abbott 2001; Kairys et al. 2001). It is suggested that the key differentiation between the majority of 'genuine' parents of SIDS babies and possible neglecters or abusers is that the former go to every length to co-operate with authorities, desperately seeking to understand and know what happened. This is problematic, however, for one can imagine a parent of a SIDS baby, feeling guilty, and if they previously had poor experiences with those in authority, their response may be more to do with fearing accusation, than trying to hide an abusive or neglecting act. Nonetheless, it is important to explore these dilemmas, for there does appear to be a possible overlap between infanticide and SIDS, and it is necessary to ensure current or future children's safety. When the infant of a mother suffering post-partum depression suddenly dies, child protection workers have to move very delicately to avoid acute distress to a woman whose 'closed' emotional response reflects her depression, made more acute by her child's death, rather than by her alleged or actual guilt (Stanton et al. 2001).

Yet there seems to be no disagreement that when faced with a sudden infant death, the professionals involved must respond to the parents with understanding, tact and sympathy, for in all probability the parents would be doubly damaged by an ill-founded accusation in the face of grief (Committee on Child Abuse and Neglect 1997; Kairys et al. 2001).

Consider the case of 'Mrs Angela Cannings', a cause célèbre in Britain, who was convicted in 2002 of murdering her third child. This followed two other apparent SIDS deaths over the previous five years, both of her children dying around 6 months old. Police returned to the case and exhumed both bodies. The woman may have killed her children during the acute phase of post-natal depression, which occurred after each of her pregnancies. There is now fear that in prison the woman (and women like her) will present as a major suicide risk (Kairys et al. 2001; Stroud 2001).

Consider too the case of 'Mrs Smith', who was referred for an atypical depression following an SIDS death of her 5-month-old. Police and social services were under enormous pressure to vigorously investigate, due to a recent high profile media case of an unequivocal abuse-related homicide of a 10-month-old baby. In the first three treatment sessions 'Mrs Smith' remained 'frozen' and there was clear indications of suicidal thinking. But when the breakthrough came, her grief was overwhelmed by the horror that 'they thought I'd murder "Anne". They thought I had killed my own baby'.

Her body was wracked by a grief-stricken sobbing which was distressing to behold and unforgettable. Moreover, in spite of the quasi-adversarial role of both police and social services, she and her husband had made every effort to co-operate, seeking to learn if 'it was something we did or didn't do'. Part of the therapy involved bringing 'Mrs Smith' to meet the two main investigators, who without external pressures were able to acknowledge 'Mrs Smith's' innocence.

The complexity surrounding 'cot deaths' has been highlighted by two major 'cause célèbre' cases. The first when Mrs Sally Clarke, a solicitor, had her original conviction overturned after serving two years in prison, when the Court of Appeal said that statistical evidence had inadvertently misled the jury, in effect inferring that 'to have lost one baby is unfortunate but to have lost two is careless [in other words, murder]'. The media's response to Mrs

Sally Clarke's acquittal was to reverse their original hostile epithets, to 'blaming' the experts. This was repeated when Mrs Trupti Patel was resoundingly found not guilty within 90 minutes of the jury retiring following a case lasting six weeks. Now the media were in full cry against 'experts' in a case 'that should never have been brought'. Indeed, the Patel's family nightmare can hardly be imagined and I recalled the deep, deep hurt of 'Mrs Smith's' unnecessary and sad depressive grief. Never has the need for in-depth evidence-based practice been more needed, for imagine the media's response, if child protection were to miss a case of multiple child homicide. I was involved in giving two interviews to TV, 'to have it in the can when the verdict is reached', both sought to explain why (a) a mother might kill or (b) what a false accusation might do to the family and how could it come about. It is very easy to become cynical about the media.

On the other hand, the matrix of social disadvantage, poverty and family disorganization, which can surround unexplained infant deaths, is strikingly illustrated by Oliver's (1983) study of 147 English families (in a small area of Wiltshire in which Oliver worked as a psychiatrist). Over two generations the 560 children born to these families (in which at least one member had a psychiatric diagnosis) were studied: 32 (5.7 per cent) of these children died in the first year of life, a death rate several thousand times the national average. Causes of death included smothering, inhaled vomit, malnutrition, gastroenteritis of unknown cause, bronchopneumonia due to lack of care, brain injuries due to hitting and shaking, and various unknown and unexplained causes including SIDS. Oliver was struck by how marginal medical and social services had been in the lives of these dead children, and inquests were rarely held. Prosecutions for what in Oliver's opinion were *prima facie* cases of unlawful killing were rare. He comments: 'Dead and discarded children disappear from record as if they had never existed ... [fortunate ones were abandoned into the care system] ... In particular dead or damaged children became erased by these mothers, especially if they were only half siblings of surviving children' (Oliver 1983: 117).

In further reports on these families Oliver (1985) observed that surviving children are particularly likely to suffer emotional, physical and sexual abuse: not the hidden abuse of the 'ordinary' family, but blatant abuse and sexual exploitation within extended, interbred families. Oliver reported that the few successful outcomes he encountered involved a child being removed at birth and placed for adoption – a solution also considered by the French writer Bonnet (1993). Truly, these sub-cultures of families experiencing and presenting with 'multiple problems' exist in all developed cultures. In cities they live in the most deprived areas of housing, and re-housing policies have created corners of 'sink estates' in which such families mix with one another, beget each other's children, and assist in their abuse and exploitation. Identification of such clusters of troubled families calls for vigorous programmes of community intervention.

(4) 'Shaken Baby Syndrome'

Another 'new syndrome' in part identified by the media, is the so-called 'Shaken Baby Syndrome' – but Oliver (1975) had identified severe brain injury resulting from shaking the infant, in his early Wiltshire series. The syndrome has acquired recent prominence from a number of high profile cases in which a baby, often under 9-months-old, has been brought to a hospital emergency room by a carer often without external signs of injury to the child. The symptoms and 'explanations' of the child's condition given by the carer are often vague, but include 'unaccountable' drowsiness, or failure to respond, and floppy body posture. On examination, there would be a range of soft neurological signs, ranging from slight dysfunction to increasing partial or full paralysis. There would often be visual disturbance, stemming from retinal haemorrhage (Dashti et al. 1999; Fulton 2000b; McCabe and Donahue 2000; Sakamoto et al. 2000).

Crucially for medical and social care services, the more obvious physical signs associated with physical child abuse are often not present. 'Explanations' of the baby falling, or being found in an odd sleeping position and somehow straining themselves against a cot side, along with the age of the baby, gave no immediate clue to what might have happened. What seems to occur in these cases is that the carer, exasperated by the baby's behaviour, holds the child firmly and shakes it violently. This can result in the unsupported head swinging around and creating a dangerous centrifugal force. The resulting damage can range from a temporary parasethesia, to subdural haemorrhage with a range of symptoms stemming from pressure on the different structures of the brain, including visual disturbances. Nearly a third of cases lead to death (Dashti et al. 1999; McCabe and Donahue 2000). The problem for the authorities is that rarely are there witnesses, and providing the assailant 'sticks to their story' of not knowing, it proves extremely difficult for courts to decide responsibility.

However, an important study by Dashti et al. (1999), reviewing two years of children's head injuries often including visual disturbances, found a distinct pattern of an excess of shaken babies aged under 2-year-olds, particularly associated with infants and babies coming from lower socio-economic group families. They urge that whenever a child under 2 is found to have head injuries, no matter how slight, the possibility of abuse should always be investigated.

Generally, however, the use of the term 'Shaken Baby Syndrome' is not very helpful, other than to describe how the baby or infant came by their injuries; the term may be a distraction from looking at the family situation as a whole. Furthermore, it is not a new phenomenon, but rather reflects greater awareness by the medical and child protection services, so that such tragedies probably happened ten and more years ago, but were not recognized as abuse. Nonetheless the situation produces yet another conundrum. When babies, infants and small children are brought for medical help for apparently inexplicable injuries or symptoms, they should have the benefit of family support, not least as a preventive measure. This needs to be sensitively done, first to avoid adding further distress to parents of an injured child, and to avoid frightening parents or carers from bringing their injured child for the speediest possible medical help.

The raised profile of the problem of 'shaken baby' deaths is reflected in recent international conferences in Britain and the USA, and the establishment of the National Center on Shaken Baby Syndrome in Utah. Wheeler (2002), a British forensic expert has made a 'best guess' on the basis of police information data that up to 200 infants a year in Britain are either killed or seriously injured through being shaken excessively. The most likely offender in this study was a non-family caretaker, who was not biologically related to the child; although stressed single parents are also known to have shaken their infant child excessively.

(5) 'Injuries' and 'accidents' – problems of child abuse and neglect?

Bull et al. (2001) analysing national US data point to the number of apparently accidental falls from windows, roof tops and balconies, killing several hundred children a year. These falls are particularly likely to occur in families marked by poverty and interpersonal disorganization, and the question arises whether neglect taking the form of failure to supervise children properly, children being pushed by other children, and actual fatal child abuse might be involved in some or indeed in many of these cases. Oliver's (1985) English series although not living in high-rise apartments, show a similar pattern of excessive 'accidental' deaths. Hobbs (1984) in Leeds studied 60 children under 2-years-old admitted to hospital with skull fractures following alleged 'accidents'. A careful psychosocial investigation established that 29 of these children had not experienced accidents, but had been hit on the head (or dropped) by caretakers – 20 of these children died, a much higher death rate than in the true accidental cases. In the non-accidental cases the fractures tended to be diffuse, with individual fractures covering a greater area of the skull. The families of these seriously abused children appeared to resemble the multiple-abusive families in Oliver's series. Hobbs (1986) also studied burns and scalds of children in Leeds, and found that a quarter of scalds were non-accidental, compared with 44 per cent of burns. The patterning of scald injuries can help identify the likelihood of abuse (Hobbs and Wynne 1994).

However, a major form of neglect leading to more than a thousand child deaths a year (nearly five times the rate of direct child homicide) is that in which children are killed in or by motor vehicles (Pritchard 2002), yet the large majority of road killings of children are preventable. These are not child abuse deaths per se, but deaths due to lack of supervision in parts of the city where children are separated from school and play spaces by heavy traffic flows. Yet, while it may be considered an invidious comparison, in the USA, annually more children die on their roads and are homicide victims, than the 3074 tragic innocent victims killed in the World Trade Center on 11 September (Pritchard and Butler 2003), and the children victims are more likely to come from the socio-economically disadvantaged, a feature found throughout the Western world (Pritchard 1991; Judge and Benzeval 1993; Zunzungegi et al. 1997; Feletti et al. 1998; Gillham et al. 1998; Sanders et al. 1999; Vock et al. 1999; Pears and Capaldi 2001).

A pattern begins to emerge of depressed families, economically poor, often socially disorganized, whose child care activities are curtailed to the point of neglect, and are sometimes marked by frank abuse. Some of these parents are likely to hit and shake their young children, and are more likely to leave them unsupervised at home or out of doors. Predatory paedophiles patrol such neighbourhoods, and when children are known to have been sexually abused by strangers, the community reaction can be one of extreme externalization, denying their own faults in collective hysteria, attacking instead the homes of the alleged 'pedos'. The public riots in depressed council estates in Portsmouth, Bristol and elsewhere (de Bruxelles 1998) are cases in point.

An additional question must be raised: why have depressed areas of the city – the 'sink estates' – and the wretched conditions of family poverty in Britain, been allowed to perpetuate themselves? This is the fault of all citizens, including ourselves, who are part of an 'institutionalized' class system.

(6) Memories of sexual abuse – real and imagined?

The French writer Marcel Proust had a sudden revelation of his childhood, remembering great details of very early events, a memory triggered by a fragrance suddenly encountered in adult life. The resulting autobiographical account, *Remembrance of Things Past* (1922), informed Proust's literary philosophy in which he defines the artist's premier aesthetic task as that of releasing the creative energies of a hitherto undiscovered unconscious memory. This leads to clinical questions: can memories of child abuse be suppressed and hidden? And what, if anything, should social and health care practitioners do in relation to these released memories? Conversely, can some memories be induced, that is, are there 'false' memories?

Consider the following case example, a first-person account of a woman responding to a national survey:

> Even though I am no longer a child or youth (I am 40), I would like to report sexual abuse as a child. The first rape occurred when I think I was approximately 18 months old. I was too little to speak and tell my mother. A second rape occurred when I was between two and three. From three to age seven, I was raped routinely, especially in the summer when I could not be kept in the house. The rapist was my father. Until age 36, I had no memory of my childhood. Growing up on a farm, I had assumed until then it had been a happy one. I knew my father as a good man, religious and a leader in our small community. When he died, freeing within me the terror and the rage against him, I started experiencing serious problems towards men. If any man showed any interest, I would 'freeze up', be paralysed inside and unable to move or speak.

This woman had never consulted a therapist, and certainly her memories of abuse were not induced by 'planted' memories. It was a matter of coincidence that, contacted in a random sample survey she volunteered these details. In several adult recall studies (screening several thousand adults for any memories of child sexual abuse) one can encounter several cases of this type. In a British study of 20 young adults who were known to have suffered severe, prolonged sexual abuse in childhood, when interviewed in their 20s at least half had, apparently, only the vaguest memories of their childhood, and no memory whatever of sexual abuse.

There is no doubt from this and other evidence, that prolonged and severe trauma which physical and sexual abuse often involves, can create memory loss in some victims. In extreme cases, victims dissociate from the abuse experience to the extent that it does become buried, accessible only in traumatic dreams and waking nightmares, and psychological states known as post-traumatic stress disorder which involve sudden flashbacks to previous trauma which the victim is unable to believe or integrate with an ongoing, stable ego. But it is also abundantly clear that over-involved, overly directive and highly anxious therapists and group settings can *induce* in individuals with symptoms of neurosis the idea that the origin of their neurosis lies in sexual abuse imposed by a parent, abuse which they have forgotten – *abuse which did not in fact occur*.

This emerges clearly from the authoritative 750-page monograph by Prendergast (1993). It is clear from the case material cited by Prendergast, including women who have sorrowfully retracted accusations against innocent parents, that memories of abuse can be induced, and indeed in a climate of 'therapeutic hysteria' often are induced. This contentious issue will not be discussed in detail other than to quote Prendergast's final paragraph:

> It will do no good to demonise recovered memory therapists in the same way that many of them have encouraged the demonisation of parents. There can be no doubt that the therapeutic community must be held *primarily responsible* for promoting this disastrous and misguided form of 'therapy'. Ultimately, however, no one *intended* harm – not the therapists, not the children, and certainly not the parents. You were all caught up in a very unfortunate, destructive phenomenon, and you need to acknowledge it, talk about it, and then get on with your lives, leaving judgmental hatred behind.
>
> (Prendergast 1993: 640) – italics in original

Shades of Arthur Miller's *The Crucible*, a play evoking seventeenth-century witchcraft trials, but which can be far exceeded by modern media's longer research.

A different kind of motivation for false allegations of sexual abuse comes when alleged victims are offered substantial cash payments from the criminal injuries compensation scheme in Britain, especially when police 'trawl' individuals who were resident in particular child care institutions sometimes years before (Webster 1998); or when substantial sums can be obtained from civil suits against institutions such as the church. Another type of distorted or false evidence can come from substantial payments by newspapers to alleged victims in high profile cases (Bowcott 2002). The case of the acquitted British premier league soccer club manager is a case in point (Craissati et al. 2002). Despite these cases, it is clear that some paedophiles have obtained positions of trust in childcare and educational settings, and have cruelly abused those in their care (Utting 1997), as seen in the minority of children's homes in the North Wales inquiry.

Another vexed area concerns battles for child custody and access following marital breakdown. While the discovery of sexual abuse can precipitate marriage breakdown, there have been a spate of cases leading to largely unsuccessful litigation in which sexual assault has been alleged by a mother after the marriage has already failed (Faller 1991a). The courts have in general not looked favourably at such allegations, though I suspect colleagues will have also found in cases of marital disharmony, both parents are likely to accuse the other either of being 'psychiatric' or a potential abuser, adding to the social worker's and counsellor's dilemmas.

(7) Dissociation following child sexual abuse

The mental mechanism of dissociation was at one time controversial, but its reality as a long-term sequel of childhood sexual abuse and other early trauma is now reasonably well established (Putnam 1997). Dissociation occurs when bodily invasion is painful, traumatic and prolonged – the trauma could be a series of painful medical procedures, or could be various kinds of physical and sexual assault. The child focuses on something outside of themselves and goes into a trance-like state in dissociating themselves from the current pain and trauma. In some individuals this dissociation becomes part of a personality system in which although the earlier trauma is not forgotten completely the individual sometimes goes into fugue states in which current actions are hardly remembered. A legacy of dissociative identity states is disturbed dreaming, anxiety, depression and post-traumatic stress syndrome (Briere 1989). Sometimes traumatic events are recreated in these fugue states and the adult may abuse their own child with no recollection of having done so. This applies, *inter alia*, to cases of MSBP. Mothers (and fathers) who abuse their child deserve a full psychosocial investigation of the possibilities of trauma in their own lives – 'healing' must apply to both victims and perpetrators, which contributes to increasingly effective child protection.

(8) Satanic abuse and moral panics

It has been asserted that conspiracies exist by which groups of evil men and women procure children (often through day care centres) for extreme acts of child mutilation, murder and sexual abuse. Concerned citizens and professionals believing that such evil conspiracies exist act to remove children from parents and arrest teachers, childcare workers and others who have had contact with the allegedly molested children. Such stories litter Western history, but invariably, it describes an 'out-group', so it might be Jews, or Albegnesians, or Knight Templar 'heretics', and so forth, who kill Christian children and drink their blood. Satanic abuse stories seem to stem from 'moral panics' about sexual abusers in the community. Wild allegations are made, but ultimately not a single case involving organized, ritual and satanic abuse has ever come to prosecution. When police undertake a careful investigation seeking evidence, none is found. Proponents of the satanic abuse case counter-argue that children whose births have never been registered are killed in satanic masses; and local undertakers and police chiefs are part of the conspiracy by which satanic abuse is concealed. And a conspiracy theory, like jealousy, 'feeds upon itself'.

In Britain Fontaine (1998) undertook a careful examination of alleged cases of satanic and ritual abuse for the Department of Health. As in earlier Dutch and US studies, not a shred of evidence for the various allegations was found. What was clear was that the alleged child victims had been interviewed by anxious adults, asking leading questions, which elicited what the inves-   tigators wished to hear. On careful investigation, however, none of the cases could be substantiated, and what had occurred was the modern version of the ancient witch-hunts.

If, and the 'if' is reiterated, ritual abuse does occur, it has a casual nature in disorganized families in which children are haphazardly used sexually by adults in families isolated from the norms and values of the rest of society (Oliver 1988). Sex rings exist too, but these are usually organized by paedophiles recruiting older children from disorganized families into pseudo-family groups in which sex between children and with adults is routinely practised, often in a group setting, which are often avenues of recruitment into prostitution and pornography (Arnaldo 2001). For a more recent review of this fraught topic, readers might well explore Sara Scott's book (2001), *The Politics of Experience of Ritual Abuse*, as she explores the problems and pitfalls of taking the concerns of an individual seriously and not adding to the panic which 'feeds upon itself'.

Child abuse is a highly topical issue which the media and politicians pontificate about, often over-simplifying the complexities. Clearly it is a major societal issue and a MORI poll in October 2002, found more people concerned about child abuse than the crisis with Saddam Hussein (*Guardian* 2002).

With such a disparate range of issues surrounding child neglect and abuse and an over-defensive professional response to irresponsible media sensationalism, not surprisingly, front-line staff find this a very challenging field, albeit rewarding, when they effectively intervene to reduce damage to children and help to break the vicious cycle. Let us now turn to a feature associated with child neglect and abuse that the media and many politicians prefer not to consider, it is so much easier to blame child protection staff.

(9) Disorders of Adult Personality and Behaviour: Personality Disorders

For many in social work, the psychiatric concept of 'Personality Disorders', or 'Psychopath' or 'Sociopath' will be controversial, not least because, such concepts are based on normative factors, which of course are largely culturally specific, unlike other 'medical' concepts such as pneumonia or diabetes, which are corporal and universal. Yet, a close reading of Noyes (1991), who reviewed a series of child abuse disasters, would to the open-minded suggest that there are people, who abuse children, sometimes with particular cruelty and violence, whose persistent pattern of behaviour fits what Western psychiatry describes as 'Disorders of Personality'. However, let it be said at the outset, the problem I have with the concept is 'personality disorder' as a disease process, which it is not, but it will be argued that it is an invaluable concept in the child protection field if it is seen as a persistent pattern of behaviour, probably mainly 'learned', and/or superimposed upon a biological predisposition. Back to the 'nurture AND nature' interaction, rather than the sterile 'nurture versus nature' debate.

The *International Classification of Diseases* (ICD) – an evidence-based diagnostic manual – is not perfect, but as yet, the best we have, defines people whose persistent behavioural patterns and characteristic lifestyles impact adversely upon others and their own lives. Crucially, the ICD acknowledges the origins of 'personality disorders' are interactive, that is, learned and genetic predisposition. Some of these patterns occur very early in the development of the child, discernible in childhood in fact, and appear to be 'a result of both constitutional factors and social experiences, while others are acquired later in life' (WHO 1992: PF60–62, p. 200). They are essentially defined by behaviour and the person's response to other people. This infers a set of social values against which the person's behaviour is being assessed, which has been acknowledged by psychiatrists since the 1970s and the ICD itself can be problematic as it can inadvertently create the impression of a too rigid set of categories (Claire 1976; WHO 1992). Indeed, it is this social dimension which makes the concept of personality disorder so very different from the major mental disorders, which although they might be seen as an extreme variation of psychic experience, the functional psychoses clearly result in behaviour which is internationally recognized as abnormal. But let us explore the psychiatric perspective, before further comment.

A key factor in understanding 'personality disorders' is that by the ICD definition, there are two broad categories, first those who were assessed as problematic from early childhood, inferring a constitutional as well as a social interaction, and the second group who develop the problematic behaviour as teenagers or young adults. In effect, this suggests that some personality disordered people were born with such a susceptibility, which was reinforced by their life experience, and the others, who developed the patterned behaviour, were more influenced by environment than any predisposing endowment. This has reasonably good supporting research evidence, for example, of a continuation of problematic behaviour in childhood, especially disorders of conduct running on into later adolescence and young adulthood (Modestin et al. 1998; Parker et al. 1999; Rutter et al. 1999; Messerschimdt 2002; Reti et al. 2002). Whilst such behaviour is problematic for those around them, there is evidence that apart from the exceptional extreme, many personality disordered people also experience a range of subjective distress as well as problems in personal and social relationships (Eher et al. 2001), which of course adds to the ethical dilemma.

The key elements appear to be marked disharmonious attitudes and behaviour which is patterned and long-standing, it is sometimes said 'they don't learn from their mistakes; the behaviour is often maladaptive and pervasive in a range of personal and social circumstances, and often associated with significant occupational problems. Such people have been described as 'psychopaths', inferring 'mental derangement', whereas in the USA, the term 'sociopath' has been coined, placing the focus on the person's behaviour towards society, rather than inferring a psychological problem. Perhaps the most useful way to look at personality disorders is to consider the condition as the end of a continuum, so whilst we can all feel selfish and behave so, we do not cross a boundary where our behaviour would be totally self-centred, with a callous disregard for others. Crucially, they seem to lack any sense of empathy for or with other people, including any children in their care (Marshall et al. 1997; Maletzky and Steinhauser 2002), whilst they often have other psychological/psychiatric co-morbidity, low self-esteem, alcohol/substance use and depression (Rutter et al. 1999; Eher et al. 2001).

Dissocial Personality Disorder is the 'typical' psychopath 'personality disorder', most likely to be involved in neglect and/or abuse of children in their care. They are characterized by an indifference to the feelings of others, often totally so, a self-centredness that makes them almost appear to be unaware that others might object to their often overt verbal and physical aggression. Often there is gross and persistent irresponsibility, with a total disregard for social norms, and especially important, an inability to sustain enduring personal relationships. They have great difficulty in tolerating even the mildest frustration with an associated very low threshold for the expression of aggression, which often ends in violence. Not only do they appear to be incapable of any remorse or feelings of guilt, or profit from previous experience, but are extremely hard to work with as they invariably blame others, with egocentric rationalizations of why he struck his female partner. For example,

> she knows I've a temper, ... I'm a proper man, you can't mess with me, ... she was winding me up, I warned her, it was her own fault and if she hadn't have gone on, the kid wouldn't have got hurt.

This 'explanation' came from 23-year-old 'Neil', on being questioned by police and social services following his brutal attack on his female partner of six months, in which he kicked and fractured the ribs of the 3-year-old child of his partner. Both his victims required hospitalization. This was typical of him as he had a string of violent convictions, from a very early age, as well as a multiplicity of other crimes, including sexual assault, and his three spells in prison did little to improve his post-discharge behaviour. We will return to the cases of 'Neil' and others like him when we explore the child protection-mental health interface. Sufficient to say the 'Dissocial personality disorder' as described by the ICD10 is found far more often amongst men, though not exclusively so. Irrespective of 'cause', experienced practitioners will recognize such patterns of behaviour in clients of most of the community agencies, especially police, probation and child protection.

Related to neglect and abuse of children might be the *Paranoid Personality Disorder*. As would be expected, this person is characterized by an excessive sensitivity to being 'got at'; suspicious, overly so, often without any reasonable justification. This can lead them into combative situations, with a tendency to bear grudges and being preoccupied with their status and concerns over 'conspiratorial' activities and their 'rights' but less so about others. Self-evidently, there appears to be a link or overlap with paranoid schizophrenia, indeed some suggest that this pattern of personality is, as it were, an unfulfilled paranoid schizophrenia (Bentall 2003).

Particularly amongst women can be found the behavioural pattern described as *Histrionic Personality Disorder*. They are characterized by high drama and self-dramatization, suggestibility, shallowness and lability effecting rapid mood swings from love and hate about the same person within minutes. They are attention seeking and may be quite coquetish, irrespective of their orientation or the therapist's gender. Crudely described as 'drama queens', they are found amongst men and women, but with a preponderance of women. Can be associated with 'dissociative disorders' with somatoform [physical] symptoms, classically the 'hysterical' conversion disorders, where they produce invalid physical symptoms, often of paralysis. Examples are 'glove and stocking' paralysis, where they do not appear to feel pain, but the numbed/paralysed area does not fit the known distribution of normal neurology. It is more often found amongst people from simpler and less educated cultures and is typically characterized by 'hysterical blindness'. It is the kind of client who on first meeting tells you that you are the 'worker/therapist' for whom they have been waiting, that at last someone understands them, they are appealingly 'childish' and the unaware might be mildly flattered by their obvious regard and hint of seductiveness. Before you know where you are, they will insist that you have promised them the earth, and how could you be so callous as to deny them what they need. If this sounds 'unprofessionally' harsh, it is not meant to be, but these people can be very manipulative, a word which most professionals seek to avoid, lest they appear to be making moral judgements. They can be helped, providing the worker is not overwhelmed by their practised art of building you up, to reject you because you have failed to live up to their fantasy expectations. In these days of litigation, the worker needs to be extremely careful and self aware that they are not drawn into the client's manipulative fantasy, which might well lead to an allegation of sexual impropriety.

'Olive', 38 years, was referred to the Child Guidance clinic because of the alleged bizarre sexual behaviour of her 6-year-old daughter. I was young and inexperienced and followed 'Olive's' story, which became more and more extreme, which the initial interview with 'Olive's' husband did not reassure, for his rejection of her allegations was initially thought to be hiding possible sexual abuse. 'I'll tell you now, it's a load of xxxx bull, she's making it up, it's one of her stories, she'll have you running around till you don't know whether you're coming or going – I've seen it before, you don't know' was the husband's dismissive response. A belated liaison with 'Olive's' GP confirmed her history of changed GP, house moves, list of bizarre complaints about schools, all of which proved to be unfounded, but characterized by 'Olive's' almost ecstatic excitement at being the centre of attention. A multidisciplinary case conference helped to clinch the 'assessment/diagnosis', as more experienced colleagues reassured me that they too had learned and suffered at the hands of an 'Olive'.

One category of particular use is that of 'borderline personality', where several of the problems of emotional instability are present in a patterned way, which often leads to intense but short lived unstable relationships, characterized by the dominant theme of the over-arching personality disorder, be it dissocial, paranoid or histrionic.

It is this imprecision which leads to criticism of the concept, and not just from those of a social science orientation (Lewis 1955; Clare 1976; Barker et al. 1998; Szasz 2002). Not least because the 'disorder' seems to be at one extreme of a continuum of ordinary personality traits, and lacks the value of a traditional medical diagnosis which excludes other conditions, for example cancer, pneumonia, which whilst possibly have psychosocial 'symptoms', can always be traced back to the underlying physical pathology. Whereas personality disorder diagnoses if anything, are over inclusive.

Yet despite the weaknesses inherent in genetic studies related to personality, that is the degree to which the environment influences any genetic predisposition (Torgersen 2000), there is considerable evidence to show that personality traits and whole patterns of personality both exist and have some genetic loading in most countries in the developed world (Ebstein et al. 2000; Nishiguchi et al. 2001; Bahlmann et al. 2002; Fu et al. 2002; Siever et al. 2002).

Moreover, many of these patterns of behaviour appear to have their origin in childhood, not just as reactive, but again with genetic weighting (Parker et al. 1999; Rutter et al. 1999; Messerschmidt 2002; Reti et al. 2002). Nonetheless, most of us from the social and behavioural sciences feel a little uncomfortable with the idea of personality disorder, in part because it suggests an intractability, and judgements are made on how 'different' the person is from a stereotyped idealized social norm. Hence to describe behaviour as a 'disorder' which is along a continuum, is criticized as a 'medicalization' by psychiatry of a spectrum of social behaviour (Pilgrim and Rogers 1993; Szasz 2002).

In part this is because we think of much unwelcome behaviour, such as theft and vandalism, as reactive to adverse circumstance. Indeed, there is little doubt that the cycle of psycho-socio-economic disadvantage is associated with a whole raft of anti-social behaviour (Audit Commission 1998), in which 'crime' might well be seen to be a 'rational alternative market response' to their disadvantage (Pritchard and Cox 1997; Pritchard 1991; Pritchard and Clooney 1994; Pritchard et al. 1998; Pritchard 2001). However, such a 'social reactive' position does not explain why the vast majority of 'poor' people do not continue in a life of crime; are not persistent thieves or vandals; are not wife-beaters and perpetrators of domestic violence and crucially *do not neglect and abuse their children.*

The value of the concept of personality (PD) disorder lies in the recognition that there are characteristic patterns of behaviour that are found in certain individuals whose lives and the lives of those around them, are disturbed, with differing degrees of distress. The 'PDs' are not like the functional psychoses, with strong biochemical markers (Ingraham and Kety 2000; Freedman et al. 2001), which differ from non-disordered people, but the pattern and form are identifiable. The degree to which the person and others around them are damaged seems to be associated with age as, for example, the violent offender becomes less violent the older he gets. It appears that the dissocial personality disordered person relatively mellows over time, or they 'grow-out of it' as they exhibit a degree of maturing (Ebstein et al. 2000; Home Office British Crime Survey 2002). What sticks hard with social workers, however, is that under the Mental Health Act 1983, the concept of personality disorder is defined as either 'treatable' or 'untreatable'. The idea of 'rejecting' a person, giving up on them, strikes hard at the social work ethic of valuing all, rejecting no one and purposeful acceptance of the individual (Plant 1978; Pritchard and Taylor 1978; Davies 2001). Yet from the field of mental health (Linehan 1993; Maletzky and Steinhauser 2002) has developed a very promising line of intervention, broadly associated with the 'cognitive behaviour therapy' model. Social workers would find this a very acceptable approach as it reflects many traditional social work values, especially as Linehan's (1993) 'dialectic behaviour therapy' in the modality, really refers to establishing a relationship with people who have little experience of positive regarding, self-esteem boosting relationships.

The concept of personality disorder can be useful when jettisoning the idea that it is an 'illness', rather than a disorder, which infers nothing about aetiology. Moreover, a simple analysis of long-term cases of any of the major social work agencies, reveals people whose pattern of behaviour has got them into trouble since childhood (Pritchard 1991; Farrington 1995; Ford et al. 1997; Ebstein et al. 2000; Pritchard and Butler 2000a, 2000b). Yet, social work has never tried to categorize behaviour with which most practitioners are familiar. It is as if we are afraid to quantify qualities of personality and behaviour, lest we appear to be judgemental. Yet there is considerable evidence to show that personality traits are part of the 'Nature – Nurture' interaction (Pinker 1998; Rutter et al. 1999; Reti et al. 2002). The danger is that we are less able or willing to determine risk of violence, be it to another adult or against a child. But of course, our clients, service users, have never fitted the textbooks, but that should not make us blind to the discernable patterns that are present. For example, the first 'extreme' dissocial 'psycho-path' I worked with was typical in every way of the ICD description except that he was 'socialized' to his group:

> 'Peter' was a charming 45-year-old industrialist, but had been sent to prep and public school, from the age of 6, then away to university and then the army, and ran his family business, and his family, with 'military discipline'. His son had been admitted to the regional adolescent unit and, on my first home visit, he 'gave the servants the afternoon off'. He expressed delight in meeting a male psychiatric social worker, an ex-serviceman to boot and his offer to talk cricket, arrange a ticket to the local football team was almost irresistible. 'Trouble is my boy can't decline his Latin verbs, damned nuisance because he's our only fella [in a family of five girls] and he's got to be able carry corn, what?' His wife who was present, hardly said a word, nor did he expect her to but one trusted one's intuition, Later it transpired that 'Peter' would drag the naked 11-year-old son from one bathroom to another, with a loofah stuffed in his mouth 'to stifle the screams' sobbed Mrs P, as father cursed him 'you will learn your Latin verbs you little xxxx bastard' as he was plunged first into a cold and then a hot bath.

I was very frightened on 'Peter's' return, as it was with great difficulty that he restrained himself from assaulting me. Eventually, we were able to ne-gotiate a new situation for the son, but 'Peter' was that rarity, a 'socialized' personality disorder, who is quite callous about other people's feelings, not one ounce of empathy, a concept that is outside his emotional ken, whose only mediation, is their social persona. Later we had some sessions with 'Peter' for his transient depression, but he rejected any further offer of help as being 'it might be useful for the purile and weak', but not for this sad man.

One could pity a man who de facto had been rejected at the age of 6 and, bullied and abused by a school residential system that Utting (1997) re-cognized can be so damaging. Change 'Peter's' background for a prison rather than boarding schools, and he would likely have been a familiar case in many statutory agency caseloads.

If social work applied some simple research methodologies to that practice knowledge which surrounds us all, we too might find benefit in recognizing patterns of behaviour, which require a very special response, particularly in the child protection-mental health interface. Crucially, the value in the concept is the 'persistence' of the behaviour, which posits the tough realization, that for the extreme 'personality disordered' person, there is little likelihood that they can change *in time to meet the child's legitimate psychosocial and physical needs*. Therefore, is there a case to argue that we should begin to think of removing children with such child carers, earlier rather than later, if we are serious about ensuring the child's interests are paramount?

No doubt, this is an issue to which we shall have to return, hopefully strengthened by research evidence to underpin such a serious decision.

6 The Societal Abuser: Re-discovering the Cycle of Poverty

The fathers have eaten a sour grape, and the children's teeth are set on edge.

(Jeremiah 31:29)

Introduction

Kempe and colleagues in their earliest studies on physical child abuse were anxious to emphasize the ubiquity of the problem across all social classes and cultures, and in consequence played down both the role of socio-economic disadvantage and the psychiatric dimension as causal factors in child abuse (Kempe et al. 1962). But as I have shown, the psychiatric-child protection interface is often a crucially important factor in helping us understand both the extremes of child abuse, as well as distortions in family environment and child socialization and care associated with various forms of child neglect and abuse, and this is often associated with poverty.

In turning to the issue of poverty I emphasize that in the vast majority of families stressed by chronic poverty, people do *not* abuse or neglect their children. Nevertheless, poverty is a major factor in the neglect and abuse of children and, within the population of the very poor, I will identify a serious type of child abuser, who usually avoids detection. Nonetheless, as we explore the cycle of poverty and child neglect and abuse, it is readily accepted that all forms can and do sometimes occur in families of affluence and social status. In these cases the pathology of mental health impairment of the abusing parent has more dominance as a causal factor.

Cycle of poverty

Virtually no child in Britain lives in the absolute poverty of many children living in the developing world (UNICEF 2000). We need therefore to focus on *relative* poverty. Since 1945 efforts have been made to diminish the absolute amount of poverty in Britain, and in a remarkable show of bi-partisanship the coalition government of 1939–45 and the Labour governments of 1945–51 accepted the Beveridge Report which identified the poverty experienced by the majority of the population. These policy innovations created the welfare state which aimed to fight the 'giants of poverty' – low income, unemployment, under-education, lack of adequate income in old age, and chronically poor health in the face of inaccessible medical services. On the basis of this report have evolved welfare benefits to provide minimum income, decent housing, national education and free health services. Winston Churchill later refused to dismantle this new provision, even though his party had originally opposed it, arguing that the 'people had chosen' and this should be honoured, perhaps reflecting his earlier liberal and 'one-nation' standards (Pritchard and Taylor 1978). Paradoxically as mass poverty has diminished, so diseases of affluence, especially amongst the young, have emerged. These are largely psychosocial disorders (Rutter and Smith 1998). The exact aetiology of these disorders is unknown, but it is clear that they have a much higher incidence in those sectors of the population suffering the most relative deprivation (Farrington 1995; Audit Commission 1996).

Thus, as the population has grown more affluent, problems of relative poverty have become more acute. Poverty has been officially recognized by successive British governments as a family having an income less than half the national average (Policy Action Team 2000). That this still matters can be seen in health statistics, which found that children (ages 0–14) of parents in receipt of welfare benefits had a death rate three times that of children of parents not on benefits (Judge and Benzeval 1993). Interestingly, this incredible and damning research was virtually ignored by the British press in 1993. However, the actual British death rates compared with the developing countries are extremely low (UNICEF 2000; WHO 2003). But in Britain today some 2900 annual deaths of children aged 0 to 14 are associated with poverty, reflecting poor peri-natal care, SIDS and other early deaths, deaths from infectious diseases, and deaths from 'accidents' – dying in fires, drowning, and being struck by motor vehicles (Judge and Benzeval 1993; Pritchard 1996b, 2002). This is not to say that these were all 'abuse' deaths: rather, poorer, older housing, overcrowding and a degraded urban environment leads to the greater likelihood of accidents and fires, as well as to poorer use of health services. Children of the manual social classes in Britain are twice as likely to die in an 'accident' as those in the non-manual classes, and the poorest two-fifths are 1.5 times as likely to be at risk of mental illness as the richest two-fifths (Rahman et al. 2000). A comprehensive UK study by Mitchell et al. (2000) confirmed the strong link between poverty and premature death rates and concluded:

> Redistribution of wealth would have the greatest absolute effect because it would improve the lives of the largest number of people.

> Eradication of child poverty [would have] the greatest relative effect (in terms of the proportion of lives saved).
>
> (Mitchell et al. 2000: 232)

This research by Mitchell and colleagues also found that the gap between rich and poor, in terms of health indicators had been *increasing* each year for the past 17 years, confirming the earlier findings stemming from the Black Report on health inequalities in Britain (Smith et al. 1990) and the later BMA (1999) study which also found a widening gap between the poorest and the richest fifth of the UK population in terms of infant health indicators. In Britain's poorest population the proportion of underweight babies and associated peri-natal mortality was amongst the highest in any developed country, higher than in countries such as Slovenia, and equivalent to that of Albania. Observing that children born in the poorest sector of the British population were 70 per cent more likely to die in the first five years of life, the report observes:

> The first five years of life are absolutely crucial to the development of children's bodies, minds and personalities. Deprivation early in life cause life-long damage, delinquency and despair ... Poorer children are more prone to accident and injury because they often have no-where to play but the street or a dangerous room such as the kitchen. They live on estates where there are broken glass, needles and other dangerous objects.
>
> (BMA 1999: 73)

The report estimates that each £1 spent on improving the conditions of child health in the early years would ultimately save £8 in later health care costs.

The problem of children growing up in families in poverty is particularly marked in Scotland, and in Glasgow 43 per cent of children under 16 grow up in households supported in whole or part by minimal income benefits from the state (NCH 2002). A further report from Scotland (OUPI 2002) indicates that the problem of relative poverty had, by November 2002, grown worse, with one-third of *all* children in Scotland living in families with incomes at or below the official poverty level. However, it should be noted that there are many islets of socio-economic poverty in England, even in such affluent areas as delightful Dorset and Hampshire (Pritchard 1991; Pritchard and Clooney 1994; Pritchard and Williams 2001).

The direct link of chronic poverty with a number of negative outcomes – poor physical and mental health, crime and social exclusion to mention but three – has at last been acknowledged by government, when it was admitted that both ill-health and crime are associated with poverty, especially inter-generational poverty (DoH 1998a; Boateng 2000). It seems that as wealth is inherited so too is socio-economic disadvantage and crime

(Farrington 1995; Graham and Bowling 1995; Rowntree Foundation 1999), which in turn is linked to educational under-achievement and the raised potential to be homeless, and to complete the cycle involving more teenage pregnancy, poorer pre- and post-natal care, poorer development and health of the child, spurring the cycle into the next generation (SEU 1998a). As Thomas et al. (1996: 6) assert, a disproportionate amount of psychiatric illness in Britain is associated with 'the politics of the underclass' and recent psychiatric studies have shown greater incidence of depression and suicide in area of high Jarman Poverty scores (Pritchard 1999; Thompson et al. 2001).

The classic study was based on the urban area of Swindon and its rural surrounds in Wiltshire where Dr Jack Oliver an eminent paediatrician, described five generations of 'mistreated children' (Oliver and Taylor 1981; Oliver 1988), which introduces the notion not just of socio-economic poverty but 'poverty of mind and spirit'. Here, successive generations of children do not experience 'good enough' positive parenting. Oliver's findings clearly parallel those from the United States (Polansky et al. 1981) on 'damaged parents'. New work with a British cohort of 14,138 children followed up from birth (Sidebotham et al. 2001) demonstrates that the cycle of abuse is as strong as ever: the significant markers for maltreatment of pre-schoolers are parents' educational failure, their youth (implying unplanned or unwanted pregnancies), the parents' own experience of child abuse and family disruption, and their negative psychiatric history.

Experienced practitioners describe parents who undoubtedly love their children, but are either so ill-equipped that they neglect them, or are so overwhelmed by a range of stressors that they are abusive. Good parenting demands altruism, putting the child before the adult. This is based upon the parent's own inner controls that help them socialize children adequately, so that the future citizen feels the indivisibility of the 'two-R's', that is rights and responsibilities, reflecting that great social dictum, 'from each according to their ability, to each according to their needs' – thus each person is under a reciprocal obligation to do their best for their children, with the wider society doing its best to assist in their optimal development.

In this ideal, but yet unachieved model, all are of equal worth as people of differing capacity who are nevertheless urged to meet the ultimate adult parental obligation of altruism. This is something that many of the 'loving' parents on the 'At Risk of Abuse' register are currently unable to do. Evolutionary psychology would suggest that the *potential* exists in all parents, but its development is impaired by their life-circumstances (Dennett 1995; Pinker 1998; Wilson 1998). This is seen in seminal work from David Barker at the University of Southampton on the 'foetal origins of adult disease' (Barker et al. 2001; Barker 2003). Barker discovered some health visitor case notes from the 1930s and realized that he could link late middle-aged adults with their early life history. Low birth weight, associated with poverty, and other bio-psychosocial factors, were shown to be associated with a wide range of disorders in adulthood, including psychiatric ones. Consequently, anything that is a barrier to this parental altruism such as socio-economic poverty and associated factors such as substance abuse, adds to the potential of child neglect or abuse. In the USA this poverty-abuse link is well demonstrated with increased child abuse rates associated with increased family poverty over a decade (Herman-Giddens et al. 1999), which may be linked to the fact that whilst British and most Western countries child homicide rates have fallen, the USA has seen a rise in their child murders, within a declining adult homicide rate (Pritchard 1996b, 2002; Pritchard and Butler 2003). In Germany, Vock et al. (1999) also found that 95 per cent of parents involved in fatal neglect had chronic alcohol and poverty problems.

This life cycle of poor parenting, educational under-achievement, delinquency, crime and early pregnancy, can be heard in the voices of victims who have passed along the cycle to become 'assailants' namely, 17- to 20-year-olds in prison, in the graphic account *Tell them so they listen* (Lyon et al. 1996). Lyon's cohort were young people in prison, the large majority of whom experienced severe socio-economic poverty and many a degree of child neglect and abuse as well. These grown-up victims of child neglect also tend to inherit poverty, even though they have often been in the care of the state for long periods of their development (Biehel et al. 1995; DoH 1998a). Although under the Children Act 1989, former 'in-care' adolescents have the right to voluntary supervision and support from social services, they still do less well socially and educationally than their age peers (Biehel et al. 1995; Pritchard and Butler 2000b), although their outcomes are better than those who were permanently excluded from school (Pritchard and Butler 2000a, 2000b). Both groups carry massive disadvantages into their adult lives, and those who have both spent periods in care and have been permanently excluded from school are doubly disadvantaged. This can be seen in young people's health and the Oliver 'intergenerational child maltreatment' effect, as Petrak et al. (2000), showed in their study of young people in Whitechapel – children 'inherited' a pattern of educational failure, neglect and abuse of their own children, and a substantially higher rate of sexually transmitted diseases, as well as a much higher risk of teenage pregnancies. And of course, permanently excluded children were far more likely to come from families in poverty than not. Their children in turn are likely to inherit, as their parents did, all the problems associated with poorer parenting and lowered life chances (Corcoran 1998; Courtney 1998).

Poverty in George Bernard Shaw's phrase, 'blights all who come into contact with it' (*Major Barbara*) and whole neighbourhoods can develop a communal sense of 'defeatism', which is reflected in the apparent willingness to accept lower standards of behaviour and aspiration in a degraded, slum-like environment. Only the ethnic minority groups forced to live in these ghettolike areas will escape this cycle; and in many parts of the country the 'sink' estates are all-white, breeding grounds for unemployment, crime and reactionary politics. In such neighbourhoods child neglect, poverty, family disturbance, substance abuse and individual psychopathology are accepted by many as the norm (Korbin et al. 2000; Thompson et al. 2001). Given this, great credit must be given to those who escape the cycle of poverty, by good fortune or by acts of will.

A valuable but depressing study comes from Scotland where it has been found that unemployment in particular, along with other indices of poverty is associated with a range of child maltreatment. The researchers found that male unemployment was associated with two-thirds of the variance in the measure of child neglect and abuse (Gillham et al. 1998). To be without work in a modern capitalist society undermines the individual's self-esteem, which for men in particular, can lead to displaced violence, which is associated with violence against the self, and often against those close to oneself (Platt 1984; Pritchard 1992b, 1996b). As unemployment rises, so does male suicide and increased child neglect and abuse (Steinberg et al. 1981; McLloyd 1990; Pritchard 1999). These findings reinforce our arguments that there is often a crucial link between adult mental health and interventions with stressed families to support and protect children.

The poverty-psychiatry interface

The link between poverty and poorer mental health is not so much directly causal as based on an interaction between the two. There is long and well established evidence to show that socio-economic disadvantage leads to the greater likelihood of mental disorder and that mental disorder leads to the person 'drifting down the social scale', as their untreated and unsupported mental health problems undermine their capacity to meet socio-economic demands (Pilgrim and Rogers 1993).

Eamon's research (2001) showed a cross-over between poverty and increased depression in the family, resulting in rises in physical punishment of children. This is associated in turn with depression in children, suicidal ideation in parents, as well as child neglect and abuse (Dimigen et al. 1999; Finzi et al. 2001; Gomez-Alcalde 2001; Grgic 2002). A significant number of children received into care because of neglect and abuse had high rates of child psychiatric problems, often reflecting parental poverty and depression (Dimigen et al. 1999). Mention has already been made of the substantial number of 'socially excluded' adolescents, who end up at the bottom of the social scale and are much more often victims of crime and physical assault than their peers, including the worst self-abuse of all, suicide (Pritchard and Cox 1997; Pritchard and Butler 2000a, 2000b).

Yeager and Lewis (2000) reviewing a decade of research on the inter-relationship of poverty, psychiatric disorder and child abuse showed that one consequence is inter-generational violence, since the physically abused child is more likely to become a physically assaultive adolescent and adult. At the extreme it was found in a 20-year follow-up that children with identifiable psychiatric problems had a substantially worse mortality outcome than did the general population (Tomison 1996), emphasizing this interactive cycle of poverty, psychiatry and physical ill-health, substance abuse, and suicide. These may be unlamented young people, but many will have fathered or mothered children before their deaths.

One recurrent theme of recent research is the link with substance abuse amongst people with mental health problems, almost a form of 'self-medication', with links to impaired parenting ability and neglect and abuse of children (Petrak et al. 2000; Finzi et al. 2001) and at the extremes of persistent alcohol problems, fatal neglect (Vock et al. 1999). The question must be raised, which came first, the poverty or the psychiatric difficulties.

Lipman et al.'s (2001) important study gives us some clue to see both the links and the differences in a comparison of children of single and married mothers. Examining a province-wide cohort from Ontario, 1471 mothers were identified. On virtually all measures, single mothers (with substantially lower incomes) came out worse than partner-supported mothers – lower incomes, greater psychiatric morbidity especially anxiety disorders and substance abuse, and substantially higher rates of child abuse in their own lives and that of their children. Adult mental health problems were experienced significantly more often in the mothers without supportive partners, linked to child neglect and abuse in their own childhood, but the presence of a psychiatric disorder in either single or married mother, implied a higher risk of child neglect and abuse, than did poverty per se. This indicates that poverty makes a problematic situation worse, giving further weight to the cyclical theme of neglect and abuse in childhood being associated with more mental health problems, and greater inability to provide adequate parenting as an adult. Once again, exact causal pathways and interaction effects are difficult to determine, but what is clear is that a stable, economically advantaged non-abusive childhood is reflected in lack of abusive and neglectful parenting. The converse is also true.

Evidence of omission

It is unlikely that the above evidence that poverty erodes the human spirit and tends to undermine parenting capacity, will come as a surprise to professionals in the field. The question is, if we know all of this, why then have we not done something definitively radical about these problems?

When Charles Dickens wrote his great novels exposing the impact of poverty on children and families, the Victorian 'public' could have argued they did not know of the appalling conditions that the urban poor experienced. It still took 30 years before England had its very basic child protection legislation; whilst the workhouses existed until 1948; and the large children's orphanages were still around until the 1960s. Indeed the plays of Joe Orton from the 1960s, reflect his experiences of child care in those days, in which he barely disguises the prevalent physical and sexual bullying.

Yet since the 1970s successive governments have known about the poverty, child-neglect and abuse interface and apart from pious words and almost symbolic crumbs to appease an occasionally aroused public, governments have failed to tackle the structural problems in a coherent and targeted way. For example in 1964 we had the Williams Report on the parlous state of children's homes, which were predominately staffed by untrained people. We had the paradox of when children were not able to live within the community, the relatively well trained and higher status field staff, handed over the damaged, disturbed and disturbing children into the hands of untrained or under-trained staff. Whilst the trained staffing ratios are a little better, Utting (1997) still complained of the residential sector being under-resourced, despite the problem being identified in the 1960s. Utting issued a major report, following the scandals of mistreatment and abuse of children in children's homes, in looking at all sectors where children 'lived-away from home', including boarding schools. Sir William is worth quoting:

> The review has been a crash course in human [mainly male] wickedness and the fallibility of social isolation. The fact that the bad are a tiny proportion should not obscure the havoc it causes the children who were there.

He goes on

> The job of looking after them would be easier and more effective if we really heard and understood what they have to tell us.
>
> (Utting 1997: 7)

In the circles that Utting moved in, this was an extremely brave report, demonstrating the greatest integrity, allied to a brilliant analytical mind, and such people merit our greatest respect, for his news would unlikely to be welcome to any government.

This mirrors Lyon et al. (1996) whose young offenders reflect back on lives damaged and limited from birth. Most experienced primary school teachers can identify lives soon to be casualties: it is known that about 8 per cent of offenders are responsible for 80 per cent of 'blue collar' crime (Audit

Commission 1998). But do we intervene early? No, hence the need to identify areas of omission, which on moral, human rights, and social and economic grounds, demand to be addressed.

We know that children from the Third World are continued victims of poverty; even where they live is further disadvantaged as their locale becomes the site for environmental degradation (Channar and Khichi 2000; Merrick 2001). A different kind of societal discrimination exists within the affluent Western world, to the extent there is systematic bias in society's arrangements for the processing and control of children from poverty backgrounds, as professional and legal delay, bureaucratic cover-up, under-resourced services are overwhelmed (Payne 2000; Coxe and Holmes 2001; Jones et al. 2001; Leventhal 2001b; Mace et al. 2001; Grgic 2002; Maxeiner 2002). This is seen again and again when so called 'independent' inquiries look for 'lessons to be learned' from the latest tragedy, invariably focusing upon the least powerful staff, the front-line workers (for example Sanders et al. 1999). This ignores the fact that actual fatalities of children in Britain are comparatively very low (Pritchard 1996a, 2002; Pritchard and Butler 2003). And the USA, who alerted the world to the consequences of child abuse against most other nations, have seen increases in their already high child homicide rates, which also coincided with reductions in a range of welfare services following the Reagan and Bush Snr years. These could well be causal connections (McLloyd 1990; McFate et al. 1995; Mischra 1999; Pritchard 2002; Pritchard and Butler 2003).

Overall, despite a built-in cycle of poverty undermining child protection efforts, the British record merits some praise. To be fair, too, the present British government, has acknowledged the importance of chronic poverty undermining good child development, educational progress, poor health and crime (Home Office 1991; Audit Commission 1998; DoH 1998b; Boateng 2000). A number of initiatives have begun, such as 'Sure Start' aimed at nursery-aged children, and 'Social Exclusion' has been recognized as a core problem related to truancy, educational-under-achievement, homelessness and so forth (SEU 1998a, 1998b, 1998c). But the scale of the problem is still not properly recognized, including the fact that proportionately more children in the UK live in relative poverty than any other European Union member state (Policy Action Team 2000). At worst this is almost treated like a state secret; at best, the news is quietly relegated to middle pages in the 'broad sheet' newspapers, and ignored by the large circulation 'popular' newspapers. This political–media interface is a point to which we shall return.

Perhaps the worst form of 'institutional neglect' involves children whose psychosocial development has already been impaired by family circumstances – those disturbed and disturbing children and adolescents who are either leaving care or have been excluded from school. First the good news: despite initial gloom at what happens to former 'In Care' young people (Biehel et al. 1995; Utting 1997), they have a considerably better outcome than do former permanently excluded-from-school young people (Pritchard and Butler 2000a). This seems to be linked to the fact that the 'In Care' group in our follow-up study do have the opportunity for supervision and support from social services, despite over-stretched budgets. The bad news is that, 'school-excluded' youths get virtually nothing (Pritchard and Butler 2000a, 2000b). Moreover, young people in prison the majority of whom have been failed by their parents and society, simply enter into a cycle of disadvantaged victim-hood, which almost guarantees their 'market alternative response' of crime to their psycho-socio-economic situation, because of their educational under-achievement they are virtually unemployable (Lyon et al. 1996; Audit Commission 1998). For example, young people aged 15–17 years in prison are continued victims of physical and sexual bullying. The McGurk et al. (2000) report is revealing. Initially set up to explore sexual abuse of young prisoners, it 'only' found 1 per cent of cases were substantiated, while another 8 per cent although probable, were not independently confirmed. But one in three had been threatened, one in five had threatened, 8 per cent had been made to do something against their will, one in six had been physically hurt. The report admitted that staff were only aware of half of the reported incidents!

The rate of prison suicide of young offenders, especially in the first few months of incarceration is a continued scandal, matched only by the suicide rate of former 'excluded-from-school' young adults (aged 16–24) and former residents of sexually victimized youths from children's homes, which is a rate 19 times that of their age peers in the general population (Pritchard 1998; Pritchard and Butler 2000b).

More good news: a school-based child and family social work service, proved to be a very successful preventive initiative, reducing truancy, de-linquency and school-exclusion (Pritchard 2001; Pritchard and Williams 2001). Indeed it was so successful that the Chief Officers of the county (re-presenting Education, Health, Police, Probation and Social Services), asked the question, what is the cost of the general failure to offer comprehensive educational and social work support for extremely disadvantaged children? They collaborated in a unique study which compared five-year cohorts of former 'In Care' (IC) and 'Excluded-from-School' (EFS) outcome, based upon the hardest evidence available – police conviction rates and regional mortality statistics. Initially, in view of Biehel and Stein's seminal work (Biehel et al. 1995), it had been expected that the IC group (n=814) would have had a far worse outcome than the EFS (n=227), not least because being received into care is so much of a last resort for children with multiple psychosocial problems.

As noted above, the IC sample, who had the benefit of social work post-leaving support did far better than the EFS group in terms of subsequent criminal carers, prison sentence and crimes of violence. Moreover, despite the elevated incidence of depression in former IC children (Tomison 1996;

Dimigen et al. 1999; Gomez-Alcalde 2001), there were no subsequent suicides. But the EFS cohort had a suicide rate 19 times that of the general population. Worse, though there was a small group of young IC men with subsequent crimes of violence, these were far less numerous than the rate in the EFS men, who had an actual murderer rate 17 times the general population.

Furthermore, whilst the EFS young adults' criminal record cost the public purse a *minimum* of £2.7 million, if they had offended at the same rate as the IC men this cost would have been almost halved. But life is never simple and front-line practitioners will know that they have a disproportionate number of former IC people in their caseloads. Both the IC and the EFS had a higher rate of being *victims* of crime, than the General Population Rate (GPR), both in terms of general and violent crimes. Moreover, the IC group had a worse record of being victims of violent and sexual crime than the EFS group, both men and women. In both groups females were especially likely to be victims of sexual assaults as young adults compared with the GPR of their age peers. Indeed, the IC victim-hood produced a rate of being an extreme victim of violence in that the IC men were murdered many times the GPR; and the ex-IC females were murdered at astonishing 73 times the GPR rate (Pritchard and Butler 2000a).

Clearly more needs to be done for longer periods for these institutionally neglected people, especially the female ex-In Care young women.

Media and its irresponsibility

Senior civil servants from the Attlee Government (1945–51) onwards have known of the commonsense and statistical associations between socio-economic disadvantage with crime, with child neglect and abuse. Unfortunately, unlike Churchill who in his Liberal days said, 'The hallmark of a civilised society is how it treats its prisoners' (quoted in Manchester 1984), modern politicians have fallen into the media-simplistic trap of the language about a 'war against crime'. The crime most are concerned about of course are 'blue collar' crimes of burglary, mugging, criminal damage, personal violence – for all victims these are distressing and damaging experiences, as this writer knows. However, insider trader dealing, corporate fraud, tax evasion and so forth do not seem to arouse the same kind of passions, though in terms, they are likely to do far more damage than, say, burglaries.

So, the reduction of crime is a political issue – how does government best protect its citizens in their homes and on the streets? This has evolved into the simplistic nonsense of who is 'toughest on crime', rather than being the toughest on the 'causes of crime', ignoring the fact that the institutionalized cycle of deprivation has a major part to play in spurring individuals to commit these minor, but irritating, property crimes.

The politically right-wing in Britain (including 'New Labour') have made great play about stamping out crime, ignoring its contributory causes. The same is true of child neglect and abuse, and blame heaped on failing parents, ignoring the facts of the cycle-of-deprivation, cycles of crime, and of child neglect and abuse. In other words, if there is no such thing as 'society', then everything is the individual's responsibility, and the rest of society has no obligations beyond prosecuting and warehousing offenders. In 2000, the number of prisoners in Britain had risen to an all-time record (Ramsbotham 2001).

Parallel to this, in our analysis, is the gross misrepresentation and over-simplification of cases of child neglect and abuse at both official and media levels. First these institutions ignore the overwhelming evidence of the cycle of child victim to abuser, which whilst not exonerating the offender, can lead to the tragic case of 'Alan' in Chapter 1. As a bereaved child he was a victim of neglect for eight years, before being incorporated into his stepfather's paedophile ring. He had always expressed regret, was never violent, but ended up killing himself.

Secondly, linked to the victim-abuser cycle, is the fact that about a third of these men, were themselves introduced, conditioned, trained or seduced into patterns of child-adult sexual activity. This finding does not of course excuse the adult's behaviour, but it does at least help us in a rational approach. It is also noted that the epidemiological finding that single events of abuse are *not* associated with long-term mental health impairment for victims. Intrusive and prolonged police surveillance, the wrong kind of social work, medical, judicial and poor management processing can often do considerable harm (Laming Report 2003).

Thirdly, and this can not be emphasized enough, whilst there is no question that sexual involvement of adults and older adolescents with children is unequivocally wrong, in the interest of better child protection we need to differentiate between types of offenders. This means that we must seek to treat the treatable, control and manage those who are not able to benefit from treatment, and with the dangerous minority, impose custodial care which may involve a life sentence or more or less permanent detention under new legislation of 'reviewable' sentences. The case for this emerges from research on offenders and is elaborated in the chapter on treatment of offenders (Pritchard and Bagley 2000).

A major problem of offering treatment to men who have not been caught up in the criminal justice system is their apprehension about coming forward. The eminent criminologist D.J. West (2000) sought to achieve some balance with regard to hysterical media campaigns when he asked the question, 'paedophilia, plague or panic?' He would not as a general or moral principle ever excuse paedophile behaviour, but he noted that many incidents are minor, as opposed to corruptive within-family abuse, or where there is a long-term misuse and corruption of an authority relationship. West pointed out that we are in danger of over-reacting and restricting children's freedom, when the media over-amplifies the problem of 'the lurking stranger'. In contrast, motorists kill more than 20 times the number of children than extra-family abusers do (Pritchard 2002). The daily toll of serious child injuries and deaths in Britain because of our fetish with the speedy and unrestricted passage of motor vehicles goes unremarked by media and government. There is more public indignation at the introduction of speed cameras than at the 'murder' of children by motor vehicles, a rate of 22 road deaths for every extra-family homicide (Pritchard 2002).

Some innovative work from the USA showed that whilst trying to teach children about child sexual abuse which was not very effective, a programme named 'Vermont Social Marketing' aimed to reach out and invite men to seek confidential, non-prosecuting treatment has proved to be of value (Paradise 2001). In part, the campaign was to inform the wider public of the victim-abuser cycle and evoke if not compassion at least some understanding of these men's predicament, and at the same time encouraging them to seek help to control their unacceptable urges. Early results are very encouraging, not least because it offers some help in breaking the cycle of victim-to-abuser, either before it starts or becomes established.

But if the media persists in demonizing actual and potential offenders as 'beasts', it would take a brave man indeed to come forward and ask for help. This type of journalism is epitomized by the inane 'name and shame' campaign of the *News of the World*. Such editors 'darketh counsel using words without wisdom' (Job 38:2) and in my opinion actually endanger the children whom they purport to want to protect. The mass circulation paper the *News of the World* called for a 'Sarah's Law' to mirror 'Megan's Law' in the USA. This was named after a child brutally murdered by a known sex-offender who was living in her community. The Government made it possible for parents to know of the presence of a former offender living in their community. Most states in the USA have now adopted a similar version. Some sectors of the UK press called for similar legislation, ignoring the opinions of the Home Office, the Department of Health and a number of judicial bodies who all argued that this would not help, and might even possibly hinder effective protection of children. The inevitable happened following the popular press campaign to 'name and shame' paedophiles giving their last known address – the tabloids' irresponsible reporting led to beatings and arson. There are four factors listed for the tabloid press of Britain to consider.

(1) Four out of five of *all* types of abuse occur within the family, so 'naming and shaming' would be irrelevant to the majority of cases.
(2) The *News of the World*'s recommendation about knowledge of whereabouts of known offenders is impracticable and may make

matters worse, as the 'treatable' will be afraid to come forward and the dangerous will go 'underground'. Moreover, why did they not risk challenging reporting restrictions imposed on the North Wales Waterhouse child abuse inquiry, when eminent names were mentioned? Their 'name and shame' policy appeared to be somewhat selective.

(3) For every child killed by a 'stranger', at least twenty are killed as pedestrians or cyclists by other 'strangers', that is, motorists – but the press do not campaign for curbs on the motorist.

(4) The majority of child neglect and abuse is associated with children living in poverty. Britain has the highest proportion of children living in relative poverty in the European Union. But the tabloid press do not campaign on ways to improve British children's relative poverty.

Politicians are themselves victims of the media, in that they rarely challenge the oversimplification of newspaper campaigns of vilification. The media image of British child protection services is generally unfavourable (Parton 1994). Despite the major reductions in our child homicide rates over the past 20 years, the child protection services invariably get only a critical press, remembering only those rare tragedies when things went wrong. Why is this damaging? Because it undermines committed front-line staff morale and deters committed professionals entering the field of child protection. Moreover, it traps politicians into simplistic approaches, despite brave assertions of change. Consider the following observation by the then Deputy Home Secretary Paul Boateng (2000), who reflecting the best of recent research wrote:

> As we enter the 21st century, there can be no more important task facing us than to ensure that no matter who they are, each young person has the best possible start in life and the opportunity to develop and achieve their full potential. ... Through a combination of poverty, family conflict, poor educational opportunities and poor services, too many find themselves apparently destined for a life of underachievement and social exclusion.

Who could disagree with such sentiments? Yet, despite the Home Office funding a major three-year preventive initiative to break this cycle, this same Home Office held back the subsequent report, for an inordinate long time, ostensibly because the report needed to be shortened but it seemed to me that they were concerned lest an obvious liberal and progressive report, be mistakenly thought to be 'soft on crime' as the following case study seems to show (Pritchard 2001; Pritchard and Williams 2001).

Services, structure, resources and cost benefit: an 'embarrassing' case study

In 1991, following a series of separate research projects for Dorset county Education, Health, Probation and Social Services, it was recognized that there was a direct inter-relationship between educational failure, health-impairment, crime and child protection. A project was designed to reach damaged and damaging families, breaking into the cycle of deprivation to improve rates of educational success, crime reduction and indirectly child protection. The project was a three-year longitudinal study of a school-based child and family social work service to be compared against standard service in primary and secondary schools in a similar, severely socio-economically disadvantaged area.

At the beginning of the period, the estate on which the project was based had the highest rate of families on the 'At Risk of Abuse' register in the county. They had the second highest rate of crime; and 40 per cent of fathers were unemployed, and 37 per cent of children belonged to single-parent families, compared with 8 per cent and 15 per cent respectively in the rest of the county. Almost a quarter, 24 per cent, of men on the estate was in recent or current contact with police or on probation, and 12 per cent of households had been a recent victim of crime. The males on the estate were 8.5 times more often on probation compared with the county general population.

The 'experimental' focus primary and secondary schools which served the estate had the benefit of an 'enhanced' service, that is, a school-based social work team to work with children and their families to reduce truancy, delinquency, drug misuse, vandalism, child neglect, school-exclusion and to improve school attendance and educational results. These variables were measured before the start of the three-year project and annually, against the 'comparative schools' from another disadvantaged estate, which was not quite as severely deprived with only 28 per cent of fathers being unemployed, and only 25 per cent in single-parent families. The estate, built in the late 1960s, predominately housed London over-spill families, and had developed a very dubious reputation. One teacher commented,

> After inner-London I thought I could manage anything – but this was an effin & blinding chair-throwing school, not a bit like the leafy suburbs I'd expected – everything had to be nailed down, not just the kids. Before the project started, it was impossible.

The estate bore all the hall-marks of inter-generational disadvantage, strongly associated with cycles of child neglect and abuse (Oliver and Taylor 1981; Oliver 1988). This was seen in the former pupils of the estate's schools, now aged 20–24 years, with 12 per cent of females and 10 per cent of males being involved with either probation or social services or both. At the start of the project 12 per cent of the project's children and their families attending primary school were involved with probation or social services, compared with only 2 per cent attending the comparative schools.

The team was led by a full-time experienced educational social worker, with a full-time teacher-social worker in the primary school and a half-time teacher-health educationalist in the secondary school. The full report, which can be obtained from the Home Office, or downloaded without cost was eventually published in December 2001 (Pritchard 2001). The results are extremely encouraging, showing dramatic reductions in educational failure and school exclusion, as well as prevention of family breakdown in the children and families in the focus, experimental schools.

On all outcomes children (and their families) in the project schools did significantly better than the comparative schools. Truancy was halved in the project secondary school, drugs, and especially hard drug misuse fell, as did fighting, bullying and vandalism. Theft from the project schools became almost unknown. There was a marked reduction in exclusions from the school, and the two project schools successfully took in a number of children who were on the point of being excluded by other schools.

The project social worker recognized that the team's role crossed the boundaries of education, crime, health and child protection – dramatically seen in the fact that the numbers of families on the 'At Risk of Abuse' register in the project area fell by more than 60 per cent during the three years, whilst in the rest of the county the figure rose by 30 per cent, reflecting a general economic recession. Moreover, half of the families on the register were self-referrals, which is more than half the battle won.

One simple but significant finding was that every parent in the project schools visited their child's school at least once in the final year for a non-disciplinary event, a remarkable indicator of a growing sense of community and involvement with education by parents, who had previously ignored the schools. The project cost £230,000 over three years, which is far higher than the usual cost of educational welfare provision. In effect we had two educational social workers for two schools, whereas the usual provision is one for between six and eight schools. So was the project too ideal and too expensive to run? No. A Cost benefit analysis, based upon hard data on school exclusion costs and the savings related to reduction in the cost of the administration of justice (including costs saved to potential victims inherent in the crime reduction figures in students from the project schools) found major savings, a minimum of 250 per cent 'savings' over and above the cost of the project. At first sight this seems extraordinary, but as the Audit Commission showed, the cost of crime in the administration of justice alone for young people runs to literally billions (Audit Commission 1996). The cohort of former 'excluded-from-school' adolescents from comparison schools cost a minimum of £2.7 million through as yet incomplete criminal careers, since the cohort's age was but 16–24 years at follow-up, it would have been cheaper to employ their own police and social work person!

The reader will have noticed the gap between the time of the project 1992–95, and the final recognition by successive Governments (March and November 1997) and the point at which the report was finally published, December 2001. The first version of a final report was with the Home Office in June 1996. Because the results had immediate practical implications, a management review synopsis was shared with the chief officers of the Dorset county departments of education, public health, probation and social service. But the author was then threatened with prosecution by Home Office who claimed full copyright over the report as the main funders! They pointed out that even discussing the results without the express permission of the Home Secretary, made the author liable to a criminal prosecution and a possible jail sentence. This seemed a little extreme as I was not exposing anything like military secrets – but the Home Office was obdurate. Peace was restored and the 'final' shortened report went to the Home Office, under the seal of confidentiality in June 1996. I was asked to provide a shorter version which was duly completed in June 1997, when it was confidentially expected that the new Government would be delighted to have the report. Consequently, I placed the words 'social work' back in the title, not least because the results showed that school quality and the children's family are the most vital factor in children's achievement, as had previous research (Rutter et al. 1979; Farrington 1995; Graham and Bowling 1995; Rutter and Smith 1998).

But nothing happened for a further year until I was requested to shorten the report even further – this was carried out in mid-1998, nearly three years after a project which showed that with adequate resources and support, we could achieve major inroads on crime, delinquency and family functioning. Why was the Home Office still so interested in suppressing our results? All our petitions to the Home Office requesting publication were ignored or diverted by bland excuses.

Individual civil servants in the Home Office thought the study important and that they were, as individuals keen to publish. This did not happen. The only reason I could discern why the Home Office were slow in publication was the misapprehension that for them to accept the report might infer that they were 'soft on crime', ignoring the second part of the maxim 'being tough on the cause of crime'. The research team had demonstrated highly cost effective ways of being 'tough on crime' which reduced youth crime and broke into the cycle of deprivation, abuse and neglect, and family dysfunction. Yet the Home Office effectively delayed the use of important but perhaps unacceptable information.

The 'Family-Teacher-Social Work Alliance' was eventually published by a new Minister of State, John Denham, in December 2001, a week before Christmas, but quietly buried in a list of 'miscellany' documents. The influence on the policy process at the level of national government of this crucial report, however, has been reflected in recent Department of Education initiatives, in particular, the new 'Children Fund' and 'Connexions' for older children. So perhaps all is not lost, save deserved credit going to dedicated front-line social workers.

Apart from occasional piety, Her Majesty and Her governments have ignored decades of evidence of the corrupting corrosion of poverty upon children's minds, bodies and spirits, which contribute in their turn to a cycle of inter-generational child maltreatment. With well-targeted investment we could save money, and reduce the miserable lives that many children inherit, as well as reducing cycles of crime, child neglect and active abuse. Not to invest in preventive services is a false economy. The UK government in its current policies, is woefully lacking, not least because it does not explain to the general public, what common sense tells them, 'give a dog a bad name', and so forth. So until we (as voters and supporters of government) accept the dictum 'suffer the little children to come unto me', but continue to ignore children being kept upon the conveyer belt of poverty, neglect and abuse that leads to crime and more abuse, we are also child neglecters at best and passive abusers at worst.

7 The Extremes of Child Abuse: Who Kills Children and The Psychiatric-Child Abuse Interface?

Introduction

From the earliest recognition of child abuse by Kempe in the 1960s, it has been realized that the extreme outcome of the physical abuse of a child can be a dead child. This transgresses one of the oldest cultural taboos and an affront to the most powerful human drives to protect one's own child. Yet in most cultures when a mother killed her child, there was some recognition that such an 'unnatural' act was so bizarre as to be 'moon struck': that is in modern terms, the act of a mentally disordered person. Indeed in British law 'infanticide' – the killing of a child under 1-year-old – was previously rather casually dealt with, on the assumption that the mother was likely to be suffering from post-natal depression, puerperal psychosis or extreme poverty with the implicit assumption that the children of the very poor were hardly worth bothering with. There is an evocative poem by W.H. Davies from the 1930s, *The Inquest* which reflects a British view that persisted well into the early 1970s. He, with 11 other male jurors, was asked to judge how a 4-month-old baby had died. The poem tells how they agonized about the tragic, pale and pathetic mother standing in the dock. Somehow she appealed to their sympathy, despite the fact they saw the baby's under-nourished body, but by inference, what else would they expect from a 'love child' in those days. But Davies showed how the unthinkable kept intruding into his deliberations, as at the end of each verse, was the stanza:

> that child's one eye which seemed to laugh, and say with glee: 'What caused my death you'll never know – Perhaps my mother murdered me?'.
>
> (Davies 1935 from *Oxford Book of Modern Verse*)

Britain's relatively uncomplicated view was rudely shattered by the Maria Colwell inquiry (1973) and it would be fair to say that modern British concepts of child protection began then. Indeed, at the beginning of the 1970s Britain had the fourth highest child homicide in the Western world, exceeding the USA and every other country other than Japan, Germany and Austria (Pritchard 1992). One key factor that Kempe originally stressed was that child neglect and abuse occurred across cultures and social classes and they deliberately downplayed any 'psychiatric' dimension (Kempe et al. 1962, 1985). Subsequent research on child homicide shows it to be a complex, multi-faceted phenomenon (Bourget and Bradford 1990; Bourget and Labelle 1992; Stroud and Pritchard 2001). The focus, however, has largely been on deaths of children linked to what Stroud (2001) accurately calls the 'child abuse-neglect syndrome' (Greenland 1987; Bourget and Bradford 1990; Noyes 1991). Indeed, child homicide has been equated with child abuse, and many have argued that it is the indicative 'tip-of-the iceberg', representing the many, relatively hidden distresses and conflicts involving children and parents (Jason 1983; Pritchard 1992a, 1996a, 2002; Stroud and Pritchard 2001), confirmed by a UNICEF report (UNICEF 2000). Thus, although child homicide is a heterogeneous phenomenon the professional response has made global child protection and intervention with distressed and abusing families the major preoccupation of the paediatric and social services (Greenland 1987; DoH 1991, 2001; Noyes 1991; Stroud and Pritchard 2001).

Multi-disciplinary, international research will be explored to avoid the usual mistake of only looking at the 'child protection' literature, for as will be shown there is an urgent need to re-discover the mental health dimension in child protection, and most such research lies in the medically and psychologically related fields.

Within family child homicide

Because of the relative rarity of child homicide it is difficult to find research studies of large samples in contemporary literature. As we will see, the majority of people who kill children are family members, predominately parents. Moreover in stark contrast to adult murder, women, mainly mothers, kill as frequently or even more often than males. Resnick's (1969) classic study contained 131 filicides (that is, people who killed a son or daughter), there were 88 maternal and 43 paternal assailants, identified from world literature on child homicide. Scott's (1973a) classification of filicide applied to 46 paternal and 39 maternal filicides. Somander and Rammer (1991) made a most valuable and useful examination of all child homicides in Sweden 1971–80, with a focus on identifying intra- and extra-familial homicides. They emphasized that extra-familial child homicide is even rarer than within-family homicide, for out of their sample of 77 child killings, only 12 were extra-familial. However, these extra-familial assailants might have actually known the child as a family friend or acquaintance. The absolute 'stranger' assailant is very unusual (Somander and Rammer 1991).

It should be noted that virtually all the research studies identified relate to filicide. There is consensus in that child homicide is committed by parents in most instances (West 1965; Harder 1967; Resnick 1969; Rodenburg 1971; Scott 1973a; d'Orban 1979; Bourget and Bradford 1990; Somander and Rammer 1991; Bourget and Labelle 1992, Pritchard and Bagley 2000). Jason (1983) appears to be the only researcher suggesting that child homicide is not predominantly intra-familial. Jason examined the FBI statistics on child homicide 1976–79 and found two patterns of child homicide: for children aged 0–3 years the homicide was intra-familial, but with children over 12 years the homicides were almost always extra-familial. This was a similar pattern found in Britain, where in all but one within-family homicide, victims were aged 7 years and younger (Pritchard and Bagley 2001), but of course in terms of numbers in the USA, Jason had a point, but proportionately based upon numbers per age group, even in the USA, parents are most often the fatal assailants.

A particularly important international study, undertaken in Britain, was that by Wilczynski and Morris (1993). They utilized the Home Office Criminal Statistics (2002) and found that over an eight-year period, 395 parents were suspected of filicide between 1982–89, with 44 per cent being mothers. However, where the victim was under the age of 1, mothers made up almost one-half (47 per cent). It appears reasonable to conclude that child homicide by a father is just as likely to occur as that by a mother (Grunfeld and Steen 1984). New research will be examined in detail, which will help to clarify this problem.

The psychiatric–child protection interface

With a few notable exceptions (Famularo et al. 1992), the psychiatric dimension in child homicide has received relatively little attention in the social care and child protection literature in recent years. Indeed, a key review of 'child abuse' in *The British Journal of Social Work* in 1998 made no mention of mental disorder whatsoever! Yet most cohort or longitudinal child homicide research published in non-social work journals indicates a significant incidence of psychiatric diagnoses among persons who kill children (Resnick 1969, 1970; Scott 1973a, 1973b; d'Orban 1979, 1990; Bourget and Bradford 1990; Bourget and Labelle 1992; Pritchard 1992a; Stroud 1997, 2001, 2003; Pritchard and Bagley 2001). In a study of 89 women remanded in Holloway Prison and charged with the killing of their child(ren), d'Orban (1979) found 16 per cent had a psychotic illness, 21 per cent had reactive depression and 43 per cent had a personality disorder. In fact, d'Orban found only 16 per cent (that is, 14 women) had no psychiatric abnormality at the time of committing the offence. Similarly, Somander and Rammer (1991) studying all 79 cases of child homicide in Sweden 1971–80 found only 10 out of 47 perpetrators were not mentally disordered when examined by a psychiatrist after the crime. The most definitive work was from Falkov (1996), who despite gaps in his data related to psychiatric diagnosis, found that 80 per cent had had some contact with specialist psychiatric services. This rate should be contrasted with that found in the British prevalence survey (Jenkins et al. 1998), which found 2.9 per cent of women and 2.1 per cent of men in the general population had a serious psychiatric problem. It is reasonable to infer that Falkov's sample had an unequivocally high rate of psychiatric difficulty, more than 26 times the general population.

Some writers have made a distinction between child abuse-neglect deaths and other child homicides (Greenland 1987), but it is important to be clear that all child killings are now being considered, and to remember that whilst all 'murders' are homicides, not all homicides are 'murder' because the assailant may be legally 'unfit to plead', or the initial 'unlawful killing' charge may be dropped to manslaughter because of 'diminished responsibility'. Moreover we are looking at what surely must be the hardest definition of the extremes of child abuse, namely a dead child for whatever reason, who later appears in national mortality statistics.

Of course, the characteristics of child abuse-neglect may be present as well as a diagnosable mental disorder. Referring to preventive measures in relation to homicide, Bourget and Labelle (1992) argue that a multi-dimensional phenomenon requires a multi-dimensional approach. By focusing upon the dimension of mental disorder rather than the child abuse-neglect syndrome, issues can become clearer, identifying situations where children are at a high risk of physical harm, as well as assisting further developing preventive strategies. Moreover, since child care/protection and psychiatric professionals are working in a climate of great public alarm and anxiety over both child homicide and the perceived dangerousness of mentally disordered persons, it seems essential that there is more accurate knowledge of the issues.

The term mental disorder is used in this discussion to mean diagnosable mental illness and personality disorders, including psychopathic (dissocial) personality disorder. The term is employed since it is the generic term used in the Mental Health Act 1983 and in the *International Classification of Diseases Version 10*, commonly written as ICD-10 (1995). Mental illness and psychopathic disorders are both specific categories of mental disorder to which the Act applies (section 1(2)(a)). The syndrome of 'alcoholism' is frequently associated with multiple-substance abuse as well as being co-morbid with various mental and personality disorders, and even the relatively moderate presence of alcoholism or drug misuse is known to make a difficult situation worse (Pritchard 1991; Pritchard et al. 1997).

Since mental disorder has long been viewed negatively and stigmatized (Fernando 1988; Miles 1989), it could be considered controversial to examine the association between mental disorder and child killing and Stroud and Pritchard (2001) were accused of stigmatizing the mentally disordered (Barnes 2000). While any right thinking person must be concerned about further stigmatizing the mentally ill, it is necessary to confront hard topics with hard evidence for the safety of both assailant and potential victim (Pritchard and Stroud 2002). For example, in 1993 Tracey Evans, who had a history of mental illness for which she had received in-patient treatment, was sent to a Regional Secure Unit after drowning her two young school-age sons in the bath (Brindle 1995) and in January 1994 Sharon Dalson was detained in Rampton after strangling her son (aged 6) and suffocating her daughter (aged 5) while experiencing delusions (Ivory 1994). Sadly, if those involved had thought through the implications of the nature of the pre-existing mental disorder, conditions known to service providers, and the potential vulnerability of children, these tragedies may not have happened.

Practitioners, however, will be aware that there are some occasions when, in acute and severe crisis, a mentally disordered person may pose a risk to another person's safety and be unable to perceive this him/herself because of the mental disorder (Mental Health Act 1983). It is apt to remind ourselves that the mentally disordered are far more at risk from themselves, as their involvement in homicide remains statistically rare, albeit higher than the general population, but these tragedies are dwarfed by their high suicide rate (Pritchard 1999, 2004).

Mental disorder and child homicide warrant a high level of professional attention not only in respect of children's safety, but also in terms of preventing the trauma that the perpetrator of such a homicide will likely experience for the rest of their lives (Bluglass 1988). To kill a child, and especially one's own child, is viewed as an 'unthinkable' act that may well ostracize the perpetrator from his/her family and community for ever (Fraser 1998; Stroud 2003). It should be emphasized that while the trend in Britain is for an increase in homicide rates (Bowden 1990; d'Orban 1990; Home Office 2002), this increase is substantially accounted for by 'normal' murders. The number of 'abnormal' murders (that is, manslaughter due to diminished responsibility, infanticide, suspect insanity, suspect committed suicide) has remained relatively constant (d'Orban 1990). Thus mounting public concern over mental disorder and violence, which has led to new legal powers (that is, the Mental Health (Patients In The Community) Act 1995) does not reflect an actual increase in fatal violence committed by mentally disordered persons, but rather reflects media and pressure group campaigns. Indeed the recent report of the National Confidential Inquiry into homicide and suicide by the mentally ill showed again that murder by mentally ill people of victims they did not know remains very rare (Appleby et al. 1999). In extrapolating from

UK mortality statistics (WHO 2001), even if we assume that a quarter of all UK homicides have a psychiatric link, the motorist kills more than 20 times as many people as does the mentally disordered person, and the 'drink-and-drive' person even more frequently. Certainly the motorist kills children at four times the rate of child homicides (Pritchard 2002).

A gender difference between 'normal' and 'abnormal' homicide, which has been explored by Wilczynski and Morris (1993), should also be noted. While 'normal' homicide of adults is predominately a male province, a significant proportion of 'abnormal' homicides are committed by women (d'Orban 1990), especially where children are concerned (d'Orban 1990; Somander and Rammer 1991; Falkov 1996; Pritchard and Bagley 2001). Violent deaths of children are rare, infrequent events (Greenland 1987; Bourget and Bradford 1990), but what is not at issue is that proportionally, babies (less than 1-year-old) and infants (aged 1–4) are proportionately more at risk, and babies in Britain are more often killed than any other age band – the next highest being the young males aged 15–24 (WHO 2003). The murderers of victims aged less than 5 are in the main family members and especially mothers. Controversy surrounds the exact number of children assigned to the 'child homicide' category: Wilczynski and Morris (1993) suggest that homicide statistics are likely to be an under-estimate because of possible misclassification of deaths as accidental, and legal difficulties in proving some 'suspicious' deaths as homicides. But this is likely to be true for all Western countries, and moreover with the unprecedented level of concern about abuse, it is probably less likely that a suspicious death is missed today than in the 1970s. New concerns about the 'shaken baby syndrome' are a case in point. Nonetheless, in an effort to highlight child deaths related to violence, in an international comparison of combing child homicides and what are known as 'Other Violent Deaths', road deaths still exceed such fatalities and England and Wales have amongst the biggest reductions in the Western world since the 1970s, whilst the USA actually increased over the 1974–99 period (Pritchard and Butler 2003).

Typologies of child homicide

A number of studies have sought to create a typology of different types of child homicide. For example, the classification 'altruistic' (Resnick 1969) covers both the mercy-killing of a severely handicapped and dying child by its parent(s) and the killing of a child by a depressed and suicidal parent who believes that he/she is saving the child from a cruel world. It can moreover, be difficult to assign one case to a specific group: for example, in d'Orban's sample, 12 subjects classified as 'battering mothers' also had a mental illness (reactive depression). 'Accidental' filicide appears a particularly misleading category and Somander and Rammer (1991) suggest that 'fatal child abuse' is a more appropriate classification, reflecting severe and heavy-handed punishments which tried to eliminate disturbing behaviour of a child, without the intention to kill but which ended in serious injury or death.

Such classifications may not be particularly useful in practice where the focus is prevention and identification of high-risk situations, as opposed to a retrospective analysis of motive or impulse. Classification by motive is useful for practitioners – in medicine, nursing, police, education and social work – to have knowledge and understanding of the psychopathology associated with child homicide. Such knowledge may alert practitioners to symptoms in their patients/clients, which may potentially post a risk to a child's safety. Stroud (1997) has given a useful tabular summary of the earlier classic child homicide studies highlighting the psychiatric dimension in child protection and I offer it here.

Different studies focus on the importance of various psychiatric disorders. For example, schizophrenia is considered a significant diagnostic category by West (1965), Resnick (1969) and Myers (1970). In contrast, d'Orban (1979) reports only four psychotic cases and Bourget and Bradford (1990) none. Likewise in a number of studies major depression with psychotic

Table 7.1 Classification of Filicides

Resnick 1969	Scott 1973a	d'Orban 1979	Bourget and Bradford 1990
N=131 88 F 43 M	N=85 39 F 46 M	N=89 all mothers	N=13 9F 4m
Altruistic, associated with suicide to relieve suffering	Elimination of unwanted child	Battering mothers	Pathalogical filicide and altruistic suicide
Acutely psychotic	Mercy killing	Mentally Ill mothers	Accidental death and battering parent
Accidental	Gross parental mental disorder	Neonatricides	Others
Unwanted child	Cause not in victim, but revenge upon partner	Retaliating mothers	Retaliatory
Spouse revenge	Victim is primary target – the battering parent	Unwanted children and mercy killing	Neonatricide and paternal filicide

Table 7.2 Psychiatric diagnoses associated with child homicide (d'Orban 1979) n=89 mothers

Type of Filicide	Personality Disorder	Reactive Depression	Psychotic Illness	'Sub-normality'	No Abnormality	Total
Battering	17	12	0	3	0	36
Mentally ill	4	6	14	0	0	24
Neoatricide	2	0	0	1	0	11
Retaliatory	8	1	0	0	0	9
Unwanted child	7	0	1	0	0	8
Mercy killing	0	0	1	0		1
Total No:	38	19	14	4	14	89
%	43%	21%	16%	4%	16%	100

Table 7.3 Resnick 1969: Psychiatric diagnoses of 131 parents charged with filicide

Diagnosis	Numbers
Schizophrenia	22
Psychosis, other	24
Non psychotic illness	15
Character disorder	12
Melancholia	11
No psychiatric diagnosis	7
Manic depressive	2
Retarded	2
Neurosis	2
Delirium	2
Epilepsy	1

features is the most common diagnosis, particularly for material perpetrators (West 1965; Harder 1967; Resnick 1969; Rodenburg 1971; Scott 1973a). Nevertheless, both d'Orban (1979) and Bourget and Bradford (1990) find personality disorders more prevalent. It should be noted that in the more recent studies, no diagnoses of Munchausen Syndrome by Proxy (factitious disorder) are made. While it may be difficult to identify clear patterns and trends from the available research data, there is consensus that there is a significant incidence of mental disorder among perpetrators.

It is important to note that research studies also find that the perpetrators of child murder often experienced significant levels of psychosocial stress. Bourget and Bradford (1990) concluded that exposure to a variety of psychosocial stressors prior to the offence was a major factor in most cases. They identified the following: family stress, marital separation or stress, unwanted or difficult pregnancies/deliveries, disabled child and serious financial problems. Likewise, d'Orban concluded that 'Most women in the study were subject to multiple adversity' (1979: 563). d'Orban found 71 per cent of subjects experienced severe marital discord, 32 per cent housing problems and 30 per cent financial difficulties, which matches a modern longitudinal study in Britain (Stroud 2003).

The stress factors identified by d'Orban (1979) and by Bourget and Bradford (1990) are of the same tenor as the major ongoing difficulties identified by Brown and Harris (1978) and Brown et al. (1990), as being of aetiological significance in depression in their longitudinal work with a cohort of working class women randomly sampled from an urban community – financial, housing and marital problems, loss of a mother, three or more children at home. It seems important to link Brown and Harris's (1978) findings to those on the psychosocial stress experienced by persons who kill children.

Although personality disorder is the leading diagnosis for 'battering' mothers in d'Orban's (1979) sample (17 of 36), reactive depression was also a diagnosis (12 of 36) in this group. Bourget and Bradford (1990) and Rodenburg (1971) suggest that personality factors, when coinciding with depressive illness, substantially increase the risk of homicide. It would also seem that psychosocial stresses are part of this equation. Consequently, there appears to be a possible interaction between personality factors, psychosocial stresses and depression, each reinforcing the other in a downward spiral of violence directed to vulnerable family members, which is of particular relevance in understanding the causes of child homicide. The evidence for this proposition appears to be strengthened by the British findings of Hawton and Roberts (1981) and Hawton et al. (1985) who studied the association between attempted suicide in mothers, and abuse of children. They found that there was well-documented evidence of serious child abuse (or risk) in 29.8 per cent of mothers who were referred to a general hospital following a suicide attempt. Likewise, Pritchard (1991) assessed data on 60 families who were on an 'At Risk' register and found high levels of psychosocial stress, with two-fifths of mothers experiencing 'some form of depression'. At this interim stage therefore it can be asserted with some confidence that the majority of *parental* assailants are or have been mentally disordered and that psychiatric disturbance is a major factor associated with the unlawful killing of a child.

Patterns of mental disorder

There appear to be several major patterns in the association between child homicide and mental disorder. Firstly, serious assaults may be directly associated with acute mental illness, that is, puerperal psychosis, depression, schizophrenia. The nature and quality of the symptoms of the illness (for example delusional beliefs) are the origins of the assault, which is deliberate and severe. If delusions are present, it is essential to determine whether the child is involved in the delusional system: practitioners, therefore, must ask about the 'unthinkable' and 'unaskable' to assess the threat of violence/ homicide (Prins 1991).

Secondly, often repeated assaults may also be directly associated with dissocial (psychopathic) personality. The assault relates to the perpetrator's 'callous unconcern' for others, a low threshold for frustration and discharge of aggression and an inability to feel remorse (WHO 1992). Mr Morris Beckford, the stepfather of Jasmine Beckford, who was found guilty of her homicide, might be considered to have facets of dissocial personality. The persistent nature of the violence he committed are evidenced by the 'multiple scars ... consistent with repeated episodes of physical abuse' from which Jasmine died (Blom-Cooper 1985).

Thirdly, assaults may be associated with a combination of factors, for example personality disorder, depression and severe environmental and psychosocial stress. There is often no deliberate intent to kill or seriously wound, and the assault occurs when a crisis precipitates a loss of control in a severely stressed individual. This type of assault equates with the child abuse syndrome. It is important that future research investigates this interactive process further.

Fourthly, severe depression has an identified association with problems of child care (Hawton and Roberts 1981; Isaac et al. 1986; Pritchard 1991; Shepherd 1994; Stroud 1997, 2003) may lead a parent to decide that they are sparing children from cruel fate when they kill those children and themselves.

The inter-related nature of the issues is illustrated by the fact that psychosocial stress associated with physical abuse is of the same tenor as the stress which is of aetiological significance in depression (Brown and Harris 1978; Brown 1987; Brown et al. 1990). Brown and Harris (1978) identified those severe, stressful life events and major ongoing difficulties as three times more common in depressed women. Ongoing difficulties were identified such as financial, housing and marital difficulties: a stressful life event might, for example, be a husband leaving home. Such factors, together with vulnerability factors such as loss of, or separation from, mother for more than one year before the age of 17 years, having more than three children at home, and chronically low self-esteem, are associated with the development of depression. It seems vital to make connections between these findings and those on the stress experienced by physically abusive parents.

An understanding of the nature of depression explains why it is difficult for abusive parents to appropriately parent their children and to manage the stress they experience. Depression is marked by a loss of interest and enjoyment, with fatigability and disturbed sleep. There is a reduction in concentration and attention (WHO 1992), with negative cognitions predominating (Fennell 1989). Beck (1973: 11) summed up the essence of depression as a 'sense that the self is worthless, the world meaningless and the future pointless'. Negative cognitions explain why abusive parents perceive stress more negatively than other parents, with a poor appraisal of their ability to meet the demands upon them (Whipple and Webster-Stratton 1991). Depression is eminently treatable with medication and cognitive therapy (Blackburn et al. 1981; Weissman et al. 1981). Depression is often wrongly equated with passivity – however, irritability and extreme agitation may well be a feature (WHO 1992) and it is worth remembering the psychodynamic concept of depression as anger turned upon the self. Depressed mothers, therefore, are identified as being more harsh, critical and likely to use physical punishment (Seagull 1987; Whipple and Webster-Stratton 1991). Ghodsian et al. (1984) found an increased frequency of physical punishment in depressed mothers, and Zuvarin (1989) found an increased risk of child abuse and physical aggression in moderately depressed mothers.

Without appropriate intervention the difficulties are self-perpetuating: the children of depressed parents are more likely to exhibit hostile and anxious behaviour (Rutter and Quinton 1984) which places additional stress on the parents, increasing the risk of abuse. Although a number of studies have found an association between anxiety and physical abuse, the role of anxiety has not been as well researched as that of depression (Whipple and Webster-Stratton 1991). Because anxiety may be a feature of depression (WHO 1992), it seems essential that future research analyses the association.

However, in the recent past, the ability of social workers to identify specific mental illness appeared no greater than chance (Huxley et al. 1987). It seems essential that the connections between childcare and mental disorder are both recognized and taken account of in practice. More recently Shepherd (1994), reviewing maternal depression and child care, makes the case for 'a mental health child care worker' in light of the indirect, but formidable evidence of the association, yet sadly in a fairly recent review which might be thought to have been 'definitive' and up-to-date, totally failed to mention most of the above literature and nothing on the mental health dimension (Munro 1998).

While social service departments are the lead authorities responsible for child protection (Home Office et al. 1991) a mistaken view has evolved that child protection is solely – or at best mainly – the province of Social Services (Noyes 1991). In fact, both the National Health Service Act 1977 and section 27 of the Children Act 1989 provide that health authorities must assist Social Services with the safe care of children. The importance of psychiatrists and general practitioners being alert to child protection issues is illustrated by research. Resnick (1969) found 40 per cent of filicidal parents were seen by a psychiatrist or other physician shortly before the crime. d'Orban (1979) reported that at the time of the offence 60 per cent of his sample were in contact, in order of frequency, with a general practitioner, psychiatrist, social worker and health visitor. Bourget and Bradford (1990) likewise found that a significant number of homicidal parents came to the attention of psychiatrists before the tragedy.

As long ago as the Beckford inquiry (Blom-Cooper 1985) it was recognized that doctors should be educated about the need for inter-agency work in child protection and notes that current medical training emphasizes doctors being in charge, listening to other professional views, but still taking decisions based upon their own medical judgment. The Cleveland Inquiry (Butler-Sloss 1988) made the same observation. It is also suggested that often a doctor's assessment of a situation depends on what he/she is told by the patient (the Lucy Gates inquiry: London Boroughs of Bexley and Greenwich 1982). Similarly, Johnston (1967) considers that psychiatrists may identify with the patient and be sympathetic with his/her problems, resulting in vital 'cues and clues' about potentially violent behaviour being missed and assessment not being based upon the reality of the situation.

Noyes (1991) points out that a theme running through the child abuse inquiries of the 1980s is the isolation of the GP and their non-involvement in the inter-agency system. It appears psychiatrists are similarly isolated and non-involved. It would seem sensible that the community psychiatric services develop a role in informing the medical professions about the association between mental health and fatal child assault. Some doctors consider that patient confidentiality prevents them alerting social services to situations of risk, but as early as 1987, the General Medical Council expressed the view that

> If a doctor has reason for believing that a child is being physically or sexually abused, not only is it permissible for the doctor to disclose information to a third party, but it is a duty of the doctor to do so.
> (The Annual Report of the General Medical Council, 1987, cited in DoH et al. 1991: 120)

This statement was 'warmly supported' by both the Department of Health and the Home Office.

It is essential that up-to-date research be carried out, identifying the psychiatric diagnoses of those who kill children. Quantifying these stresses and detecting any link to depressive illness appears to be highly important. Shepherd (1994) points out that research on mental disorder has been carried out largely separate from child care issues: it seems the psychiatric and social work professionals must make good this omission and undertake more collaborative research. It is important that existing and future research findings are utilized in informing preventive practice.

Parental stress and the interaction with mental health difficulties

It is well documented that many physically abusive parents face multiple adversity with high levels of psychosocial stress (d'Orban 1979; Justice et al. 1985; Pritchard 1991; Gibbons et al. 1995; Waterhouse et al. 1995). Issues of parental mental health have been subsumed in discussions of the role of stress generally, rather than there being analysis of the nature, effect and consequence of the diagnoses, and their interaction with stress factors. But it is likely that all are compounded within the context of poverty and negative socio-economic factors, such as unemployment, low income, housing difficulties and poor educational attainment. It is equally well-documented that most abusing parents experienced high levels of stress as children, including having been abused as a child and experiencing parental separation, by virtue of being in care. There is also an association of perpetrating serious physical abuse, with poor marital relationships and family violence victimization, parental criminal offences and substance abuse (d'Orban 1979; Korbin 1986; Egeland et al. 1988; Pritchard 1991; Whipple and Webster-Stratton 1991; Famularo et al. 1992; Gibbons et al. 1995; Langeland and Dijkstra 1995; Waterhouse et al. 1995).

However, not every parent experiencing severe socio-economic hardship or life stress abuses their children. It appears that it is the additional presence of negative mental health factors which plays a significant and critical role in the association between stress and abuse (Pritchard 1991). Egeland et al. (1988), for example, found that psychological differences, that is, anxiety implying definite psychiatric morbidity, and negative personality characteristics, explained why some highly stressed mothers were easily frustrated, annoyed and quick to respond in a hostile and aggressive fashion, and were less competent in understanding and relating to their children.

Significant levels of mental health problems have been found among physically abusive parents. In a British study of 60 families on an 'At Risk of Abuse' register it was found that two-fifths of mothers experienced some form of depression, with low self-esteem and some attempted suicide (Pritchard 1991): this reflects the findings of Hawton et al. (1985), discussed earlier. Whipple and Webster-Stratton (1991), in a study of 123 families referred to a parenting clinic, found that only the abusive mothers had a clinical level of depression: they also had higher levels of state anxiety than non-abusive mothers. Famularo et al. (1992) reviewed the cases of 54 maltreating mothers and found 40.7 per cent had a mood (that is, depressive) disorder compared to 5.4 per cent in a control group. More recently, Gibbons et al. (1995), in a detailed study of families referred to eight social service departments because of suspected abuse, found parental mental illness (unspecified) to be a factor in 13 per cent of cases: in one Outer London Borough the percentage rose to 25 per cent.

Personality difficulties have been identified as a significant factor in adults who abuse. Justice et al. (1985) found physically abusive parents, compared with non-abusive parents who experienced equally high levels of psychosocial stress, were significantly more likely to use violence as a response to stress, or to attempt to 'solve' a problem. Pritchard (1991) found abusive parents were hostile (42 per cent), unco-operative (57 per cent), unmotivated (93 per cent) and with unrealistic expectations (62 per cent). Equally, Famularo et al. (1992) found 64.8 per cent of maltreating mothers had a personality disorder, compared with 29.7 per cent of non-abusing mothers.

Issues of gender difference require consideration. The research quoted thus far is based mainly on mothers, even though in physical abuse male and female parents are approximately equally represented (Martin 1984; Pritchard 1991; Langeland and Dijkstra 1995). A clear picture of differences between male and female diagnoses cannot be obtained. This omission in the published research leaves a potentially erroneous image that an abusive parent is an economically poor, lone, depressed mother. It also raises the question whether socio-cultural assumptions have been made, with an abusive female being seen as the norm. It has been suggested that such bias operates in psychiatry, with women being diagnosed as disordered in disproportionate numbers (Scott 1973a). Considering that fathers are likely to be facing the same negative socio-economic circumstances as women, why is so little known about their mental health? Given that unemployment leads to declining self-respect and despair (Jahoda 1979) and that there is an association between suicide, depression and male unemployment (Platt 1984; Pritchard 1988, 1999), it is possible that there is an increase in both depression and propensity to violence in fathers. It is essential that research, employing clear diagnostic criteria, clarifies the situation.

Personality factors

Personality disorder as a diagnostic category is traditionally viewed by social welfare professionals with suspicion, if not hostility, because of its negative implications for change and personal development. However, in the light of the adverse childhood experiences of many physically abusive parents it is not surprising that personality development has been affected. Rutter and Quinton (1984) found parental hostility; irritability and aggression/violence were important factors in the development of conduct disorder and psychiatric disturbance in children. Personality disorder covers a wide range of types of personal and social functioning (WHO 1992): it is important to be

aware that the term does not solely relate to dissocial/psychopathic personality, which is, to reiterate, directly associated with a risk of serious physical
abuse, as is evidenced by the death of Jasmine Beckford (Blom-Cooper 1985).
It is suggested that physically abusive parents may have personality difficulties relating to impulse control and a tendency to act without consideration
of the consequences: equally, a lack of emotional stability may result in a
sudden loss of temper. Adverse childhood experiences, it is suggested, may
well lead to the so-called 'borderline' type of personality, which is characterized by a disturbed self image, chronic feelings of emptiness, emotional
instability and is associated with self-harm (WHO 1992). Obviously, such
traits will render the individual prone to depression.

Personality difficulties prevent physically abusing parents from utilizing
support systems and this differentiates them from non-abusing parents
(Seagull 1987). Egeland et al. (1988) found maltreating mothers were suspicious, defensive and rigid, and they found it difficult to maintain relationships and seek help. Depression may well play a part in this defensiveness: low
self esteem and feelings of worthlessness may well contribute to hostility
when parenting is identified as lacking. This hostility and lack of co-operation
poses a great challenge to professionals.

A greater awareness about personality difficulties and the role they play
in physical abuse is needed. It appears important that identifying different
types of personality problems becomes less of an anathema for child welfare
workers, in assessing the areas of difficulty that can guide intervention: psychological strategies such as anger management can effect positive change.
Equally, supportive counselling may assist individuals experiencing the distress associated with the 'borderline personality' syndrome (Briere 1989). It is
important that such interventions are considered when there is risk of physical abuse.

Who kills children?

The answer to this question has been posed in a British study, published in a
leading American journal, which was the first ever cohort study of child
homicide assailants over a decade (Pritchard and Bagley 2001). Theoretical
models were eschewed in this study which focused directly upon 'outcome'
behaviour, namely those who were found responsible for the death of the
child, based upon decisions of the Crown Court but in some instances, the
Coroner's court.

The cohort of a decade of child homicides occurred within a general
population of some 2.6 million people, over a ten-year period. During this
time in the two English counties studied, 33 children were killed by 27
assailants, 14 women (all mothers) and 13 men, a similar gender ratio found

in other studies (Resnick 1969; d'Orban 1990; Somander and Rammer 1991). Again, similar to other international research, 82 per cent of assailants were within-family murderers, while the remaining five extra-family assailants were all men. All but one of the latter was known to the child and only one was a total stranger. There was also one undetected assailant, apparently extra-familial, in which sexual abuse also occurred but self-evidently, we can say nothing further about the assailant. The children's ages, compared between within-family and extra-family murderers are shown in Table 7.4.

Table 7.4 A Decade of Child Homicide: Age of Victims by Gender

Category	Boys	Girls	Total
Victims	20	13	33
Intra-family 0–7 years 8–16 years	15 1	11 1	26 2
Extra-family 0–7 years 8–16 years	0 4	0 1	0 5

[Age by intra-family and extra-family: χ-squared = 16.8519 P < 0.00001]

Of the 28 children who were killed within their family, 26 were aged 7 and under, whereas the extra-family homicides were all aged 8 and over, the oldest being a girl of 14. This within-family versus extra-family pattern was statistically, highly significant. This is an important indicator when assessing risk, namely the younger the child within the family, the greater the risk of death. However, it may be that older children may equally be as severely assaulted as younger, but they are more likely to physically survive their injuries.

The assailants could all be 'categorized' in the following four categories. First were those who were 'mentally ill', defined as having contact with specialist psychiatric services (Jenkins et al. 1998), or being found unfit to plead. Second were the 'Violent Offenders', defined by having a previous conviction for inter-personal violence. Third were the 'Neglecter/Abusers', defined by being on the 'At Risk of Abuse' register of the local authority and lastly were the 'extra-family' assailants, who were also sexually assaultive, men in all cases, had previous convictions for sex offences against children.

The division of assailants into within- and extra-familial is of practical benefit, especially when it comes to attempts to make assessments about 'dangerousness'. Table 7.5 lists the assailants under these four categories: the majority of family abusers were mothers (52 per cent), of whom 57 per cent were mentally ill. Indeed, the most frequent category of assailant was the 'mentally ill' 44 per cent, as all four natural fathers who killed a child were also mentally ill. In four cases in which the 'stepfather-cohabitee' had previous convictions for violence, they were joint 'defendants' with the child's mother, but the courts could not decide, which of either parent was guilty, so both were convicted of the child's murder. However, in three cases, the male received a far longer sentence indicating the most likely leader of the final assault against the child. These four mothers were or had been on the 'At Risk of Abuse' register. Two other 'At Risk of Abuse' mothers, however, killed their children singly, but more with neglect and fecklessness, than with marked violence. One of these mothers was described by her GP as depressed, but she never consulted psychiatric services, so she was not included in the 'mentally-ill mothers' group.

Table 7.5 Ten Years of Child Homicide by Gender, 'Category of Assailant' and Within-Family [n=22] versus Extra Family Assailants [n=7]

Categories and age	Males n=13	Females n=14	Total n=27
Within-family n = 22 Mothers [1 stepmother]	0	14	14 (52%)
Fathers	4	0	4 (15%)
Step-parent cohabitee [joint]	4	0	4 (15%)
Category of assailant Mentally ill [Aged M24–69 F18–34]	4	8	12 (44%)
'Neglect and abuse' [Aged F18–24]	0	6 [4 joint]	6 (22%)
Violent offender [Aged M18–37]	4 [all joint]	0	4 (15%)
Extra-family [n = 5]	5	0	5 (19%)
Category Child sex abuser CSA only Multi-criminal, CSA	0 5		0 5 (19%)

All five extra-family assailants were child sex abusers. However, it is important to note that they already fell into the most dangerous category of sex abusers, having previous convictions for non-sexual crime, but most importantly, for previous crimes against the person, designating this category as the 'Violent Multi-Criminal Child Sex Abuser' (Pritchard and Bagley 2000). Such men are self-evidently the most dangerous, but fortunately, they are a small minority of the general run of men convicted for sex offences against children (Simon et al. 1992; Waterhouse et al. 1995; Pritchard and Bagley

2001). In a related study it was found that none of the men who were 'sex only' child sex abusers, killed a child, or had ever physically harmed a child. This is not to exonerate or belittle the seriousness of 'sex only' abusers: rather, this finding adds to judgments about 'dangerousness', and highlights who poses the greatest physical danger to children. Recognizing that we can differentiate between type of abusers facilitates the taking of very hard but necessary decisions about preventive detention on grounds of future risk of very serious offending.

Estimating dangerousness

The reader may comment that despite this cohort spanning ten years, with only 27 assailants, could serious generalizations be made? Indeed, following an earlier review of national child homicides in Britain and other countries (Pritchard 1992a), the use of child homicide statistics were also so criticized (McDonald 1995; Lindsay and Trocme 1995), because even national numbers, averaging 50 per annum are, fortunately, rather rare in Western countries (Pritchard 2002). However, crucially, these critics forget that in studying the rarity of child homicide assailants, one is not looking at rates within the total population for potential killers, as invariably they belong to the four 'special categories' identified (Pritchard 1996a; Pritchard and Bagley 2000, 2001). Moreover, as Grubin (1994) showed, in a study of adult sex murders there is important information to be gleaned from studies on samples as small as 20 assailants. The majority of child murderers come from small, 'special' groups of populations at risk. If we take these numbers and apply a common sense approach to statistics, important indicators can be demonstrated for assessing comparative risk of dangerousness, which was independently said to be the value of this epidemiological approach (Shah and De 1998).

To determine an epidemiological rate of child homicide, one is using not the general population as potential perpetrators, but rather the four 'special samples'. These are: mentally ill assailants; 'neglecting and abusing' parents; men with history of criminal violence; and male child sex abusers. To establish the rate in the special populations at risk, divide the number of events, murder, by the numbers of actual or potential assailants. The following formula is used to estimate mortality rates per hundred thousand (pht), per annum (p.a.):

$$\text{Rates pht} = \frac{d}{p} \times \frac{100,000}{y}$$

where 'd' is the total number of murders [deaths], occurring in 'y', years, and 'p', is the estimated population for each cohort. For illustrative purposes only, it will be artificially *assumed* that all child homicides in England and Wales in

1995 were committed by a male, who killed just one child. Extrapolating from the 1995 mortality statistics (WHO 2003) there were 43 child homicides, and 15,950,000 men aged 19–64 years – the age range of the British assailants, who are the at-risk group for calculating the estimated General Population Rate (GPR) of potential killers. This works out as follows:

$$\text{GPR} = \frac{43}{15,950,000} \times \frac{100,000}{1} = 0.27 \text{ pht}$$

Thus a random sample of 370,930 men would be required to reach the estimated statistical 'expected' rate of one child murderer. Such numbers need to be borne in mind when considering the size of the special groups and the number of child murderers they contained.

This epidemiological approach was applied to two counties' child homicide rates, using the best official data available to determine the potential size of the special groups. The mentally ill within the general population was estimated from the British Prevalence survey (Jenkins et al. 1998). The 'Violent Males' were based upon the actual number of men convicted of such an offence, from police records. The 'Neglecting/Abusing' mother was based upon the numbers on the two counties' social service 'At Risk' registers; and the male child sex abuser, by the sex-only and violent-multi-criminal child abuser type, figures gathered from a two-year cohort of police records (Pritchard and Bagley 2000). Whilst the rates which emerged are still an estimate, they are probably the strongest data for these populations as yet assembled. When approaching the numbers of assailants from this perspective, we get a very different picture of dangerousness.

Table 7.6 shows the 'special groups' estimated to be in the general population, and this gives us the potential pool of assailants, who are at risk of killing a child. In terms of frequency, the 'Mentally-ill mother' was responsible for 30 per cent of all the child homicides, exceeding the neglecter/abusing mothers, especially when we note that only two such women killed when not aided or abetted by a male partner with a previous record for violence.

Based upon the notional 'normal' mother who killed, the rate would be 0.5 per 100,000 (pht) p.a., whereas the 'Mentally-ill Mother' (MIM) killed at 20 times this rate at 10 pht. In ascending level of 'dangerousness', based upon the epidemiological rates of child homicide, the 'single' mother on the 'At Risk' register, killed at nearly three times the MIM rate, at 28 pht. The male violent offender killed at more than four times the MIM, and when partnered by such a man, the mother on the 'At Risk of Abuse' register mother killed at eight times the MIM rate.

By far the most dangerous were those extra-family child sex abuser assailants, one of whom was a multi-criminal sex abuser, killing at a rate of 204 pht; the remaining violent multi-criminal child sexual abuser, killed at

Table 7.6   Estimated frequency of child homicide assailants by 'status', rates per 100,000 (pht)

Assailants by Age	Males estimated population *	Females estimated population *	Assailant rates per 100,000 p.a
Mentally ill [1] **Male:** 24–69 yrs 2.1% **Female:** 18–34 yrs 2.9%	Pop: 13,419 4 assailants	Pop: 8,022 8 assailants	3 pht p.a. 10 pht p.a.
Neglect [2] [SSD] **With cohabitee** **Without cohabitee**		723 p.a. 6 assailants	83 pht p.a. 28 pht p.a.
Violent offender [3] [Police]	901 p.a 4 assailants		44 pht p.a.
All male CSA [4]	187 p.a [5 assailants]		267 pht p.a.
Sex only CSA [50%]	93 p.a. 0		0
Multi-crime CSA [26%]	49 p.a [1 assailant]		204 pht p.a.
Violent and multi-crime CSA [24%]	46 p.a 4 assailants		869 pht p.a.

Sources [1] Jenkins et al. (1998); [2] Social Service Department register; [3] Police records, [4] Child Sexual Abuser study. *1991 General Population 18–75+ Males 750,890 Females 853,399 OPCS

more than 80 times that of the mentally ill mother, at a rate of 869 pht. To put this in context, some 1 per cent of this group go on to kill a child, which is vastly different from the notional 'ordinary' male rate of 0.00026 per cent. Put another way, out of a potential sample of violent multi-criminal sexual abusers, estimated to be 46 men per annum, at risk, over a ten year period they killed four children. But to find one 'random' male child killer from the general population requires more than 370,000 men, 8043 times the sample of these most dangerous child sex abusers. By any criteria, this type of man is very dangerous, hence the rationale for the idea of indeterminate, 'review-able' sentences (Pritchard and Bagley 2001).

All the mentally ill fathers who killed, also died by their own hand. A quarter of all the mentally ill mothers committed suicide. One of the 'At risk of Abuse' mothers, made a serious attempt on her life, but survived. *None* of the multi-criminal and violent child sex abuse murderers killed themselves, or attempted to do so. On the other hand, amongst the two-year cohort of child sex abusers, 3 per cent of the 'sex only ' offenders (men who were essentially 'non violent' offenders) killed themselves. A surprising finding was that whilst victims of child sex abuse as adults had significantly higher suicide rates than the general population, it was not as high as in those with a background of mental illness. Moreover, all the women and the majority of men who had been victims of child sexual abuse also had a concurrent mental disorder, as defined by having contact with the specialist psychiatric services. Remarkably, the current perpetrators of child sex abuse had a suicide rate that was even *higher* than that of the mentally ill. Yet none of these men had committed any violence, or any other crime besides sexual assault, nor had they any prior contact with the psychiatric services: but their deaths, occurring around the point of disclosure or trial, suggested that there was profound remorse and shame, not shared by the violently multi-criminal perpetrator of CSA (Pritchard and King 2004).

There are implications for intervention from this study, for on the one hand it makes it easier (although morally questionable) to agree for indeterminate sentences for the violent child sex abuser, whilst on the other, to argue for an outreach approach to assist men who come forward for treatment, to help them control their behaviour, rather than instituting immediate criminal proceedings. Let me try to illuminate these findings from some case examples.

These ethical dilemmas are illustrated by the case of 'Ulrich', a 50-year-old professional man with a previous history of depression which, with the support he received from his wife, had been successfully treated. Unfortunately the marriage ended, and 'Ulrich' lived alone and was very isolated, also losing key links with his supportive GP. His depression returned, with increasing paranoid ideas of persecution and unworthiness. A brief visit to a new GP resulted in a perfunctory investigation. Apart from the prescribed anti-depressants no follow-up, nor any counselling support was offered. 'Ulrich' deteriorated and he was convinced that the world was going to end and that his two children were in real danger: to 'protect' them he strangled them and then hung himself. Apart from the obvious tragedy, the sad aspect of this case was the fact that he was amenable to treatment, and with a properly integrated approach to mental health, that is, to a bio-psychosocial integrated treatment model, these murders could well have been avoided.

Consider 'Vaz', a 55-year-old Asian businessman, very much a pillar of the local community. Over a six-month period his behaviour and interpersonal relationships began to deteriorate markedly, as he began to speak of fearful conspiracies. Paradoxically, he became a victim of inverse racism, since as his behaviour became more odd, fellow businessmen were very reluctant to encourage him either to seek help, or to respond honestly to his question, 'Do you think I'm going mad?', when he patently was. He had the briefest and most indirect contact with the formal services at an inter-ethnic community initiative, when he spoke about 'aliens' and being 'watched by malevolent' beings. The professional interpreted this as racial harassment.

His wife sought informal help and advice from her community, but she did not tell her friends just how bizarre her husband's behaviour was becoming. More importantly, 'Vaz' began to talk about 'death as the only way out' which was anathema to his culture. Again because of the marked cultural stigma about suicide and mental health, neither wife nor male members of the 'Vaz' family, sought outside help. He brought all his family together and poisoned his four children, his wife and then himself. From the journal he kept it was obvious that he was suffering from an acute episode of paranoid schizophrenia, with marked delusions and hallucinations. They, concerned 'Shaitan' taking over the world, that his blood was slowly being poisoned, because he alone was aware of what was happening. Therefore, he alone could save the world, by sacrificing himself and his family to prove that there was one good, uncorrupted man in this corrupted world.

Both the above cases initially at least, seem far away from the work of the child protection teams: yet as the above results show, the mental health dimension is often the single biggest factor in protecting children from severe abuse and neglect.

Consider 'Winnie' an 18-year-old, with a history of neglect and abuse, broken foster-care placements and intermittent spells in residential care up to the age of 11. As a very young teenager she quickly gravitated to substance abuse and was sexually active, culminating in two pregnancy terminations, associated with her permanent exclusion from school. Her mother, herself a victim of the cycle of neglect and abuse, had virtually abdicated any parental role with any of her teenaged children. The two hour a week contact sessions with the home education service were woefully inadequate and when 'Winnie' was 15 she was eligible to 'leave-school' and both she and the Education Authority, were happy to move on, despite 'Winnie's' reading-age being barely that of a 10-year-old. Whilst technically she had a 'learning difficulty', whether this was innate and/or acquired, meant that she was virtually unemployable. As has been shown, there is no follow-up service for the 'excluded-from-school' adolescent (Pritchard and Butler 2000a, 2000b), and as 'Winnie' was not directly under the supervision of social services, she drifted into a lifestyle of drugs, drink and 'informal' sex-working.

She allowed her third pregnancy to go full term as she hoped that she and the father might form a family. This did not work, in part because the baby was underweight, as 'Winnie' had failed to complete ante-natal care and refused or was unable to reduce her smoking. The father left within a month, leaving 'Winnie' to attempt to cope with a small, fretful, demanding baby. Her response was to 'self-medicate' by more drink and drugs to 'ease her mind'. Social service involvement initially improved the situation, but there was a gap in supervision, and her escapist drink and drugs compounded her physical neglect of her baby. Neighbours expressed concern at her leaving the child overnight when she went out for 'work' or pleasure. She resolutely denied this to her new social worker but unfortunately after giving the baby a small dose of opiates to 'help her sleep' – and 'keep the neighbours off my back', 'Winnie' irresponsibly went 'clubbing' leaving the baby alone from 6pm until next morning, to find her dead on her return. 'Winnie' was found guilty of manslaughter, as it was realized that this 'child–woman' was crucially incompetent and unfit for parental responsibility, and in the last analysis was not a malevolent child killer.

'Yvonne' aged 32 had had a turbulent childhood, an alcoholic father who physically abused all his other four younger children and their mother. This led to 'Yvonne' being taken into care, aged 10, when her mother was admitted to psychiatric hospital and her father deserted the family. 'Yvonne' had a very poor self-image, was an under-achiever at school and was unhappy in a number of foster placements, all of which broke down, followed by short spells in residential care. She returned home at 14 to her mother and two of the other children. However, the mother's mental state was such that 'Yvonne' was needed to be more of a support to the mother, than the mother was to 'Yvonne'. As a young adult she was shy, with eating difficulties, anxious and very much a victim to predatory males, who exploited her and then moved on, often after indulging their physical and sexual aggression on someone even less able to cope than themselves.

Her three pregnancies were difficult, followed by apparent depression, though she successfully delivered a daughter after the third pregnancy. The father immediately left. Nonetheless, for four years she had been successfully supported by a social worker and all appeared to be progressing reasonably well. Unfortunately, when the social worker left, because of the 'progress' made, 'Yvonne' was not reallocated to a new worker by social services. Once again 'Yvonne' was isolated and felt abandoned. She began to neglect herself and her little girl and to compound matters, her GP retired and the new practice were unsympathetic, and told her to 'pull herself together and stop being a victim all your life'. 'Yvonne' became very miserable and obviously seriously depressed. She administered a massive overdose to herself and her child because 'nobody cares – I'm not worth it'.

This tragic case is doubly poignant because the very success of the social worker ultimately became a negative factor, since there is evidence that one factor associated with actual suicide of mentally disturbed people is the sudden absence of a supportive person, either when the person's key worker goes on leave or is reassigned, or leaves for another job (King et al. 2001). We do matter to our clients and when we inadequately 'close down' a case, there can be serious consequences. Hence it is crucial to plan either the closure of a case, or to hand over the case in a way that involves the full support of the client. Crucially in the case of 'Yvonne' there was a failure at least at team leader level, both in respect of transferring responsibility and in appreciating the importance of the child protection interface. As all practitioners know, hindsight gives perfect vision, but had the team leader's supervision been based upon 'evidence-based practice' neither 'Yvonne' nor her child need have died.

'Zack', 24, had been in care as a child following violence and sexual abuse at home, which was compounded in residential care where he was bullied and exploited as a 'pretty boy'. Apart from a three year period in primary school where he responded well to two concerned and skilled primary teachers, his 'criminal' career' from the age of 10, was downhill all the way. He was lost in a large comprehensive school serving two disadvantaged estates, where both pupils and staff struggled to survive, with low morale matching low resource. Privately an OFSTED inspector had called it a 'sink school for a sink estate'. 'Zack' was a tearaway, an obvious educational under-achiever although as a 10-year-old, he had a certain manipulative charm. By his mid-teens however, he had decided that life was tough and he had to be tougher, for violence was his everyday experience and he was undoubtedly badly bullied. He became a member of a bullying and extortion gang of alienated youths who preyed upon other pupils. By 15 he was leading it, willing to threaten anyone with a knife, and simply ruled by terror. He had become a very unprepossessing young man with a very bad local reputation.

His family had disintegrated and on a number of occasions he and his mates beat up his mother's current cohabitee. Quickly his delinquency included all the usual problems, including theft, criminal damage, drug misuse and a charge of rape, which was dropped because the victim was too afraid to testify. All his relationships proved to be short term and invariably with other unstable young people. The 'sympathy' he deserved as an abused and exploited 8-year-old, had been used up, as he preyed upon feckless young women from a similarly deprived and damaged background. They seemed to think that he would protect them, despite the fact that he had two spells in prison, one for violence, where following drugs and drink, he severely physically assaulted a youth.

He had been with one particular partner for six months, which was about his maximum time for being tolerated. She was 30 years old, with four children, the youngest a little more than 9 months old, under-nourished and not thriving. 'Zack' and his partner were not co-operating with social services, who were concerned mainly about the 11- and 9-year-old girls. Amidst drugs and drink, the baby died, virtually shaken to death because 'she insisted on crying'. Each 'adult' blamed the other. They were initially jointly charged with murder, but in the end the courts accepted pleas of manslaughter from both. The mother received a short custodial sentence, in part because she was exhibiting real remorse, and was clearly under the domination of 'Zack' whom she sought to please in everything. 'Zack' received a long sentence, reflecting the court's view of where the responsibility lay. The tragedy was the classic case of 'bolting the door' too late.

The frustrating thing about this catastrophe was that it was foreseeable. A young, isolated, disadvantaged young woman typically finds the company of an equally damaged young man, with a propensity to violence – recognizable as 'socially excluded' and has been so since childhood. Such individuals are both disproportionately victims and the perpetrators of crime (SEU 2000; Pritchard and Butler 2000a, 2000b).

Despite the success in calculating rates of child murder in specific at-risk subgroups, because child homicide is statistically so rare (a very large number of those in the risk groups do not kill or injure children), it is virtually impossible to devise predictive guidelines, or describe typical child homicide assailants. Indeed, there is a strong element of the 'accidental' when child abuse goes to the extreme. Nonetheless, the above cases are not dissimilar to many on a child protection team's caseload, be they in social services, police, health visiting, medicine or education. Indeed, any professional from one of these disciplines could have been involved in any of these cases. As will be explored at the end of this chapter, there is evidence to strongly suggest, that as their disciplines have been working more closely together over the last decade or so, the 'extremes' of child abuse are actually being reduced (Pritchard 1996a, 2002; Pritchard and Butler 2003). Crucially, of all the 'indicators', the all-prevailing ones seem to be a previous history of criminal violence and/or severe depression associated with paranoid ideas – both of which should set all the 'alarm bells ringing'.

Extra-family assailants

'Alpha' aged 30, was a big, burly man with numerous convictions for property crime, violence against the person and sex offences against both children and adults. By any definition he was a 'sociopath' in the sense that irrespective of his own damaged childhood, he showed no sense of understanding or sympathizing with another's perspective and created mayhem wherever he appeared, including causing serious road traffic offences and 'accidents'. He had been banned from driving but he would still steal a car to 'take him home' and was not averse to wrecking it afterwards.

He was very much a 'loner', and appeared to be incapable of forming close relationships with adults of either gender, and often resorted to sex-workers, to whom he showed quite serious violence, but none pressed charges. He had already served eight years in custody, and this and his educational failure made him unemployable. His life of crime was in one sense a rational 'economic alternative' and he was involved in drug trafficking and also used hard drugs and alcohol, during which times he became extremely violent. He gloried in his reputation as a 'bad-tempered lout', and he tried to dominate or bully all those around him. He had already one serious rape charge against a women, as well as two 'minor' offences of indecent assault of young girls in the local park. Two male friends of his rape victim beat him up when he was leaving a nightclub in a very drunken state. Next day, he went to a locale popular with children, abducted a 10-year-old girl, and in his fear and rage at her struggle, strangled and then sexually assaulted her. At his trial he suggested he did not appreciate that the child was so young and complained that he thought she was 'on the game'.

'Beta', a 28-year-old unemployed carpenter, roamed the Internet for sado-masochistic pornography. Despite being well technically qualified, his short fuse made him a difficult colleague and he had been frequently dismissed, often after either threatening, or actually committing an assault against work mates or his employer, when his thefts were discovered. Little is known about his background as he was extremely secretive. However, he was known as a bully throughout his school days, and there had been complaints from his early teens that he had sexually interfered with younger boys. At the time he had a short spell of 'treatment' for his inappropriate sexual behaviour, but in those days it had not been taken very seriously, seen more as a 'phase' and 'sexual experimentation', rather than a possible precursor of child sexual abuse. What had been missed was that there was a distinct pattern. He always went for younger boys, aged between 8 and 10, which as a 14-year-old, was a considerable gap. Also, the complainants mentioned his physical bullying which were virtual 'mini-tortures'.

By the year of the tragedy he had more than 20 property crimes, and two short periods in prison for actual bodily harm. This included his only known adult sexual crime, against a very slightly built 18-year-old youth, who was unwilling to press charges for 'grievous bodily harm', in part because he required hospitalization, but was too ashamed to admit de facto male rape. 'Beta' had been cautioned twice for apparently soliciting young boys, whom he was clumsily trying to groom: they complained that he hurt them, rather than about his sexual fondling. Later the police found that he possessed hundreds of videos of sado-masochistic abuse of young boys. He had made a contact with a 9-year-old from a nearby disadvantaged estate, who was eager for attention. He went with 'Beta' who callously killed him to 'shut him up', when he tried to escape the sadistic torture. 'Beta' showed no remorse whatsoever at his trial.

Such cases as those of 'Alpha' and 'Beta' evoke a sense of great sadness, not only at the terrible and meaningless brutality against the children, but at our sense of helplessness. It may be thought that 'Alpha' and 'Beta' were past the point of effective preventative intervention: so what do we do? Some may feel that such men have laid aside their humanity, whilst for others, such a view is a counsel of despair. But such cases as these have reluctantly led me to accept the need for 'reviewable' sentences, in effect, indeterminate sentences, until such people can be deemed to be safe to live amongst us (Pritchard and Bagley 2001). These and other ethical issues, will be explored later.

Suicide amongst the abusers

Yet matters remain complex, as I explore the other end of the spectrum of violence, namely, those 'sex only' offenders, who committed no violence (other than the sexual assault itself), but turned their 'violence' against themselves, indicating a significant degree of remorse and/or shame at their behaviour. Table 7.7 shows the subsequent suicide rate of people involved in a decade of child homicides and a two-year cohort of male child sex abusers (Pritchard and Bagley 2001), contrasted with all suicides in the region. In the general population there were 757 male and 260 female suicides, giving an annual overall rate of 15.3 pht men and 4.8 pht women, equivalent to 0.016 per cent and 0.005 per cent respectively.

However, within the cohort of homicide assailants, *all* of the mentally ill

Table 7.7   Completed suicides amongst a decade of child murderers and a two-year cohort of child sex abusers

Category	Male suicides	Female suicides	Suicide rate %
General population rates * All regional suicides per 100,000 p.a.	757 15.3 pht	260 4.8 pht	Male 0.015% Female 0.005%
Child killer Mentally ill [all aged <54]	4	2	100% fathers 25% mothers
Neglect and abuse		1	17% p.a.
Violent offender	0		0
Multi-criminal child sex abuser	0		0
2 year child sex abuse cohort			
Multi-criminal and violent [n=46 p.a.]	0		0
Multi-criminal- but no violence [n=49 p.a.]	1		1.02% p.a.
Child sex abuse sex only [n=93 p.a.]	6	0	3.23% p.a.

* Source: Wessex Regional Suicide Register

fathers who killed their children also killed themselves, that is 6600 times the general population. And 25 per cent of the mentally ill mothers, died by their own hand, or 5000 times the general population. One 'neglecting' mother killed herself, which is notionally 3400 times the general population rate. But *none* of the violent multi-criminal child sex abusers who killed a child committed suicide. In marked contrast, however, three in 100 of the non-violent, 'sex only' child abusers committed suicide, which is 200 times the general population rate. In contrast 0.18 per cent of mentally-disordered people killed themselves, which means that the non-violent 'sex-only' abuser killed themselves at more than 16 times the rate of mentally disordered people.

This shows the uncomfortable fact that the least physically damaging abusers are at considerably greater risk of self-killing, than are the physically dangerous. The violent multi-criminal extremists, are clearly dangerously damaged individuals, with chaotic lifestyles, detrimental in their violent behaviours to all around them. It is as much as their inability to control their aggression, as their sexual preying upon children and weaker people, that is the key area to differentiate them from the majority of child abusers. These results came as a surprise and led to a comparison of 'child-sexual-abuse-related-suicide' (CSARS) in the six-year regional suicide cohort, compared with the usually most frequent category associated with suicide, 'mental-disorder-related' (MDR) suicide.

Based upon detailed and extensive coroner's records, it was possible to identify both 'victims' and 'perpetrators' of child sexual abuse. It has to be admitted that both categories are likely to be underestimates, which is an artifact working *against* statistical significance (see Table 7.8).

Table 7.8   Comparison of Mentally Disordered versus Child – Abuse related suicides (Victims and Offenders versus General Population rates per 100,000)

Group and sex		Number	Per 100,000 *	Times GPR	P value
Mentally	M	167	182	12:1	<0.0000
disordered	F	96	72	10:1	<0.0000
CSA	M	4	12	2.5:1	<0.01
victims	F	5	34	2.2:1	<0.05
CSA offenders	M	16	613	40:1	<0.0000
CSA offender within-family	M	7	377	25:1	<0.0000
CSA offenders extra-family	M	9	1190	78:1	<0.0000

*Average annual suicide rate per 100,000 cohort population

Extracting the identified 'CSA Victims', the women had a suicide rate equivalent to 12 pht, that is, more than 2.5 times the general population. Male CSA victims, perhaps surprisingly, had an even higher suicide rate than did female victims at 34 pht, more than twice the general population rate. However, extracting the 'mental-disorder-related suicides' (MDR) from the total in the region, it was found that the MDR males and females had statistically significantly higher rates than the CSA victims, more than five and six times respectively.

The largest surprise came when the male CSA *perpetrators* were compared with the male MDR: as they had a suicide rate more than three times that of the mentally disordered group (Table 7.9).

Table 7.9   Comparison of CSAR v MDR Suicides by Gender, Victim and Perpetrator Groups

Groups	$\chi^{2}*$	P value
Male CSA Victims versus Male MDR	17.4805	<0.000
Female CSA Victims versus Female MDR	16.6349	<0.000
Female CSA Victims versus Male Victims	2.6596	n.sig
Male CSAR Victims versus CSA Perpetrators	51.2581	<0.000
Intra- versus Extra-Family CSA Perpetrators	0.7983	n.sig
Male MDR versus CSA Perpetrators	24.4284	<0.000

All $\chi^{2}*$ 1 d.f. CSAR = Child Sexual Abuse.
MDR = Mentally disturbed risk group.

When this suicide rate of de facto 'sex only' offenders, was viewed against other child sexual abuse victims, and mental-disorder-related suicides, it gives us pause to reflect. All these men died at or around the point of disclosure and trial. And of course, nothing is known about any sense of guilt they may have felt about their victims, but there appears to be evidence of a sense of shame, if only at the potential social disgrace. Nonetheless, these are elements with which to work to prevent such people offending against children. It is suggested that if public attitudes were less hostile, they might risk seeking the help of the treatment agencies, such as general psychiatry, their GP or the specialist services.

Discussing this latter research with colleagues and looking at the limits to the study, it was agreed that 'ethically uncomfortable research' such as this is a major challenge for therapists and researchers who seek to help and understand child abusers.

8 Professional Iatrogenesis: The 'Helping Hand Strikes Again'

Introduction

In the field of the human services there are few more complex dilemmas than child protection. Not surprisingly therefore wrong decisions are sometimes made. Yet despite an often negative media, child protection services almost always succeed in preventing serious events of child abuse (Pritchard 2002; Pritchard and Butler 2003). Occasionally mistakes, inadequacies and on some occasions, incompetent practice occurs. The consequence can be that the so-called 'helping hand strikes again' and the child and family we would assist are inadvertently damaged (Newberger 1983). In a text on suicide, case examples were explored in which I had not been very successful, but had learned important lessons (Pritchard 1999). I should hasten to add, whilst there was no formal negligence related to these deaths, factors such as worker fatigue, too many cases to deal with and inadequate information, meant that I had been less effective than was necessary. When this was published, numerous letters followed from practice colleagues who appreciated the acknowledgment of the tough reality of mental health practice. Now, nothing is tougher than child protection – but we need to confront the issues surrounding the inadvertent failure to intervene effectively.

The word iatrogenesis comes from the Greek *'iatro'*, physician, and *'genesis'*, to cause – the word is usually used to describe those medical situations in which the physician inadvertently causes the patient pain or disease. Sociology texts, for example Pilgrim and Rogers (1993) point the finger at these medical practitioners, the 'arrogant profession'. Indeed, in both child protection and psychiatry direct practice we are invariably operating with only partial information, often in constant flux. This is sometimes known as 'flying by the seat of one's pants'. Fortunately absolute, fatal failures in these professions are statistically very rare.

Yet we have to face the fact that the system and the people in the system designed enhance and protect the lives of children, sometimes damages those children by either acts of commission, or more often, omission and we need to learn from these mistakes in order to explore 'professional iatrogenesis' in child protection.

Profession iatrogenesis in child protection

Iatrogenesis occurs in two broad categories, the *macro* where the major system fails by either omission or commission; and the *micro*, where an individual is responsible for the damage.

The high proportion of British children living in relative poverty has already been highlighted, and even after a Labour government, the trend appears to continue to grow, despite pious phrases and the setting of policy goals. For every year that this poverty persists, children are dying needlessly from illness and 'accidents', as well as being abused and neglected, at the very least by the sins of omission including the lack of resources to break into the family cycle of socio-economic disadvantage, which is associated with active abuse (Gillham et al. 1998; Lipman et al. 2001; Merrick 2001).

This knowledge should create an equal 'moral panic' to that which often follows child fatalities in the child protection system (Atmore 1999) – as Merrick (2001) says, children are being discarded in 'waste baskets' by an iatrogenic system. Public and professional concern is of course justified at unnecessary fatalities when, as Lyon et al. (1996) put it we should 'tell it as it is'. Since the inquiry into the death of Maria Colwell in 1973 there have been at least 35 fatality inquiries into the killings of children known to social services. The flaws exposed in health, social service, educational and police systems for monitoring and preventing fatal abuse failed in all of these cases, with the recommendations of each report usually ignored in subsequent practice, invariably because the pious words are not backed by resources and properly supervised caseloads. A report issued by the inspectorates of police, health, probation and social services, *Safeguarding Children* (Ford and Frean 2002), points to continued lack of co-ordination between services, failure of any worker or service to take responsibility, and of service systems overstretched to the point of chaos by underfunding and lack of staff.

Children and adolescents living in run-down estates quickly perpetuate and repeat the problems of the parents in a manner described as 'snakes and ladders' (MacDonald et al. 2000). The problems of children and families associated with poor housing or transient homeless (Beggs 2001) are features associated with 'Children At Risk of Abuse' (Pritchard 1991) and we are all guilty when we fail to break the inter-generational cycle of mishandling of children (Oliver 1985; Langeland and Dijkstra 1995; Social Exclusion Unit 1998a, 1998b, 1998c). Knowing of these chronic cycles of poverty, neglect and abuse implies that many sectors of society – media, politicians and many citizens – are in inadvertent collusion as they tolerate the failure to meet children's needs in the tenth richest economy in the world.

The Audit Commission, not immediately associated with 'left-wing' causes has written a scathing report on the fiscal cost of failing to break into the cycle of pyscho-socio-economic disadvantaged, and the associated child neglect and abuse, and crime (Audit Commission 1996). Their findings were supported by several other studies (Steinberg et al. 1981; McLloyd 1990; Pritchard 1991, 1993; DoH 1998b; Gillham et al. 1998; Boateng 2000; Policy Action Team 2000; Lipman et al. 2001).

Just how big a problem this is can be found in the official statistics of children involved with social services. The latest figures available on the number of children being 'looked after' by English local authorities, show a serious rate increase. Rising from 45 per 100,000 in 1996 to 52 per 100,000 in 2001 (DoH 2002). Whilst in England and Wales alone, there were 376,000 youngsters on their caseloads as 'social care cases', including 223,000 with current and pressing problems (Berger 1999). If we assumed the worst and doubled the number of WHO reported child homicides in England and Wales (approximately 50 p.a.) and assume that all were at some stage on the case-loads of social services, this would yield a death rate of 0.04 per cent, that is, about 4 in 1000 cases known to social services. While such a rate is disturbing, the rates are well below the 'fatal mistakes' of medicine which are frequently around 1 per cent.

But what of the 'iatrogenic institutions' in the field of child neglect abuse.

The media

We must all be dismayed by endless media scapegoating of over-stretched professionals in the child protection system. Of course, the need for constant vigilance is understood in regard to professional negligence – especially the cant and hypocrisy of professional politicians, who have over the last few decades failed many of our most vulnerable children. Unfortunately, identifying the guilty men and women who are responsible for the chronic underfunding of child protection services rarely helps front-line staff, who are often pushed into dangerous and often non-productive defensive practice. It is much easier to remove a child at risk from their family, rather than trying to heal or support that family. But children who drift through affectionless childcare settings can become victims of the process described by Steinhauer (1984) as 'how to succeed in the business of creating psychopaths without trying'. In this process, bonds of affection and attachment are frequently broken through changes in childcare arrangements occasionally leading to the emergence of a young adult who is an affectionless psychopath.

Despite being a relatively media-friendly academic, I am appalled at the media's frequent inaccurate reporting and the occasional deliberate distortion of facts is breathtaking. For example, I gave the *Daily Mail* chief health cor-respondent a very detailed interview concerning a recently published paper showing that the UK had amongst the lowest rate of GDP expenditure on health in the Western world, which was associated with having the lowest cancer survival rates (Evans and Pritchard 2001). The 'shock' element, which some medical editors shied away from, was that whilst Black Americans had a 25 per cent worse survival rate than did White Americans, which would surprise no one, the UK figures were slightly *worse* than those for Black Americans (Evans and Pritchard 2001). The *Daily Mail* dutifully carried a very fair outline of the paper, but totally distorted the piece, in the headline used by blaming the NHS not the under-funding, 'What to expect from the NHS if you have cancer' which is typical of the way they often blame child protection staff for failing to prevent the unpreventable – a further twist in the cycle of inter-generational mishandling of children (Oliver and Taylor 1981).

The tabloids exercise the prerogative of harlots over the ages, power without responsibility. The *News of the World*, for example, took a press release on some research showing that former excluded-from-school adolescents get no statutory form of support, despite invariably coming from disturbed and disturbing backgrounds with a suicide rate 19 times that of the general population (Pritchard and Butler 2000b). These damaged, socially unsupported and educational under-achieving young adults were virtually unemployable and were over-involved in unacceptable crime and violence, de facto an alternative 'market-response' to their situation, and were already begetting their own children, perpetuating cycles of poverty and failure. But instead of highlighting the missed opportunities to reach these people when they were children, the headline declared 'Truants turn into killers', referring to the disproportionately high murder rate of this group (Pritchard and Butler 2000a), ignoring the fact, that they were also more often victims of violence than the general population and that very few truants actually committed murder (Pritchard and Butler 2000b).

The more recent cases of mothers being wrongly accused of killing more than one child, Mrs Sally Clarke and Mrs Trupti Patel, created a very hostile media response to those in child protection in June 2003. Whilst it is self-evident that our compassion should go out to the Clarke and Patel families, the cynical behind the scenes of shooting two alternative 'reactions' prior to the verdict, tells its own story. What the reporter found confusing was that my 'expert' evidence differed little in each presentation. There was compassion either way, first for the bereaved family potentially mourning the loss of a child and a falsely stigmatized parent, and second, for the potentially mentally disordered mother, who on becoming aware of what she had done, would be a profound suicide risk (Stroud 2003). Perhaps one positive outcome may be that politicians will have to be more careful before jumping on a media band-wagon and encourage more inter-disciplinary reviews of future multiple tragedies, before the services are pressurized to resort to law.

The persistent press attacks on the child protection system often unfairly focus on social work rather than medicine – classically seen in the Victoria

Climbié case – which has resulted in serious crises of recruitment for crucial staff, adding to the burdens of all concerned with child protection. Indeed, if social workers are not blamed for failing to protect children, then they are accused of being interfering 'busy body do-gooders' and 'kid-snatchers'.

The maliciousness of the *News of The World*'s call for 'Sarah's/Megan's Law' of disclosure has already been highlighted, which is counter-productive because it hinders efforts to reach and treat potential offenders, and therefore exposes children to further abuse. Yet, they persist in their 'campaign' in the face of condemnation from all the authoritative bodies associated with protecting children, making a difficult situation worse.

A lone but welcome voice, crying in the wilderness has been Richard Webster's book on the enormous pressure the media have placed upon staff and agencies concerned with children leading almost certainly to the false conviction of men on child sexual abuse charges (Webster 1998). I admire and fear for the vast majority of staff in childcare institutions who daily risk their reputations trying to serve the needs of our most disturbed and disturbing youngsters. The pioneering journalism of Woffinden and Webster (2002) for the *Guardian* newspaper has in fact exposed a system of childcare and social services whose moral panic did great wrong to the alleged victims, and to the alleged perpetrators. Two daycare workers, a man and a woman, were falsely accused of satanic-like practices in Newcastle-upon-Tyne, claiming that the two workers were removing children from the day care for substantial parts of the day and subjecting them to physical and sexual abuse including making wounds on the children's bodies. The local council panicked and fired the alleged assailants, who were pilloried by the *Daily Mail* which declared that

> Children as young as two were repeatedly molested by staff and ... supplied to paedophiles for filmed sex sessions ... In scenes of almost unimaginable horror, rapist paedophiles dressed as clowns or animals slashed terrified toddlers with knives.

Terrible allegations if true and meriting the strongest condemnation.

The press-inspired mob tracked down the two alleged assailants and beat them. They fled. In the interim a botched report commissioned by the social services committee concluded that there had been abuse, despite the complete absence of physical evidence and denials by children themselves. Indeed, a criminal case against the two workers was dismissed for lack of evidence. Aided by Richard Webster the two childcare workers sued the authors of the Newcastle report for libel, and were completely exonerated by the trial judge who awarded them substantial damages.

Woffinden and Webster (2002: 26) concluded that:

More than a decade after Cleveland, and the publication of the Butler-Sloss report which warned against the suspension of disbelief among professionals, and specifically pointed to 'the complex forces which can affect judgement and action in dealing with emotionally powerful material', all the same mistakes were repeated in the same part of the country.

This is not to deny that there are tragic cases of the worst kind of abuse, when those charged with the special care of vulnerable children exploit their position but simply to indicate that the constant intrusion of the media into child protection cases does little to benefit children and usually has the effect of making a difficult job even harder to do.

System/agency iatrogenesis

Among the macro issues are those in which various agencies and systems inadvertently damage those whom they should protect. All must agree with the one major and effective finding from the Department of Health, on the need for closer collaboration of children's agencies (DoH 1991, 1995, 1998b, 2001). As in medicine, the one common factor across all disciplines when things go wrong, is the breakdown in communication. I have taught generations of social work and medical students the simple fact that it is the professional's responsibility to communicate and inform their client/patient of all relevant issues and responsibilities, of both worker and client. We have to be able to cross generation, gender, ethnic and crucially, social class boundaries, in order to understand our client's difficulties, strengths and needs, but it is our responsiblity not the client's, indeed, a measure of professional competence is our ability to communicate with all, especially the damaged and vulnerable.

In defensive systems this fluency of communication is often sacrificed for the sake of bureaucratic convenience, ritual and power. When things go wrong, each department and agency seeks to defend itself against potential criticism at best, trying to ring fence their domains of finance and power. These are common themes found in inquiries over the years, and are almost perennial in large organizations, irrespective of their nature (Noyes 1991; Stacy 2000). Sometimes too there is class and ethnic bias against clients by agencies (Davidson 2001).

Newberger (1983) in coining the phrase 'the helping hand strikes again' described the unintentional but often substantial damage that can be done to families when suspicions of abuse are handled according to stereotypes and bureaucratic panic. The sad episodes in Cleveland, the Orkneys and the 'Satanic' panics are of recent memory, and examples of the helping hand which snatched children from innocent parents on the basis of rumour, panic and myth. These were media-assisted panics.

An interesting example from America of social work decisions driven by moral panics involved the so-called 'recovered memory syndrome' (Prendergast 1993). When tapes of these sessions were reviewed it was clear that, quite inadvertently 30 therapists had de facto caused false memories in their disturbed but vulnerable patients (Scheflin and Brown 1999). Conversely, Lab et al. (2000) showed that often the child protection system either fails to explore or under-estimates the effect that sex abuse has upon young men. In part this may be because the young men are less likely to admit to being seduced or indeed raped as children and adolescents – but this can be a major factor underlying mental health in 5 to 10 per cent of some men (Meltzer et al. 1995; Tomison 1996; Lab et al. 2000). At least three-quarters of victims of convicted sex offenders are female (Waterhouse et al. 1995; Pritchard and Bagley 2000) but there is actually a higher level of suicidal ideation, suicide attempts and completed suicides associated with child sex abuse amongst men than in women (Pritchard and King 2004). These findings are supported by those of Lab et al. (2000), that child protection systems are not always as fully aware of the sexual assault of boys as they might be. It is stressed that the enquiries and procedures of professionals in these areas should be informed by evidence, in assessing relative risks and possibilities in a careful, dispassionate way.

The American Academy of Paediatrics has expressed the strongest concern about the lack of resources in dealing with unexpected infant and child deaths (Kairys et al. 1999). The past two decades in America have seen a marked increase in child homicide rates, as chartered by the WHO – now the USA, compared with the rest of the Western world has the largest proportional increase in children's homicide in the West, and easily the highest rate throughout the developed world (Pritchard 2002; Pritchard and Butler 2003).

Another problematic 'systemic failure' in a child protection field was identified during fieldwork in a study of a two-year cohort of police records on 434 men charged with a sexual offence against a child. It was found that sometimes the child victim became more disturbed as the legal juggernaut rolled on, than as a result of the incident itself. This was frequently true in cases where the child did not know or have a relationship with the perpetrator. It appeared that in 11 per cent of cases the legal and medical process was more damaging to the child than the abuse itself. This finding has some support (Lauritsen et al. 2000), especially in regard to intrusive medical examinations, which most would find distressing. The finding led to a 'qualitative' defined category of 'victim damaged by system'. This was based upon the transcript of the *child's* description of what happened to them, at both the offence and the subsequent investigation, which included either a detailed in-depth verbal and/or a medical examination, in which a number showed their distress. Within this group some 7 per cent of the children were clearly more disturbed and hurt by the enquiries and the legal proceedings, but typical of the complexity of these situations, a further 4 per cent of victims were doubly 'hurt' by the abuse they suffered and the following investigation, in particular by the medical examination. It may be then that the 'system' can overreact to the detriment of the particular child? No one would envy the child protection teams, police or the prosecutors in trying to determine the best course.

At the time of writing social work and social care related to 'child protection' may be under serious review with rumours of a new configuration of child protection system, rightly based upon even closer collaboration between the services, especially 'social work', health and the police. Unquestionably one of the great improvements reducing child homicide was the 'working together' initiatives (DoH 1991). However, the new General Social Care Council (GSCC) set up to oversee the whole range of 'social care' should be careful not to repeat the mistakes of its predecessor, and may be in danger of repeating the errors of the former Central Council Social Work Education and Training (CCETSW), which could well be another system failure in waiting?

In a very clear exposition of the GSCC's perspective, its director, Lynne Bennett (2002) emphasized its 'user focus' and 'user involvement'. This is laudable, but who is the primary 'user' when our intervention may well be objected to by the recipients, namely neglecting parents or abusers in 'treatment'? Moreover, the GSCC seems to be concerned fundamentally with 'standards', but standards to do what? It is argued that the key failure of CCETSW, was its inability to *place effective practice at the centre of social work education*, in comparison with practice standards, which are now at the core of the best medical education. We should teach and seek to practise whenever possible, *evidence-based practice*. There is the new Social Care Institute of Excellence, which has the primary responsibility for furthering 'what works', but this seems a dangerous division of responsibility. Social work has confronted this tension between care and control for years, resolved by the dictum 'we sometimes have to control because we care'. But in the field of child protection this is fraught concept, since whilst the neglecting or abusing parent or extra-familial abuser can legitimately be in 'treatment' with us as a prerequisite to protecting the child, there is a dichotomy of interests. Hence the GSCC should place evidence-based practice at its core, a role which it seems reluctant to take on.

In part, the social work academy must also be included in this catalogue of professional iatrogenesis, for it too has failed to undertake or educate practitioners in key outcome research. For example, it can be shown that 'good social work works', bringing about positive change in people's lives (Pritchard 1991, 1996a, 1996b, 2001; Ford et al. 1997; Pritchard and Butler 2000a, 2000b; Pritchard and Williams 2001; Pritchard et al. 2003). Yet a perusal of the *British Journal of Social Work*, shows a staggering paucity of outcome studies. Social scientists are still fond of slating the arrogance of medicine (Pilgrim and Rogers 1993) and whilst this may occur in a minority of cases, their education is now 'evidence based' – would that social work and social care were the same. This lack of focus has left the front-line practitioner exposed and scapegoated, as media and managers often seek to blame individuals, rather than their failure to consider a system that has under-funded and frankly under-trained key staff. Only the incredible personal dedication of front-line staff has kept the system going for as the *Guardian*, almost grudgingly reported, three-quarters of clients of social service express satisfaction with the service they received, only GPs having similar results (Pritchard et al. 2003).

Micro-level iatrogenesis

It is an unfortunate fact that all the professions involved with children can either deliberately or inadvertently be iatrogenic to children and as the Laming Report shows (2003) this is often compounded by managers, who rather than listening to clients and their harrassed front-line worker, listen instead to the allure and siren voice of senior management – to cope at all cost, and one can always pass the buck downwards.

Medicine: It would be fair to say that twenty years or more ago, the idea of a physician actively abusing their position with children would have been unthinkable. Yet there was a case prior to 1970 when *prima facie* evidence was presented of a physician sexually abusing a patient. But children were failed simply because no one would believe the implication of the doctor's actions and I only learned years later that this doctor had abused not only our young client, but many other young men as well.

Paediatricians, like us all, invariably make some mistakes, and those identified by the Victoria Climbié inquiry are but one example (Laming Report 2003). Rather worryingly Vulliamy and Sullivan (2000) from the USA report that training about child neglect and abuse is still an issue for many paediatricians, as they appear to be reluctant to break 'patient confidentiality'. This calls into question the whole controversy surrounding 'mandatory reporting'. There was a case of a man who sought therapy for depression, revealing that he had sexual relations with a 13-year-old cousin many, many years before, when he was in his late teens. The therapist felt mandated by law to reveal this, and his client received a four-year jail sentence.

From paediatrics comes the severest criticism of medicine in relation to child protection, and Hobbs and Wynne (2002) complain of their profession's relative 'neglect of neglect'. This includes both GPs and paediatricians; and they make the point that a lack of lateral thinking about the potentially vulnerable child, leads some medical professionals to make understandable but none the less damaging mistakes.

Some may find the next iatrogenic group surprising, but there are grounds for being somewhat critical of adult psychiatrists. Very often one hears consultants saying that their primary concern must be their patient's mental state, and not the wider implications of the patient's behaviour in the community. But in teaching medical students for some years, it has been argued that the psychiatrist should routinely ask the question: are there children linked to the patient; and does the patient's psychiatric problem pose any risk to the safety of these children? Study after international study has found not only that extremes of child abuse are committed mainly by parents, but also that a substantial number of them are mentally disordered (d'Orban 1990; Bourget and Labelle 1992; Falkov 1996; Pritchard and Bagley 2001; Stroud 2001, 2003).

Why does this happen, when most mental disorder can be treated quite effectively? It is probably because most psychiatrists do not ask the crucial questions about children, or are reluctant to refer the case for social work consultation. Conversely, it has been known that social services 'panic' in the face of a mental disorder, seeking only to intervene using a section of the Mental Health Act. It is reiterated, that most mental disorder is treatable and containable in the community (Warner 2000; Kingdon and Turkington 2002; Pritchard 2004), and is by no means an automatic ground for taking the child into care. Yet, the link between psychiatric disturbance and child abuse has long been known (Hawton and Roberts 1981), but apparently still ignored. Furthermore, reflecting on what is known about mental disorder and child homicide, one must agree with Stroud (2001, 2003): that if both psychiatrists and the child protection services thought laterally, across their disciplinary boundaries, a substantial number of children killed by a mentally ill parent might well be saved?

The individual 'blindness' of some professional psychiatrists about family implications of an adult's illness can be seen, disturbingly, in an otherwise outstanding piece of research, the *Confidential National Inquiry into Mental Illness Related Deaths* (Appleby et al. 1999; Shaw et al. 1999). This team surveyed all forms of violent deaths over a two-year period including suicide, murder (victim and perpetrator) and all other violent deaths, yet amazingly the inquiry failed to ask two simple and obvious questions, namely, the age and relationship of the victim to the assailant (Shaw et al. 1999). This meant that the vitally important work of Falkov (1996) on numbers of children killed could not be systematically examined. This 'professional blindness' is much less likely to happen in the practice and research of cognitive behavioural therapy orientated psychiatrists, who have a truly 'integrated' view of modern clinical psychiatric practice (Warner 2000; Kingdon and Turkington 2002; Pritchard 2004).

Criminal justice system

In an infamous but brilliantly produced BBC2 programme *Tracking Britain's Sex Abusers* (July 2002), viewers saw a Mr Levine who led a small but vicious ring of child abusers, trying to claim that their concern for young girls was to compensate them for their often affectionless families, claiming that as they did no physical harm, they were enhancing the lives of 6- to 9-year-old girls! This was, as the programme amply demonstrated, a travesty of the truth. The programme was worth seeing not least to show how hard it is for the police to gain a conviction, and the difficulty of obtaining a sentence which is both just and offers protection to future children. Perhaps some lawyers in the 'performance of their legal duties', protecting the 'rights' of defendants, are also guilty of a certain professional iatrogenesis. In the case of Levine, his now grown-up niece gave graphic evidence of the hurt and distress caused by Levine's systematic and callous sexual abuse. Yet clever work by his lawyer resulted in crucial evidence not being heard, and some charges being dropped leading to a derisory sentence of six years, of which Levine, a serial child molester with previous convictions, will likely serve only four.

We can only speculate how it was that the killer of Sarah Payne had earlier only received a four-year sentence for his previous very serious sex offence against two girls of similar age to Sarah, offences which included abduction. Did the lawyers involved not consider the harm to future children which this man posed?

Speight and Wynne (2000) make some very interesting comments about the civil courts considering the fate of children in contested child welfare cases. Despite the best efforts of social workers, there appear to be longer delays in obtaining court decisions about children than before. In part this is because judges are seeking more precise evidence on physical abuse. But they fail to grasp the 'time reality' of children: a month's delay is long, six-months may seem like a life-sentence in limbo.

Perhaps the biggest culprit of iatrogenesis in the criminal justice system is the prison service. Again and again, damaged, disturbed and disturbing young adults are incarcerated but the opportunity to educate and treat them is lost – iatrogenesis by omission. Worse, sometimes young offenders are themselves victims of physical and sexual abuse whilst in prison, though this has been challenged by the Home Office. A recent study reported that 'only' 1 per cent of 15–17-year-old inmates were victims of sexual assault, but acknowledged that the staff were unaware of at least half the possible events of assaults on young inmates (McGurk et al. 2000)!

The churches and voluntary associations

At first sight these types of organizations may appear distant from the child protection field. But both institutions have figured large, in different ways, in the media and merit at least a brief comment. First of all are the scandals that have emerged regarding priests, and lay brothers in Catholic childcare agencies, whose sexual abuse of children is deplorable. These men who were particularly and doctrinally expected to uphold the highest standards of morality; instead have abandoned celibacy for the basest kind of sexual obsession (Haywood and Grossman 1994; Haywood et al. 1996).

With regard to the charities and voluntary organizations, ordinarily one might assume that they would work co-operatively with social services, in the continued pursuit of social justice for children. Sadly, some charities err on the side of sensational and distorted advertising in the search for funds, without offering a measurable or meaningful service in return. The most obvious example is the NSPCC.

Their campaign to shock the public into supporting services for children gives the message that there is little effective work done by official child protection services, and that somehow the NSPCC will step in to rescue children – an implication which is a travesty of truth. Indeed my first international comparative study was stimulated by an NSPCC advertisement which claimed 'send us £15' as a child a day dies from abuse. This proved to be a puzzling claim, since the number of children who die violent deaths at the hands of others in Britain is more like one a week. When the figures were examined it was found that the numbers of British children dying in this way was steadily falling (Pritchard 1992a). This was challenged by the NSPCC (Creighton 1993) but following the NSPCC method of analysing the data, the earlier positive international results, that England and Wales rates were better than most other Western countries, were confirmed (Pritchard 1993, 1996a, 2002; Pritchard and Butler 2003). Whilst controversy continues to surround 'final' child homicide figures, as the Office of National Statistics website (2002) admits (*www.ONS.gov.org.uk*), the NSPCC in their public advertisements and publicity material continue, albeit unintentionally, to undermine efforts of front-line practitioners, feeding a hostile media image of child protection, implying persistent failure. The critique of the NSPCC is that they are not pushing an evidence-based appeal, for as this book has shown, the key features of the neglect and abuse of children are the inter-generational factors, predominately linked to psycho-socio-economic poverty, and the interface of mental health with child protection. Why does the NSPCC, with its moral fervour and the independent status of a voluntary agency, not campaign for reducing relative child poverty in Britain, for improving educational services to children, and for improving social and mental health services to families in general?

Most children's charities have avoided the sensationalism of the NSPCC, who devote more than 40 per cent of their annual budget to 'campaigning' rather than to direct services, the highest administration cost of any of the children's charities. Consequently it was disappointing to find that at the Barnardo's British campaign in late 2002 using child models as preteen prostitutes, implying that Barnardo's was involved in 'rescuing' such children. In fact, research on child victims of sexual abuse, including extensive research on adolescent prostitutes suggests that the 9-year-old hooker is largely a figment of imagination or a gross exaggeration of those rare cases. It would be interesting to see whether Barnardo's could give figures on ages of such cases they dealt with. As in a two-year cohort of 374 convicted men, only five cases of children abused by multiple perpetrators were found, which might be thought to be child 'prostitution'. Self-evidently, five too many, but not the norm in Britain. The Barnardo's campaign, involving costly TV and newspaper advertisements, moves public attention away from the key areas where we need to intervene. To be fair to Barnardo's their recent adverts highlighting the damage of babies born into poverty proved to be too accurate for some 'delicate' political stomachs. We know where the *majority* of serious child abusers come from – they have been trapped in the inter-generational cycle of psycho-socio-economic disadvantage, and it is upon this cycle that concerned charities should focus. One must object to over-simplistic presentation of such a complex and dangerous area, with the inadvertent consequence of wrongly focused political response to the problem, and the inadvertent undermining of the morale of dedicated front-line staff.

Child protection services

The cases where social workers and residential staff have abused children, physically, emotionally and sexually, caused everyone in the field the greatest distress. Some of the worst known cases concerned the children's home abuse cases in North Wales, where at least two if not four of 24 children's home were infiltrated by sex-abusing men. These men are especially reprehensible, and there are no accurate words to express contempt for such betrayals.

All that can be said is that the majority of the children's homes in North Wales did their very best for the children in their care. But the abusers' behaviour also damaged the morale and spirit of their innocent colleagues. Of all the criticism of front-line child protection staff, the most measured has come from mainly paediatric sources in papers by Sanders et al. (1999) and Speight and Wynne (2000).

The danger is that too much attention is paid to procedures rather than to actual practice which serves the child's best interest. In reflecting on mistakes in current practice, it will be valuable to reflect on four areas:

(1) There are problems of procedure in intra- as well as inter-agency communication. In part this is because there is too much defensive paper work dictated by management and legal systems.

(2) In the process of time-limited social work with children and families, assessments are always difficult, not least because one is trying to establish a trusting relationship with the client. However, the practitioner really has to contemplate the unpalatable. Just as psychiatrists should ask about children, social workers should consider whether there is a mental health dimension in each case. And very often, there is. We should then ask what is the best form of intervention?

(3) Another problem in the social work process concerns partnerships between parents and their social workers. Sometimes we expect or hope for more from parents than they can deliver, in the time the child needs. This time factor cannot be over-stressed. Unfortunately some adult clients have a 'personality disorder', a more or less set pattern of anti-social traits, and they are not likely to change in the time required for them to meet the child's developmental needs. Therefore, child protection should be more, not less, ready to consider earlier separations, to give the child a chance to attach with new and possibly permanent alternative carers. Self-evidently of course, there needs to be adequate resources to provide the necessary psychosocial 'parental' compensatory care such children will need.

(4) In the process of social work and social care staff have a responsibility for their own professional development. Most professionals, be they medics, lawyers or social workers, read less and less professional material after training, other than the job adverts. Whilst one can be critical of the social work academy for not inculcating habits of updating in our basic training, in the last analysis it is the individual's responsibility to maintain their optimum professional practice. Of course, it is hard to keep up to date and certainly employers should have a systematic structure that enables staff to achieve this, but this will only happen if we, through our professional organizations, demand that it happens. Whilst some core skills are universal in the human care services, techniques and approaches are constantly changing, hopefully for the better. Each individual worker must best equip themselves to meet the needs of their clients. It is a tough but necessary message. This is not a message from an ivory tower, for one

of the reasons I maintain a practice link, is to be in touch with the fears and uncertainties of practice, as well as its joys.

All professionals make mistakes: I certainly have and admitted when this happened, people died which with the advantage of hindsight, might have been prevented (Pritchard 1999). Consequently I have total sympathy with both clients and front-line staff. Social care is contained in Lord Seebohm's great vision, of a *personal* social service, and is the primary task of all in child protection and the human services. Consequently, *all* management and administration should be geared to these functions of enhancing personal service for clients.

Every area of our institutions concerned with human service should be examined and if they cannot directly or indirectly show how the activity 'adds value' to the primary task of the organization in delivering an integrated personal social service, then such activities are unnecessary and a luxury that cannot be afforded.

None the less, let us not fall into the trap set by media. It is not social workers, doctors, police, teachers or even managers of the child protection services, who slight, reject, neglect or/and abuse children, but predominately their carers. Notwithstanding these carers' own damaged antecedents it can be said with Karl Jaspers, the existentialist philosopher and psychiatrist, 'illness I can treat, but to life, only make an appeal'.

Let us now turn to the 'treatment' of abusers, for there are beginning to be some positive findings and encouragement. Remember, good social work works.

9 Strategies for Reducing Child Abuse and Sexual Offending: Processing and Therapy

How Big A Problem? Trying to Calculate the Numbers

Before considering preventive and intervention programmes let us consider how big the problem is of male abusers facing Britain.

As with all newly discovered conditions, initially estimates go through the roof, for example early estimates based upon reports of victims ranges from 5–60 per cent females and 5–24 per cent males (Leventhal 1998), which on reflection would suggest for females for examples at the higher estimates, 'abuse' is statistically a majority experience. Such numbers rapidly decline when a firmer definition of what is meant by abuse is used (Finkelhor 1994; Gorey and Leslie 1997; Leventhal 1998). Pritchard and King (2004) attempted to estimate the number of 'serious' offenders in a region of Britain based upon the firmest evidence available, that is the number of men charged with such an offence, whilst recognising that not all serious abuse is known to the authorities (Waterhouse et al. 1995, Leventhal 1998. However, in the USA it was confirmed and corroborated that 0.3 per cent of girls and 0.14 per cent of boys were victims of some form of abuse, that is 30 in 10,000 girls and 14 in 10,000 boys. At first sight such proportions seem derisory until one appreciates that this is equivalent to 257,000 children up to the age of 14. Indeed, Leventhal (1998) gets close to this number when he asserts that 'we know' that there are approximately 250,000 male abusers living in our communities, though of course many extra-family offenders assault more than one child. However, the immediate flaw here is that we have NO idea how many emotional and physically within-family abusing females there might be. So whatever estimates we can deduce from current research, we have virtually ignored the female contribution.

To correct for this let us take the minimum number of females on the 'At Risk of Abuse' register, which extrapolating from regional numbers (Pritchard and King 2004) would yield a rate of 0.15 per cent, that is 15 in 1000 who are essentially within-family abusers, and in that sense the most serious, yields a minimum of 15,130 women aged 16–44 in the UK annually, a formidable 'caseload'.

Returning to male abusers based upon the regional study of the number of sex offenders, not necessarily the most serious in terms of consequence because two-thirds were found to be extra-family abusers (Pritchard and Bagley 2000). As it is known that the majority of abuse with the more serious consequence comes from with-family abuse, virtually reversing the ratio of 3:1 within-family to extra-family male abusers. Based on convictions this was 0.021 per cent of the general population but Pritchard and King (2004), to account for the bias of under-reporting within-family abuse, used a 2.5:1 multiplier and produced a *minimum* rate of 0.053 per cent. Some may feel this is a very small figure, yet based upon UK population of men between 18–74 years this yields an estimate of 10,628 men. However, victim reports suggest this really is a minimal figure but how can prevalence of abuse be determined in such a problematic area?

If we turn to psychiatric morbidity and accept some early estimates of women who have developed a mental disorder who were also abused, these estimates range from 10 to 30 per cent (Hawton et al. 1985; Mullen et al. 1993; Coll et al. 1998; Felitti et al. 1998; Read 1998). Taking the mid estimate to control and allow for the effects of within-family abuse and based upon the level of serious mental disorder in the community (Jenkins et al. 1999) this is equivalent nationally to a rate of 0.58 per cent, yielding an astonishing figure of 124,670 female victims.

However, the tightest estimates of males being victims of abuse is virtually 1:3 (Gorey and Leslie 1997; Leventhal 1998) but this possibly under-estimates the within-family abuse because more males are victims of child homicide than are females in every Western country (Pritchard and Butler 2003). But with this qualification in mind and assuming an adverse mental health sequela, based upon prevalence of serious mental disorder amongst males, 1.9 per cent, this would yield 0.193 per cent, and in the UK add a further 38,700 victims, a total of 163,370 victims of a range of serious abuse.

But within-family abuse, it is quite likely that more than one child is abuse, which complicates the calculation.

So, based upon 10,628 convicted males (0.053 per cent) and 15,131 women (0.15 per cent) on the 'At Risk of Abuse' register, there are a *minimum of* 25,750 adults involved in all forms of abuse of children.

Taking the victim route to estimate the numbers of abusers in the UK, there were 163,370 severely abused young people related to subsequent mental disorder, as what might be thought of as a *medium* figure.

However, basing the estimate on victims thought to be sufficiently abused as for there to be subsequent sequel in late adolescence or adulthood, 3 per cent of females and 1 per cent males, yields 224,940 victims of whom the majority will have experienced within-family abuse is a staggering figure. To off-set those abusers about whom we know nothing, let us take this figures as *probable*. However, if we 'correct' for the male population most likely to abuse children because of their within-family access, this yields 0.87 per cent of the age-related adult population are abusing between 3 and 4 per cent of our children during any one year. It is a disturbing estimate, more so, because it was cautiously arrived at.

Let us turn to the preventive and treatment initiatives extant for his cohort of probable abusers.

Prevention and intervention

The primary task of this book is to contribute to the reduction of child abuse. It is appreciated that some of the positions taken, such as the insistence upon identifying systemic as well as individual and family factors in abuser motivation, may be controversial. This approach was necessary, however, in order to develop a comprehensive approach in understanding the origins and causes of the problem of child neglect and abuse, in order to offer both preventive and intervention strategies. It is to this end, therefore, proposals are made for breaking the cycle of abuse, whether it is associated with individuals or systems, or both.

In undertaking research on child sex abusers it was necessary to have waded through hundreds of detailed interview reports, giving accounts of the grossest and cruellest of acts perpetrated against children. It is easy to express anger and outrage at these assaults, and no one could fail to be impressed at how calm and fair and restrained police colleagues have been in dealing with these offenders – in marked contrast to the punitive hysteria expressed by some sections of the media. This reflects the view of the British psychiatrist Tyrell Furniss (1991), who argued cogently for the suspension of judgment while we study such men and women:

> To express sympathy and understanding for sexual abusers often provokes strong irrational and angry response amongst the public and professionals alike. This response originates from a confusion in which we feel that understanding abusers and showing empathy, means people feel that understanding abusers and showing empathy means making apologies for them and blaming the child. The distinction between interactional and structural elements of responsibility, participation and guilt in child sexual abuse allows us to show empathy and to try and understand why fathers and stepfathers and others become sexual abusers. In the process we may learn about traumatic life events in the abuser's own history, including possible severe physical and sexual abuse in their own childhood. Showing

empathy and understanding does not take away one iota from their full responsibility for the abuse they have committed.

(Furniss 1991: 14)

In this spirit, one of the key elements of offending, namely the victim to abuser cycle, is explored.

The victim to abuser cycle – cycles of violence and neglect

One puzzle in understanding why adults and adolescents physically abuse and neglect children, is why those who themselves have been abused go on to be abusers. In the case of intermittent but often severe neglect, often coupled with casual but sometimes severe physical punishments, there seems to be a process of social learning in which the child models their behaviour on that of the parent. Other things being equal, violent parents are likely to socialize violent and neglecting children, indeed, there will be a tendency to repeat one or all of the three schematic mishandling of child, be it neglect, physical, emotional or sexual abuse. Researchers have expressed various degrees of pessimism about breaking into this cycle. De Mause (1997), who adds a psycho-dynamic dimension to the processes of social learning, is somewhat pessimistic about bringing about change.

Kolko (1992) reviewing data from a very large sample of American children and their parents, observed that children may often replicate the interpersonal and child-rearing styles learned from their parents – but the exceptions who break the cycle of violence and neglect are important. 'Resilient children' who are not overcome by patterns of family violence and the chronic poverty of mismanagement of resources include those with a higher IQ, and those who have had a stable attachment to at least one parent figure or other adult who was not neglectful or abusing (Rutter 1985, 1987, 1999).

The work of Straus and colleagues (Straus and Kantor 1994) cited earlier shows that children who have been subject to frequent and severe corporal punishment are more likely to become depressed, violent and alcoholic as adults. The exact modes of transmission are unclear and certainly not all children from abusing homes become abusing, disorganized adults. Nevertheless the statistically significant link is there, and has to be explained. Certainly, the social learning model appears to be the most plausible at this stage of research (Muller et al. 1995; Moore et al. 1999; Geer et al. 2001).

Other theories are available to explain the link, including the failure of pathologically organized families to socialize children in ways that help their later social adaptation (Neugebauer 2000). The link between family abuse and pathology with abusive and disorganized behaviours in adults who have grown up in such families, presents challenges for developmental psychologists who try and explain the links established by epidemiologists. In one carefully designed American study, a history of childhood neglect nearly doubled the chance of an adult being arrested for a violent offence (Widom 1989). Why is this?

What we can be firm about at the present level of knowledge, is that there are good grounds for society, government, social service and other agencies, to try to ensure that the large majority of children grow up in families not stressed by poverty, violence, disorganization and weak attachments to parent figures. Some politicians are adept at 'blaming the parents', without taking into account the cycle of socio-economic poverty, as well as 'psychological poverty' they have inherited.

It should be added that not all studies have shown that abusing and neglecting families produce any statistically significant excess of children who go on to repeat their parent's physically abusive behaviour (Tomison 1996). A critical examination of the methodology of the available English-language studies by Ertem et al. (2000) found that only ten had used control groups; whereas many studies did not meet strict methodological criteria (for example controlling for the effects of social class). One study did meet the fullest methodological criteria (that of Egeland et al. 1988) and this study suggests that children of physically abusing parents are, compared to groups in the general population matched on all other factors, 12.6 times more likely to become physically abusing parents themselves. Subsequent US research (Coxe and Holmes 2001; Pears and Capaldi 2001) supports this finding, suggesting that physically abused children who go on to be abusing parents are significantly more likely to be depressed or suffer Post-Traumatic-Stress-Disorder (PTSD). This implies that the overly strict or physically abusive families may have been dysfunctional in various ways, including faulty interpersonal relationships and disordered attachment patterns.

Case history research has supported the idea that weak and disordered attachments between parent and child occurs in physically maltreating families, and it is these disturbances of attachments, rather than the physical blows as such, which lay the seed of parenting dysfunction in some abused children (Oliver 1985, 1988; Kaufman and Zigler 1987). This is reflected in the classic biblical text 'the fathers have eaten a sour grape, and the children's teeth are set on edge' (Jeremiah 31:29).

The inter-generational transmission of sexual abuse – adolescents

Findings on adolescents are important, since at least 20 per cent of sexual offending begins in adolescence; and the earlier that intervention takes place, the greater the possibility for permanent cure or control of such motivations

(Prendergast 1993; Le Grand and Martin 2001; Rasmussen 2001). This research shattered some of the early comfortable myths of youngsters 'just experimenting', especially if there are more than four or five years between the 'lead' adolescent and their partner. The victim-to-abuser cycle represents a special case in trying to understand motivations for deviant behaviour. After all, to achieve orgasm with another person is a very powerful 'reinforcer', and it would be easy for an adolescent to learn to become overly involved in such behaviour. Such results are a sufficient motivation for intensive efforts to reach these damaged youngsters in a positive and humane way but raises the question of how many 'child abusers' are there in the general population? This is an issue for which an answer will be attempted when the review is completed. Skuse et al. (1998) in one of the few British studies on adolescent abusers, found that experiencing or witnessing family violence discriminated sexually assaultive boys, from matched controls, both groups having experienced sexual abuse. This implies that it is not the abuse as such, but its combination with family violence and dysfunction that led the boys to act out their sexual victimization by abusing others. This study found no link between the type and duration of the sexual assaults experienced and going on to be an offender. In Canadian research on 60 institutionalized adolescents Bagley (1992) found that early neurological history reflected in subtle CNS impairment, and social maladaption including difficult peer relations, predicted the later development of sexual offending in adolescents. But the maladaption was of the anxious, withdrawn type of behaviour – youths who were physically aggressive towards others were actually less likely to be sexually assaultive. Within the sexual abusers was a small sub-group who had when younger manifested 'encopresis' (soiling), and some were fire-setters – none of the controls fell into these categories. One boy had burned down his home, killing his stepsister. Three quarters of the sexually assaultive youth had been sexually abused either in their dysfunctional family or in the community, or in both settings compared with some 10 per cent of controls. Reviewing the literature, Bagley and Thurston concluded

> Adolescents who sexually assault children are often socially isolated, with internalised symptoms (anxiety, depression, suicidality). They are likely to come from dysfunctional families marked by alcoholism and emotional abuse, and are particularly likely to have sexually abused themselves. Early neurological problems may also be associated with sexual offending by adolescents. Adolescent males who enter the victim-to-abuser cycle tend to have come from emotionally neglectful or abusive homes and have experienced 'traumatic bonding' with their own abuser. Treatment programmes for adolescents in this cycle must avoid the 'poor me' syndrome in which adolescent offenders avoid responsibility for their sexual assault of

others ... Sexually assaulting others is seen as a desperate attempt to regain feelings of personal power and esteem: this must be addressed in therapy ... Group treatment models can be particularly successful with teenage survivors of CSA. Groups aim to reduce social isolation, reduce guilt, give feelings of empowerment, give social skills training ... enhance self-esteem and enable members to engage in therapeutic arts programmes.

(Bagley and Thurston 1996: 66–67)

One other controversial finding should be mentioned. In their review of the psychological effects of adult-juvenile sexual relations in boys, Bauserman and Rind (1997) found that boys were much less likely than girls to be traumatized by the abuse. It is possible that there is a sub-group of offenders who go on, as adults, to sexually use boys because of the pleasure they felt in their early relationships, which they are now recreating, in some idealized form. It could be that some boys, otherwise undamaged by the abuse, have nevertheless bonded strongly with the adult abuser to the extent that they have absorbed or identified with his role, and go on to recreate such relationships in their own adult lives. This kind of behavioural fixation is similar to that experienced by Vladimir Nabokov in his early adolescence (deep romantic love for an age peer), which led to the development of his obsessive 'Lolita syndrome', which permeated much of his adult writing, which is now viewed far less sanguinely than before. There is an additional question however: since many adolescents have romantic and sometimes sexual relationships with peers, why do not many more become fixated on sexual partners or objects who are adolescent in age? There must be an additional factor at work – it might be thought, though without direct evidence, that fixation only occurs in individuals with poorly developed social skills which makes it difficult for them to achieve or maintain adult sexual and romantic relationships. Or there is a traumatic loss and separation from the idyllic fields of childhood – in Nabokov's case the loss of his family estates following the Russian revolution.

It should be noted that there is a special kind of sexual behaviour in which young children act out sexually with peers in flagrant and aggressive ways, which goes well beyond simple peer play. It is very likely that these children are victims of recent or ongoing sexual abuse by an older person, and immediate investigation and therapy is required in these cases (Hunter 1995).

Finally, comment must be made on the special situation of the United States, one of the few countries in the world which still executes juveniles and for this and other reasons has failed to sign the UN Convention On The Rights of The Child. Lewis and her colleagues (Lewis et al. 1988), carried out detailed psycho-medical investigations of juveniles waiting on death row, sentenced for brutal murders which often also involved rape. This was, for most, the first time that such investigations had been carried out, and none of the findings had been presented in court. Most of the boys, who came from disorganized, lower-class families had been brutalized in their childhoods, suffering beatings, burns and skull fractures, and many had resulting neurological abnormalities. Some had been brutally sodomized on numerous occasions. When given a brief medical examination for court purposes their overwhelming claim was the macho, 'I'm normal Doc.' As of 2003, America is still executing young men who committed murder as juveniles, keeping them alive until after their 18th birthday when sentence can be carried out. The US appears so desensitized to such violence that they are either indifferent or unaware of their substantially higher rate of personal violent deaths within their society (Evans and Pritchard 2001). For example, compared with the horror of 11 September toll of 3074 innocent victims, an examination of the most recent WHO (2003) mortality statistics for the USA shows that for every 9/11 victim, more than 5 Americans were murdered, 9 committed suicide and more than 13 were killed on US roads (Evans and Pritchard 2001; Pritchard 2002; WHO 2003). Indeed, annually more US children are victims of homicide and road deaths, than were lost in the atrocity of 11 September (Pritchard 2002; Pritchard and Butler 2003). But of course, the majority of these deaths did not occur all at once, were not on television, and were the very opposite of 'politically' useful statistics.

Victim-to-abuser cycle: a perspective on adult sexual offenders

The first point to be made is that this effect is gender specific. Kolvin et al. (2001) in a British study of adults at risk of offending, found that of 747 males the rate of being an adult child sex offender was 35 per cent for the previously abused, and 11 per cent for the non-abused. But in their series they could only locate one woman who had been both a victim of sexual abuse, and an adult perpetrator. This finding reflects the fact that overall women from whatever background are much less likely to be perpetrators of sexual abuse, compared with males. Presumably, there is some psycho-biological mechanism at work here, with women much less likely to exhibit sexual aggression against vulnerable members of society. Indeed, in a two-year cohort of all adults charged with a sexual offence against a child in two southern English counties, out of the 440 persons, only four were women and only one went on to be formally prosecuted (Pritchard and Bagley 2000), whereas in relation to intra-family child homicide, women were the more frequent assailants (Pritchard and Bagley 2001; Stroud 2003).

Men who have been subjected to incest in their family of origin are much more likely than others to go on to be violent rapists. In one American study of imprisoned men no less than one half of the violent rapists (with adult victims), had experienced protracted incest involving a female family member, before puberty (McCormack et al. 1992). Women are more likely than men to have experienced sexual assault within their families of origin, but their later psychological maladjustment tends to involve internalized rather than externalized patterns of behaviour in the form of depression, suicidality and eating disorders (Cappell and Heiner 1990; Pritchard 1999; Stanley and Penhale 1999).

In a community mental health study of 750 men aged 18 to 27 located in random cluster samples, using a computerized response format to ensure anonymity, it was established that 52 men had experienced unwanted, prolonged sexual contact up to age 16. The men were asked about sexual interest in or contact with minors. In the sample as a whole the strongest correlations were those of sexual interest or contact with males aged 12 to 15 with scores on Briere's (1989) *Trauma Symptom Checklist*, and with prior sexual abuse. The combination of these two factors (trauma symptoms and prior CSA) predicted 65 per cent of men with sexual interest in or contact with minors. Further exploration of these data suggested that 'traumatic bonding' to the abuser was a major factor in the transition from being a victim to becoming an abuser. Many of these young men had also come from emotionally and physically abusive homes, which accounted for their alienation from their own family members, making them 'easy prey' for paedophile abusers. It can be argued that these findings imply a humanistic approach to working with offenders, since many of these men come from home backgrounds which through various devious routes, have contributed to them becoming offenders. Therapy must however involve acceptance of liability for becoming an adult abuser, and the man must be helped to face down and exorcise the ghosts of the past.

Treatment of child sex abusers: findings of research literature

(1) The cycle of psycho-socio-economic poverty

Whilst reiterating that the vast majority of disadvantaged people do not neglect their children, the harsh reality is that whilst the key factor in people abusing children is psychological, abuse is more likely to occur in those problematic situations, in the presence of chronic and inherited socio-economic poverty. The following studies show the importance of the victim-abuser cycle, which has to be broken to prevent current offending, and further generation of victims.

In Britain a longitudinal study of 14,138 children (Sidebotham et al. 2001) has yielded useful findings on the backgrounds of parents who mal-treated their young children in various ways: mothers (compared to controls) had lower educational attainment, sexual abuse in their own childhoods, were aged less than 20 when becoming mothers, grew up in a father-absent household, and had a previous referrals for mental health problems as children or adults. Fathers too, were young, had often grown up in care, and were educational underachievers. They had often been victims of physical abuse and had a substance-abusing parent, and a depressed mother. An interesting finding is that mother's history of sexual abuse was related to her physical abuse and neglect of the child. In Canada the finding that male adult rapists were more often than other types offender, to have been sexually molested as children was replicated by Dhawan and Marshall (1996).

It is noteworthy that in the authoritative review by Hanson and Bussiere (1998) although generally poor emotional interactions in childhood predicted recidivism, having been a victim of sexual abuse did not, although it might predict the first and probably only offence. Ryan (2002) argued that there are no easy or single answers of why children and youth who have suffered sexual abuse, go on to impose this experience on others. While 'affectionless bond-ing' based on excessive parental control strategies may be implicated in some cases it is by no means a complete answer (Craissati et al. 2002). Craissati's carefully controlled study compared adolescent CSA victims who did and did not go to become sexual abusers themselves. Those who did become abusers had a longer and more intrusive sexual relationship with their own abuser, compared with the non-offending group. Overall, the authors concluded, a 'social learning approach' is supported by these findings. Nevertheless, the model is only partially successful in explaining outcomes, and if adolescent offenders are to be more successfully treated, more research is needed.

The big issue in breaking into the cycle is to develop a *motivation* for the abuser to change (Moore et al. 1999; LeGrand and Martin 2001; Terry and Mitchell 2001). This is true at both the socio-political 'macro' level as well as for the individual.

(2) Treating adolescents

In Ireland, O'Reilly et al. (2001) developed an 11-step group-based module for helping adolescent sex offenders to accept responsibility and change their behaviour, which LeGrand and Martin (2001) stress should include dealing with resistance to disclosure, and also deal with any accompanying underlying depression. In Britain significant developments have involved initiatives by the probation service, including skill training for workers in running groups (Monk 1998; Collier 1999). It is acknowledged that only a minority of known offen-ders are able to participate in such groups, and also that some men drop out of treatment, a factor associated with recidivism (Launay 2001). Indeed, the problem of not being able to motivate the offender to want to change, almost creates two distinct groups, the treatable and non-treatable (Browne and O'Connor 2000; Moore et al. 1999; Launay 2001; Terry and Mitchell 2001).

Aaron Bentovim (2002) a leading British psychiatrist has published an authoritative review on his own and others' work in this area on preventing sexually abused young people from becoming abusers, and addresses the psychological problems of young people who offend sexually (Bentovim 1995; Skuse et al. 1998; Watkins and Bentovim 2000). Four groups were studied cross-sectionally and longitudinally:

(i) Boys aged 11 to 16 who had been CSA victims, with no evidence of being perpetuators of CSA;
(ii) Boys who had been CSA victims but who had begun to be perpetrators of CSA;
(iii) Boys with no prior CSA but who nevertheless had begun to offend sexually; and
(iv) Boys with anti-social behaviours but with no prior CSA and no evidence of being sexually assaultive.

The important conclusions from this research were:

> There were similarities in the lives of boys who abused sexually but who had no history of sexual abuse themselves. They grew up in a family context where they were exposed to a climate of violence in the home. In addition, their mothers had themselves been subject to extensive sexual and physical abuse not only in their own childhood, but also in adult life. These boys were exposed not only to a climate of physical violence, but also to sexual violence, which may have had a similar effect to being sexually abused themselves ... we hypothesised that experiencing physical violence directly or being exposed to a climate of violence subjects a child to prolonged fear and stress, often for long periods of childhood development. This will adversely affect key developmental tasks and personality development through early childhood, middle childhood, adolescence and adult life ... Discontinuities of care, living in turn with various parents and step-parents, or being in local authority care could lead to a profound feeling of rejection. This had a bearing on the formation of attachments, and may result in the lack of secure relationships with an adult ... We felt that these boys were having the worst of both worlds, suffering both disruption of care and violence. They were missing confiding relationships that could have protective effects.
>
> (Bentovim 2002: 665)

Bentovim (2002) also provides a detailed and extremely valuable outline of the therapeutic interventions for sexually abused and sexually abusive children and adolescents developed at the Great Ormond Hospital for Sick Children, London. A high degree of denial of responsibility (74 per cent) was found on initial assessment – which is attributed to growing up in abusive and enmeshed families, in which no one takes responsibility for anything, and blaming others is paramount and the norm. In addition, boys who had escaped these family systems and had been abused outside of their homes feared the loss of the pseudo-freedom, which their detached lifestyle gave them. Only 44 per cent of mothers supported their children in the phase of abuse revelation, and not surprisingly, 60 per cent of the victims and/or perpetrators were removed into care situations.

Therapy first involves an individual counsellor who tries to recreate a positive attachment bond with the young person in order to repair:

> ... avoidant disorganised attachments. There needs to be the fostering of acceptance between the therapist and the child and sensitivity to the attachment style of the child, rather than expecting a uniform response. There should be a reasonable degree of warmth and responsiveness, but not too intense; otherwise the child may be reminded of an abusive context that groomed him or her to accept inappropriate sexual activity.
>
> (Bentovim 2002: 670)

Further elements of therapy involve 'management of emotional dysregulation' in the young person, and cognitive-behaviour therapy (Jones and Ramchandamin 1999) has proved valuable in this respect. Groups of young people diminish feelings of isolation and denial, and create peer support. Any parent who supports the youth, must themselves also be supported.

> The treatment aims of helping children and young people develop a positive sense of self which will prevent the victim-offender cycle includes developing a correct attribution for events, creating a healing alternative story, and becoming safe from retraumatisation and the abuse of others.
>
> (Bentovim 2002: 671)

No long-term evaluation of this therapeutic approach is offered, but a Canadian family treatment programme (Bagley and LaChance 2000) which is similar in several ways to the Great Ormond Street approach, found evidence of the success of programmes such as this. This programme was private in nature and was funded by fee-paying government agencies who referred cases for individual, dyadic and whole-family counselling. The study focused on 27 referred individuals and their families, and 30 similar cases who were not, because of funding limitations, referred. The programme showed highly significant increases in self-esteem scores in the treated adolescents compared with controls; 40 per cent of controls and 8 per cent of the treated group were subject to further sexual abuse. While entering the victim-abuser cycle was not measured in this study, it seems likely that the successfully treated group would not themselves become offenders.

Further work in Ireland on group treatment approaches for sexually abusive adolescents (O'Reilly et al. 2001) adds to confidence in the group treatment model for adolescents in the victim-abuser cycle. Developments in cognitive behavioural therapy also offer a promising outcome, which will be discussed later (Grossman et al. 1999; Lehne et al. 2000; Rasmussen 2001; Ward et al. 2002).

(3) Learning disability

One group of potential young offenders not yet mentioned, because they have different underlying problems, are those with a learning disability. Recent research from the USA (Timms and Goreczny 2002) and Scotland (Lindsay 2002) have characterized the nature of these young people if they become sex offenders. Such youth are in the unfortunate position of having the sexual drives of adolescence but not the intellectual and social skills to negotiate the kinds of sexual access enjoyed by their non-disabled peers. Learning disabled youth may clumsily seek sex in ways that may appear as assaultive, or they may seek the company of much younger peers with whom they have intellectual equality. Interventions include cognitive behavioural therapy and social skills training for socially acceptable behaviours, perhaps allied to the use of masturbatory outlets (Timms and Goreczny 2002). There is still much ambiguity in society about child and adolescent masturbation, with feelings of guilt imposed in religious families. It is accepted that some interpret the Bible to believe that masturbation is prohibited by scripture, and for some this is problematic, but it can provide a useful alternative sexual outlet for boys and men who would otherwise engage in some deviant actions. But then so was fornication and adultery (Leviticus 18:20; Deuteronomy 22:23), which present members of the Royal Family are self-   confessed practitioners, whilst this part of the Bible, the Old Testament, approved of slavery (Leviticus 25:44–46) and sanctioned ethnic cleansing/ genocide (Deuteronomy 1:8, 3:33–34 and 20:16)!

Lindsay (2002) however has challenged the rather unquestioning view of the greater potential for sexual misbehaviour by learning disabled youngsters, not least because the problems of institutionalization and de-institutionalization have been ignored in estimating the apparent over-representation of learning-disabled people in offender groups. It does appear that they may be less discriminating in their victims, and, like their non-disabled peers, may be more likely to offend if they too have had a history of abuse. She urges caution with this group, not least to avoid further stigmatization, and recommends an integrative treatment approach, including the pharmacological, behavioural, educational as well as the cognitive treatments.

(4) Psychological factors – attachment, empathy, motivation in treatable versus non-treatable offenders

Hudson and Ward (1997) have offered new work on attachment problems in sexual abuse survivors. Men with 'fearful' attachment styles were, concurrently the most lonely and often approached their underage victims seeking affection. But men with fearful and dismissive attachment styles expressed the most anger, and were more likely to engage in aggressive assaults, including assaults against adults as well as minors (Ward et al. 1996). Understanding a man's disordered attachment style, stemming from his own dysfunctional childhood, could be an important aspect of trauma repair in helping men to seem more mature relationships. It is clear that family dysfunction associated with the offender's own sexual victimization should be addressed in therapy and rehabilitation (Romano and De Luca 1997). These US findings are supported by British research (Manocha and Mezey 1998). Further Australian research by Lee et al. (2002) also confirms that childhood experiences of emotional and physical abuse are part of the pattern of disrupted attachments, which lead men into deviant sexual patterns in adulthood. Clearly some offenders who have never experienced their childhoods in ways, which were developmentally normal, try and recreate relationships of childhood in establishing what Finkelhor (1994) called 'emotional congruence' with their victims (Wilson 1999). However, in Wilson's research incest offenders attempted to elevate their female victims into an adult-type role in serving their sexual needs.

Research has confirmed that incest offenders are easier to treat successfully than men with fixated attachments (often of a 'homosexual' nature), this latter group having higher recidivism rates (Greenberg et al. 2000). Further taxonomic research has shown that adult sex offenders are indeed a heterogeneous group, with different types requiring quite different treatment and intervention approaches (Pritchard and Bagley 2000). Fixated offenders target victims of a particular age and sex, and this fixation makes diversion programmes difficult. In these fixated offenders, an exclusive focus on children's sexuality and number of prior offences and convictions are strong predictors of further offending (Prentky et al. 1997).

Further research using the newly emerging personality dimensions called 'the big five' found as expected, that incest offenders were more neurotic, less outgoing and socially skilled, and were less likely to be conscientious (that is, were more likely to ignore moral rules regarding behaviour).

Research needs to explain why some sex offenders are unable to empathize with their victims, a reflection of their general inability to express or feel empathy, a factor that must be addressed in treatment programmes (Marshall et al. 1997). The crucial intervening personality factor may be sociopathy (Maker et al. 1999). Unfortunately sociopathy and anti-social personality disorders are difficult conditions to treat and may underlie conditions such as sexual murder (Grubin 1994), and seemingly senseless acts of wanton murder with and without added rape of child victims. The British cases of Michael Stone (who impulsively killed a mother and child with a hammer without sexual assault) and Roy Whiting (who killed an 8-year-old girl in Sussex in a notorious case of kidnap and apparent sexual assault) are cases in point.

Waterhouse et al. (1994) in classifying Scottish prisoners identified a type of sociopathic, conscienceless offender whose patterns of brutal violence seemed to reflect their own brutalized childhood. These strands are drawn together in the theoretical review of cases by MacCulloch et al. (2000) in trying to understand 'the sadistic murderer syndrome'. The elements of their explanatory model is that the man was severely abused as a child, and stemming from chronic anxiety fostered by childhood emotional, physical and sexual abuse develops states of ego-defensive aggression, and aggressive sexual arousal. An internal working model develops in which sadistic sexual fantasy plays a major part, leading in some cases to sadistic sexual behaviour.

Fortunately the number of such murderers available for study is small, and in Britain they are housed in special hospitals such as Rampton and Broadmoor. It appears that many of these murderers are untreatable, and lengthy and perhaps lifelong imprisonment, albeit in the setting of special hospital, is inevitable.

One of the greatest difficulties for all of us in trying to understand child abusers, is how they fail to empathize with their victims, seen in the extreme in the case of the notorious 'Mr Levine', whose self-justification was offensive. This problem of changing the offender's motivation to want to change, is probably the core aim for most 'psychological' treatment models (Tierney and McCabe 2002). In the most successful programmes, up to 80 per cent do not re-offend two years after treatment – but this is linked with this motivational change, as found in two separate research programmes, both linked to cognitive behavioural therapy (Grossman et al. 1999; Terry and Mitchell 2001; Tierney and McCabe 2002). This requires the abuser to stop seeing their victims as objects, and end their rationalization and irrespective of their own backgrounds, accept responsibility for their actions. Day (1999) urges the treatment services to seek to understand the views of the offender, for unless we see where they are coming from, our efforts may be futile. Ward (2002) develops this 'client focus' in a humanitarian and practical approach when he raises the question about the offender's morale. He reminds us that the abuser, often has clear psychiatric co-morbidity (Raymond et al. 1999; Hoyer et al. 2000), which requires treatment, and also means that the abuser has a history of psychosocial failure. Consequently the therapist need to inject the notion of their possibility of living a 'good life', which requires our belief in the client that they can improve and change (Pritchard 2004). Frankly, this can be difficult, especially with what appears to be for some an intractable lack of motivation to change. This has led Grossman et al. (1999) to ask the question 'are sex offenders treatable?' With cautious optimism, the following section seeks to answer that question.

(5) Intervening with child sex abusers

Hanson and Bussiere (1998) have undertaken a comprehensive meta-analysis of 61 follow-up studies of sexual offenders, involving 23,304 men who had sexually assaulted adults or minors, or both. Thirty of the studies came from the USA; sixteen from Canada; ten from the UK; and three each from Australasia and Scandinavia. Measurement of re-offending was based either on re-arrest rates, or on confidential admission of further offences. The further sexual crime rate was surprisingly low, at 13.4 per cent. Significant predictors of sexual re-offending (usually involving a minor) across several or all of the studies reviewed were being younger and never married; having had a poor relationship with mother; lower social class; employment instability; prior sexual offences; had victimized strangers and/or extra familial members; had begun sexual offending as an adolescent; sexual interest in boys; MMPI personality disorders; and failure to complete a treatment programme. Very surprisingly however, in these samples 'contrary to popular belief, being sexually abused as a child was not associated with increased risk' (Hanson and Bussiere 1998: 353). Many of the men in these programmes had other, non-sexual offences, and a prior history of non-sexual violent offences was also associated with sexual recidivism. Overall, the men in these programmes who failed to respond to treatment appear to resemble the multi-criminal violent offenders identified in the English study of convicted child sex abusers (Pritchard and Bagley 2000). Overall, the recidivism rate in generally violent men (diagnosed psychopathic) with an established pattern of sexual assaults against both adults and minors was about 50 per cent (Rice et al. 1991), self-evidently the most dangerous, especially if they are within-family abusers.

Cognitive behavioural therapy: a way forward?

In the British programmes cognitive behavioural therapy (CBT) has been shown to be the most effective in giving men social skills and psychosocial careers, which do not involve offending. Interestingly, Nurcombe et al. (2000) in a meta-analysis of intervention and outcome studies, saw CBT as the core of the most effective form of intervention, but with others, felt that a combined approach, of CBT, group therapy and pharmacological treatments were best (Ward et al. 2002). The CBT approaches have been found most effective with younger offenders (Rasmussen 2001) in helping them accept their personal responsibility. But Nurcombe et al. (2000) emphasize the importance of specific treatment packages to deal with the individual profile of the offender, and Hoyer et al. (2000) suggests seeing some offenders as having a primary problem with 'impulse control', which is more likely to be dealt with by a combined cognitive and pharmacological approach. Equally, in cases where there is psychiatric co-morbidity, there is a need to deal with the complicating psychiatric problem (Raymond et al. 1999; Wood 2000), not least because CBT is found to be one of the most effective elements in an integrated model to treat mentally disordered people (Warner 2000; Kingdon and Turkington 2002).

Later work, reviewing 25 years of CBT with 7275 sexual offenders by Maletzky and Steinhauser (2002), shows the most promise but with mixed success. They were able to trace a remarkable 62 per cent over the period five years after initiating treatment. Overall, frankly the less serious child sex offenders, the exhibitionists had far lower re-offending rates than the intractable 'paedophile', especially the homosexual orientated, or those involved in violence and/or rape. A key feature associated with poor outcome was early termination of treatment by the offender, which was especially high for the violent/rapist man. So we need more effort and understanding to improve outcomes that ensure children are protected.

However, it is clear that punitive programmes such as simple imprisonment are likely to elicit counter-anger and further offending behaviour in the average sexual offender (Grubin 2000). Only a small proportion of the sexual offenders who have not killed their victim are so irredeemable that more or less permanent imprisonment, or detention under the new Mental Health Act (Birmingham 2002) is necessary, but should never be ruled out, not least because especially with violence, the strongest indicator of further violence, is having a history of violence. Indeed, reviewable sentences, in effect indeterminate sentences have been recommended for the multi-criminal and violent abuser until they can prove that they can live amongst us. Some may consider this harsh but it is not so much for revenge but first an attempt to protect potential future victims because in one sense these men have laid aside their humanity. Therefore until they can prove their safety, they stay not for revenge but rather in Milton's words 'They also serve who stand and wait' and in this sense until we have the knowledge and techniques to ensure children's safety, they have a humanitarian obligation to 'serve'.

There is an accumulation of useful knowledge on assessing men who sexually abuse in Britain (Briggs et al. 1998). Advances in treatment and evaluation programmes in the USA are well summarized in the papers in the edited volumes of Lawes et al. (2000) and Coleman and Miner (2000). There is emerging a welcome bio-psychological perspective which draws into the treatment network a range of professionals – forensic psychologists and psychiatrists, health professionals, and social service and parole workers. It is now clear that re-offending can be greatly reduced by cognitive behavioural, medical and social service interventions. Especially in the case of juvenile offenders, diversionary programmes, which are non-custodial, can be highly successful (Campbell and Lerew 2002). All that is lacking, in the British case, is the political will and the funding to initiate these programmes on a comprehensive scale. They are much cheaper than continued years of imprisonment, and can also save the pain to victims caused by further offending.

One word of caution, it is self-evident that the effective protection of children rests upon 'evidence based' practice. Unfortunately Nurcombe and his colleagues could only find seven studies, which matched the rigorous criteria of 'random controlled trials' (RCT) which is the evidence-based practice objective in medicine (Nurcombe et al. 2000). Of the seven, all but two studies showed better outcome results than either 'treatment as usual' or 'no-treatment' groups. However, these results are complicated by the fact that some offenders did not complete the treatment programme because of an inability to resolve the problem of motivation to change. Hence we have to face the fact that at the present state of practice evidence, it seems that there are two distinct groups, the 'treatable' and at the present state of knowledge and practice, 'untreatable' abusers. Not an easy position to be in, especially when easy sound bite answers are desperately sought by all – politicians, managers, the public and the media.

Development of offender programmes in Britain and North America

The state of prisons and special hospitals in Britain leaves a great deal to be desired (Ramsbotham 2001). Many are crowded; they are under-funded; and therapy programmes for groups such as sex offenders have to vie with funding for educational and recreational programmes. Suicide rates in prisoners are high, and many men and women who would benefit from psychiatric intervention do not receive it (Pritchard et al. 1997). Indeed, rates of mental illness in prisoners are much higher than in the general population – many offend because of psychiatric disturbance, and prison is clearly not the best place for them. Rates of childhood physical, sexual and emotional abuse are much higher in prisoners than in the general population (Ramsbotham 2001).

In Britain there are some 2500 individuals (mostly men) with a diagnosis of severe anti-social personality disorder in jail, some 25 of these (all men) having 'whole life tariff'. In the special hospitals are another 450 men and women with severe personality disorder, which has been associated with violent physical and sexual attacks on others. The average bill for a prisoner for one year is about £27,000. Crowded in amongst the regular prisoners are asylum seekers, refugees, and individuals aged under 18s. By late 2003 the number of UK prisoners had risen to a record high of 72,000. Whilst this is nothing to be proud of, it is worth noting that if Britain imprisoned men and women at the same rate as the USA, there would (according to Ramsbotham's 2001 estimate) be at least 400,000 people imprisoned in the UK.

While Britain lags behind the USA in locking up its population (despite having 250,000 current or previously convicted sex offenders in the community (Lothstein 2001), it lags in providing therapeutic innovations for sex offenders, including men who have offended against children. Most sex offenders in UK jails are offered no therapy programmes whatever. It is in the community that 'pathfinder programmes' have been set up (Grubin 1999, 2000), based on co-operation between probation, health services and police. Despite the fact that these programmes offer at a maximum 50 hours of treatment as opposed to the 150 hours 'really needed' they are associated with a one-third reduction in the expected recidivism rate if the men had received no treatment at all (Grubin 2000). Offering a full 150 hour programme over a year would cost some £15,000 per offender which is much cheaper than the more ineffective option of imprisonment alone, costing some £27,000 a year (Grubin 2000). The British community programmes are, unfortunately, under attack and closing through reduced funding (Travis 2002).

This issue of treatment of sex offenders in prisons is a problem throughout the Western world, not only in terms of sheer numbers, but also with regard to the artificiality of the setting, when the goal of treatment is to enable the man to live in the community in a non-offending role (Shapiro et al. 2001; Stone et al. 2000; Wood 2000; Lothstein 2001; Bauriedl 2002). An important British study utilizing a behaviourally based but integrated approach of 'relapse prevention', focused upon aiding the offender to recognize and then avoid the 'pathways' to offending. Again motivation was everything and whilst some were able to learn to avoid potential triggers to offending by developing through avoidance and coping strategies, a significant group did not (Launay 2001).

Pharmacological treatments for sex abusers, which are controversial, are still being criticized for dealing with only 'symptom' control, as well as ethical issues, even though the use of androgens do appear to reduce sex drive (Grossman et al. 1999; Lehne et al. 2000; Nurcombe et al. 2000; Stone et al. 2000). Recently concern has been expressed about a range of side effects, including a possible increase in prostate cancer (Seifert 2000). Moreover, clinical experience of working with people who are paralysed indicated that, as one client put it, 'sex is in the head' for despite his inability to function sexually, he felt especially frustrated because he still felt the emotional desire. This is probably the case with sex abusers, so again motivation is everything.

There is another potential problem in successfully treating sex offenders, namely the Internet. Buttell and Carney (2001) suggest that most treatment providers are unaware of the potentially negative impact of the Internet because of the relative ease with which offenders can reinforce their addictive, compulsive or impulse control disorders, by viewing the quite horrendous Internet material spewed out by criminal organizations outside the European Union. It may be that any treatment or probation order should include some form of monitoring of former offenders' computer use.

(7) Law and social services

The first question is: is child abuse decreasing? Certainly, in Britain the severe physical abuse as judged by the number of murders of young children is declining (Pritchard 1996a, 2002). In Canada there is evidence of a decline in the amount of sexual abuse recalled by adults in random surveys of community adults. It has been found that older women recalled more sexual abuse in their childhoods, and younger women (especially those aged 18 to 20) significantly fewer extended periods of abuse. This could be because child sexual abuse is now a clear item on the public agenda, and professionals are willing to listen to the complaints of children being abused (Atmore 1999), so that when an abusive event occurs, a front-line worker (a teacher or someone on a telephone help line) can intervene to have the abuse stopped. In addition, offenders (actual and potential) may, through the publicity given to studies of the nature and impact of abuse realize that sexual contact between adults and children is likely to be harmful, and also that children now have the means to 'blow the whistle' on the abuser. It is interesting to note that a report from the British organization ChildLine in October 2002 reported that of the many calls from children about sexual abuse the average time between abuse beginning and their call for help was now six weeks, as opposed to six months when ChildLine was established 15 years ago. In addition, the number of calls to this organization has increased dramatically. This is information, which the potential abuser (unless he is a person whose impulses are totally out of control) may take to heart.

In America there is an interesting debate on the question of 'why is sexual abuse declining?' (Jones at al. 2001; Leventhal 2001a; Chadwick 2002). What is happening is that reports of such abuse to mandated state agencies of CSA are declining over time. The debate concerns whether this is an artefact of procedure and statistical recording, perhaps that parents and children are now more reluctant to report such abuse, or, whether the change reflects a real decline in the amount of CSA in recent years. Chadwick (2002) calls for careful epidemiological and hospital-based clinical monitoring to try and establish whether the decline is real. The case for careful, periodic surveys of young adults randomly sampled from the general population asking them to review childhood abuse in their lives would be valuable. Hopefully, the younger respondents would recall less abuse. This would indicate that not only are we reducing the extremes of child abuse in most Western countries, for example, a dead child (Pritchard 1996a, 2002; Pritchard and Butler 2003), but this would indicate we are beginning to make an impact on the abuser/ abusing cycle.

As discussed elsewhere in this book community notification of offenders is a controversial approach (known in the USA as 'Megan's Law' – Petrosino and Petrosino 1999) and has been advocated in Britain as a means of protecting children from the further predations of a convicted offender released into a community. This has been rejected by successive Home Secretaries. The law would require that the names of any offenders living locally should be publicly available, so that families, schools and other agencies could protect their children against the potential threat of such men. This might work if the community, perhaps through the agency of a community church, could exercise benign control and care of the released offender. But newspaper campaigns in Britain releasing the names of known paedophiles thought to be living in a particular area have ended in disaster, with public riots and campaigns of vilification. Physical attacks and even the burning down of homes which the actual offender had moved from long before have occurred. It is probable that placing a man on the register of known sex offenders, requiring him to report regularly his whereabouts to the police and in any programme of mandated therapy or community correction, should be sufficient for most, but ideally we need effective evidence-based interventions and this is still far off.

(8) The importance of agency co-operation in a combined bio-psychosocial approach to work with offenders and victims

In 1996 a national commission of inquiry in Britain published a two-volume report *Childhood Matters* (Hobbs and Heywood 1997) taking evidence from over 10,000 people, including many who had been abused as children. It was clear from the report that many physically, emotionally and sexually abused children were 'slipping through the net', and many abusers were undetected and undeterred. Amongst the 80 recommendations of the report was the advocacy of 'greater integration between social services, education, and health authorities' (Hobbs and Heywood 1997: 97). The recommendations of this key report have been almost entirely ignored, and Britain under a new government moved into an era of further under-funding and disorganization of health and social services.

Writing four years later the British paediatricians Speight and Wynne (2000) reported on their survey of health professionals working with children. Many were 'close to despair' about the current state of child protection, a system in which social workers operating under the current Children Act allowed many children to return home to further abuse and neglect. It appears that the nature of the biological relationship was of more importance for many social services rather than the actual quality of care the child received from his or her mother or father, all in the name of 'keeping the family together' at all costs:

> In the absence of evidence, this resurgence of blood link ideology should be regarded as based on nothing stronger than a mixture of sentiment, political convenience, superstition, and wishful thinking ... The end result is that when and if the child finally comes into care he or she is emotionally damaged, older, and consequently harder to place.
>
> (Speight and Wynne 2000: 195)

The publication by the Department of Health of a new *Framework for the Assessment of Children in Need and their Families* (Hutton 2000) has not made any noticeable impact on policy or practice in the field of child protection. These criticisms of the child protection system have not, unfortunately, been entirely misplaced. At its worst, there has been poor practice, with an ignorance of significant signs of risk, poor recording and inadequate sharing of information between the various professionals, and failure of any particular agency to accept responsibility. In the case of Victoria Climbié (Laming Report 2003) a commission of inquiry heard that police, social services, paediatricians and the NSPCC all failed to intervene effectively in a case in which the signs of horrific, ongoing abuse were manifest. Indeed, one of these aforementioned agencies actually fabricated information given to the inquiry, while another concealed vital information!

A further report, *Tomorrow's Children* issued by the Association of Directors of Social Services (2003) argued that substantially more focused and integrated intervention by police, nursing and medical services and professions with training in child abuse, as well as schools and the voluntary sector is needed to address these preventable cases in which children are murdered by a caretaker (Leadbetter 2002). However, will this important policy document meet the same fate as the major report *Childhood Matters?* Time will tell.

Ideal frameworks for the investigation and prevention of child abuse cases can be proposed (for example, Peterson and Brown 1994; Williams and Pritchard 2004) but without political support and adequate funding, these proposals will drain into the sand. The knowledge base for the integration and vigorous action of health, social service and police professionals in preventing child abuse has been established (Wynne 1997). But, as is the case in providing comprehensive treatment services for child abusers, there is currently neither political will nor adequate funding for supporting these initiatives.

Despite such criticisms however, it can be argued that the dismal picture fails to account for the very good child protection by the vast majority of social workers. Indeed, it is re-iterated that even if we doubled the worst estimate of children dying from abuse (NSPCC 2002), and believed the worst media excesses about social services and assumed all child homicides came from the 58,900 children formally 'looked-after' by English local authorities (DoH 2002), this would yield a rate of 0.17 per cent deaths of children in social services care. Such a rate would be heralded as successful in many if not most branches of medicine.

Nonetheless, it would be easy to feel despondent and overwhelmed by the difficulties those intractable abusers appear to present. However, there are two mentoring approaches worth considering (Zimrin 1984; Eckenrode et al. 2000). The first offers an integrated research model and is associated first with initial prevention. The second aims to break into the cycle of psycho-socio-economic poverty (Pritchard 2001; Pritchard and Williams 2001; Sure Start 2002; Williams and Pritchard 2004). Both models are appropriate to quality social work practice and more important respond to the 'agenda' of parents and families struggling to overcome their psycho-socio-economically impoverished lives. One important feature relevant to every aspect of human services is the speed and availability of help to people in chronic and/or crisis situations (Pritchard 1991, 1998, 1999, 2001, 2004; Pritchard et al. 1997; Pritchard and Williams 2001).

Zimrin (1984) in the USA recognized this and provided, alongside a de facto counselling service for families on the 'At Risk of Abuse' register, a family support worker. The 'family support worker' (FSW), often a would-be social work student gaining experience before their professional course, worked in collaboration with the supervising social worker. Crucially, they were allocated a realistic caseload, so that the majority of FSW could visit their clients daily, and in times of particular stress, more than once a day. The quality of relationship between the often damaged adults and the FSW increased, even though ostensibly, the FSW work was 'practical'. It was their availability, plus the almost tangential 'monitoring' of the family situation, in that the presence or the impending visit by 'an outsider' was a deterrent as well as a positive support. Indeed, whilst Zimrin's overall study found positive outcomes with social workers utilizing an integrated 'family approach', those with the closer FSW input did significantly better.

This success mirrors a more recent longitudinal RCT study exploring the value of a 'Home Visitation' service up to the index child's second birthday. In British terms, the worker was a cross between a social worker and a health visitor (Eckenrode et al. 2000). The home visited families did consistently better, that is, they had less need for care, and had far fewer incidents of abuse than those families receiving standard care. Crucially, the greater the amount of contact again appeared to be a major factor, helping reversed the isolation and poor self-esteem of many of the adults. However, in the presence of persistent domestic violence, in the first 12 months of follow-up, mother's physical abuse of her child tended to re-occur, if the violent male continued to live within the family. This reminds us that an important predictor of within-family child abuse is the presence of domestic violence against the mother (Rumm et al. 2000). A wider application of this social work model would, if partner violence were also addressed, likely to be highly cost effective in preventing the abuse of children and the evolution of the victim-abuser cycle.

Another model came from the USA and is being currently introduced in some areas of need in the UK, namely 'Sure Start' a child and family service for the under 5s. This is linked with new government initiatives (Children Fund and Connexions), and providing they are not under-funded and are properly targeted and evaluated, one can be confident that they will bring about a significant reduction in child neglect and abuse.

This confidence is based upon recent British work, which was a three-year longitudinal comparative study of a school-based family-child social work service, compared to the standard service (Pritchard 2001; Pritchard et al. 1998; Williams and Pritchard 2004). In a nutshell, this concerned good quality social work, professionally well supported, but with optimum resources, which enabled the team to meet any family crisis, usually on the day of contact and seldom more than 24 hours later.

The project was an extension of the integrated preventive model of Rose and Marshal (1975) and Rutter et al. (1979) who showed that a school-based programme could make a difference in reducing a range of psychosocial pathology.

The intervention was not just direct social work with 'problematic' children and families, but also group work within the school, and crucially, supportive supervision of teaching staff to maximize their professional input. As a Head in one of the two schools (dealing with a total of nearly 2000 children from the most severely socio-economically deprived part of the county) put it, when the project started they were fire-fighting. The second year stopped the crises becoming emergencies. By the end of the third year, they were heading off the crises.

The outcome was that the project school did significantly better than the two matched 'standard schools' on all measures, including major reductions in truancy, delinquency, drug misuse, and in particular, there was a major reduction in families needing to be placed on the 'At Risk of Abuse' register. And where it occurred, the majority were self-referrals. Almost embarrassing was the level of fiscal savings based upon a conservative cost-benefit analysis, as the project more than paid for itself in terms of reduced vandalism, theft and more importantly, a reduction in the need to exclude children from school.

Here is a normative model that seeks to reach child and family within their own communities, using a non-stigmatized 'universal' service – the school. Its impact crossed disciplinary boundaries and brought benefits to all relevant services as it helped to break the link between inter-generational cycle of psycho-socio-economic poverty and educational alienation. There are grounds for optimism at the most important and basic level, that of prevention.

Conclusions

In the mid-1990s, the quality of research literature on intervention, compared with literature on the nature of child sexual abuse and its effects on victims, was sparse. At the time of writing, despite this book's extensive bibliography, as Newcomb and Locke (2001) has shown, relatively, there is still a dearth of outcome studies on child abusers, and child sexual offenders. None the less, we are in a better position to draw together the main themes identified from the research reviewed above. The traditional three-fold model of effective practice is still best. The primacy of prevention: stopping abuse before it takes place, either via 'treatment' interventions or deterring or appealing to potential offenders; treating abuse victims and detected adolescent offenders, to prevent long-term mental health problems and reduce the evolution of the victimization cycle; and efficient and humane treatment of adult offenders, to reduce or prevent their recidivism.

Drawing together the different type of intervention studies, at the present state of knowledge we can come to the following broad conclusions:

(1) Recognize the all-pervasive psycho-socio-economic poverty dimension in child neglect and abuse. Consequently we need social policy initiatives to reduce relative child poverty and accept the reality of decades of research on cycles of deprivation and abuse, which has

shown that 'The fathers have eaten a sour grape and the children's teeth are set on edge' (Jeremiah 31:29). The stark choice for society is simple. Every generation of children we fail, 'sows dragon's teeth' for the near future in terms of more crime, social disruption and the speedy turning of the screw for the next generation. Apart from the moral imperative for the necessary 'compensatory' policies, is the incredible fiscal cost of failure to prevent the cycle of deprivation, which runs into billions annually (Audit Commission 1996, 1998).

Related to policy issues is the need for the law to respond to the required task of prevention and intervention, rather than focusing only upon control. Hence, law should enhance the ability for the service to reach those men who would benefit from treatment, thus helping reduce future child neglect and abuse.

(2) A normative, integrative and preventive service is the ideal. The earlier the better such as the 'Sure Start' initiatives which intervene virtually at pre-birth level in order to offer a compensatory support service for vulnerable children and parents. This should be followed on by school-based service, such as the Home Office project (Pritchard 2001; Williams and Pritchard 2004), in which the emphasis is upon a normative setting, avoiding the stigmatization and reducing parental resistance. Crucially, it aims to intervene not only to stop the 'crises becoming emergencies' but also 'to head off the crises'. Early indications are that such approaches are being favoured by the Department of Education and Skills, in conjunction with the Department of Health and the Home Office, via such initiatives as 'Children's Fund' and 'Connexions'. The latter is now being extended towards damaged youth whose psycho-socio-economic inheritance has often contributed to their educational alienation, making them virtually unemployable. This leads to social exclusion and social disruption and for the females in particular, early and often inadequate parenthood.

(3) Child protection is essentially multi-disciplinary and needs to address all aspects of the problem, namely prevention of child abuse and/or intervention to stop current neglect and abuse and the necessary continued maintenance of parental functioning over time. It is seldom acknowledged that some of these very damaged parents are going to need long-term support, not just crisis work. The messages from the 'home visitation' type activities are plain, namely that in sustaining relationship to assist parents extend their ability to relate to others, many will also need practical support until they are able to take control over their own lives.

(4) Rediscover the psychiatric dimension in child neglect and abuse. In this model, an integrated child protection service is not panicked by

the presence of a mental disorder, nor would the signs of severe illness missed by social workers, and neither does adult psychiatry ignore the patient's children's need. This requires therefore an adequate funding of psychiatric services, not the much heralded new mental health legislation which although necessary, implies that the certification and detention of a wider sector of the mentally ill (those with anti-social behaviours, and various personality disorders) is a major innovation in mental health services. Real initiatives belong in the community, not in the psychiatric unit of the secure hospital.

As early as 1992, a massive but hidden shift of resources from mental health took place, to make good inadequate funding of acute surgical services (Pritchard 1992b; Pritchard et al. 1996c). Until the Chancellor's new monies for the NHS work through the system, the adult psychiatric services will continue to function sub-optimally. What is so frustrating is that with adequate integrated bio-psycho-social treatment models, most mental disorders can be more than adequate relieved in the community (Warner 2000; Kingdon and Turkington 2002; Pritchard 2004).

(5) Moving directly to consider the individual sex abuser, we need to first overcome the offender's denial of the offence. This requires that we counter the offender's minimization of its impact upon his victim as an important first step in the treatment of sex offenders with child and adolescent victims. We must directly address and change their motivation.

(6) Many first-time offenders, if they were a single within-family victim, can be treated in the community and will not re-offend. This needs a co-operative judicial system, which places an offender on probation, on the condition that he enters therapy and assists in therapy for the victim and his family. A family systems approach may be successful in this respect. However, careful follow-up studies of this and other treatment regimes for offenders are quite rare. An evaluation of a Canadian programme based on Giarretto's humanistic principles of treatment for the whole victim, which stressed the primacy of the victim's needs, was quite successful, with very low rates of recidivism in comparison with untreated controls who had a known re-offence rate of 30 per cent (Bagley and LaChance 2000).

(7) For men sentenced to prison terms, therapy to prevent re-offending is important. If there is no treatment in prison, the man may be discharged without modification of deviant sexual motivation, and the probability of recidivism is about 50 per cent in fixated, paedophile offenders. Prison treatment programmes cost relatively little, and could be highly cost effective. The combination of group therapy to reduce denial and increase self-acceptance, individualized cognitive

behavioural therapy, and drug treatments in some cases is associated with reconviction rates of between 10 and 20 per cent.

(8) In addition to lack of treatment in prison, other predictors of re-offending are having been a CSA victim, beginning to abuse children whilst a teenager, offences involving predatory approaches to many children or adolescents outside of the offender's family, never married, and number of previous convictions. Some men can be treated successfully despite the existence of many risk factors, but others appear to be untreatable by available therapies. Taxonomic studies could help identify sub-groups requiring more specific types of treatment.

(9) Classification of sex offenders indicates several different groups for whom different treatment and control strategies are necessary: adolescent boys (and sometimes girls) from disrupted and abusive families; regressed paedophiles who abuse a family member; fixated or career paedophiles; casual abusers with multi-criminal careers; and sociopathic abusers who abuse cruelly, without conscience, empathy or remorse. There is some evidence that some men in this latter group are neurologically damaged. These men are probably untreatable, and may have to be detained more or less permanently in special hospitals. All of the other groups are treatable, the regressed offenders having the best prognosis. Even the fixated offender can have recidivism rates as low as 10 to 20 per cent with prolonged, focused treatment and careful monitoring of progress.

(10) For the 'untreatable' men, especially if they have a record of generalized violence, as well as sex offences, then for the safety of our children sadly, it is recommend they have indeterminate but reviewable sentences (or containment in a secure hospital). This should not mean that they have been abandoned in the prison system, but rather they should be encouraged to take part in new modules of intervention which offer the best prospect of aiding them to control their violence and their unacceptable sexual behaviour. This challenges us to develop research based treatment initiatives to reach the 'untreatable' abuser, with the aim of giving them the hope that they can lead a 'good life' (Ward 2002) and that they can ultimately return to society as equal human beings.

Understanding and empathy for men and women who abuse children emotionally, physically and sexually is not to condone such abuse, but is part of a strategy to prevent further abuse taking place, constructing models for prevention strategies. A key factor in intervention is to prevent the victim-abuser cycle, part of a cycle of deprivation in which family neglect and abuse is associated with disordered emotional attachments between adults and children. But the victim-abuser cycle is by no means inevitable, and some two-thirds of abused and neglected children do not go on to become abusers. These are the unsung heroes of child abuse, individuals and families who despite their disrupted childhoods do not become adult abusers.

Babyhood, or indeed, better family planning, is the key to any preventive intervention programme, summarized in the cliché we need 'better family planning more than we need better social work'. Of course, we require both. Adolescence is possibly the last best chance to develop a highly effective preventive intervention, before sexually coercive behaviour has developed. Humane and sympathetic treatment models employing a mix of methods including group treatment and cognitive behavioural therapy can restore a sense of identity, which respects both the self and others.

While models of treatment are now well established, in Britain these programmes are sparse and under-funded, too short, and without follow-up monitoring and if my estimate of a probable number of abusers is even close to accurate – in excess of 220,000 – there is much to be done.

Punitive prison sentences may remove a man from circulation but, without associated treatment for all but those with severe anti-social personality disorder, they are likely to be counterproductive so far as recidivism is concerned.

The combined bio-psychosocial approach to treatment and prevention of offending is acknowledged as the one most likely to succeed, but this approach implies in the co-operation between health and social services that is not as well developed as it could and should be.

The problems facing practitioners, managers and policy makers alike, are the many and conflicting pressures upon the service. On the one hand is the media demands for over-simplistic answers, and at the other end of the continuum, is the pressure with which front-line practitioners are most concerned, the inability to meet the needs of vulnerable and exposed children, within the child's subjective time span. More can and should be done for the damaged adults who abuse children, but sadly at the present state of knowledge, they are unlikely to change sufficiently quickly to meet the children's needs – hence the clash of interests which invariably surround child protection and psychiatric practice.

Dilemmas abound but one key way forward is to recognize the need to differentiate between the risks to children and urgently tidy up our language and our conceptual framework, so that we are not as it were, mixing up a slight headache with meningitis. But we need the public's confidence, which demands properly evaluated intervention programmes for current offenders. Indeed, we need targeted intervention to break the cycle of victim-abuser – on the one hand, anti-child poverty programmes and on the other, more proactive intervention with current parents, even if it means early removal of a child into an adoptive home, as early adoption can have highly successful outcomes for children who would otherwise have very negative psychosocial outcomes in adolescence (DoH 2001).

Hence we need to control *earlier* because we care. The way to determine this is to keep at the forefront of our deliberations the child's continued welfare. If they are left to be mishandled by inadequate parents, we merely condemn them and often their own children, to a repetition of neglect and abuse. Therefore if we consider the parent/s to be 'personality disordered', they are *unlikely to change within the time frame necessary to meet the child's basic psychosocial needs*. Therefore remove earlier and compensate with adequately trained and long-term supported foster or adoptive care. It cannot be re-iterated enough that the majority of serious abusers are within-family abusers and any policy to protect children should be based essentially upon a normative 'support the family' policy, not child protection per se. For it is prevention that will make the biggest impact upon vulnerable children, with their often equally vulnerable, damaged and damaging parent figures.

Hence, in whatever style or combination of family children are cared for, we can adopted Utting's (1997) clarion call of 'all our children', and make 'children and families' the core of all governmental social policies.

At the time of writing the Green Paper (2003) 'Every Child Matters' sought to bring up-to-date the practice and organization issues surrounding current and future child protection services. It makes many excellent suggestions, but I fear that in its inevitable focus upon agency process, it has missed the key preventive issue. Namely that if we are to reach children we need to focus upon the 'abusers'. The suggestion that the child mental health services might help break the cycle of adolescent victim-to-abuser is very welcome. However, this misses the core psychiatric dimension, namely adult psychiatry and mentally disordered adults, especially parent figures. In the study of a decade of child homicides (Pritchard and Bagley 2001), I am confident that if the social workers had considered the adult psychiatric concept of 'personality disorder', a number of children would have been saved. I am even more sure, that if the adult psychiatrists had asked themselves, 'has my patient child responsibilities or involved with a child?' then half the mental-disorder-related homicides might not have occurred. The disturbed parent/guardian is at the core of the child protection-psychiatric interface, and can be effectively treated to the benefit of both the patient and the child. It is hoped that the Green Paper consultation will consider this research-based recommendation.

It is accepted that some tough issues have been considered and whilst I certainly do not have all the answers, it is hoped that you have found this to be a helpful contribution to your consideration of child protection issues. Whilst it is appreciated that you may well have a different perspective and emphasis, it is hoped that we can share the same vision for all our children, seeing them but at just one stage of their human pilgrimage and with Wordsworth (from *The Prelude*) we say,

I speak about a race of real children,
Not too good or too wise, but bounded up by love and hate.
Oh may their early joys be nature and in books
And Knowledge, rightly honoured by that word,
Not purchased by the loss of power.

Bibliography

Abbott, M. (2001) Distinguishing SIDS from child abuse fatalities, *Paediatrics*, 108: 1237.

Adshead, G., Brooke, D., Samuels, M., Jenner, S. and Southall, D. (2000) Maternal behaviors associated with smothering: a preliminary descriptive study, *Child Abuse and Neglect*, 24: 1175–1183.

Alexander, P. (1992) Application of attachment theory to the study of sexual abuse, *Journal of Consulting and Clinical Psychology*, 60: 185–197.

Alexander, P., Anderson, C., Brand, B. et al. (1998) Adult attachment and long-term effects in survivors of incest, *Child Abuse and Neglect*, 22: 45–61.

Alexander, P. and Schaeffer, C. (1994) A typology of incestuous families based on cluster analysis, *Journal of Family Psychology*, 8: 458–470.

Al-Lamki, M. (2000) Munchausen syndrome by proxy, *Saudi Medical Journal*, 21: 482–486.

Anderson, P.L., Tiro, J.A., Webb-Price, J. and Kaslow, N.J. (2002) Addictive impact of childhood emotional, physical and sexual abuse on suicide attempts among low-income African American women, *Suicide Life Threatening Behaviour*, 32: 131–138.

Andrews, B., Brown, G.W. and Creasey, L. (1990) Intergenerational links between psychiatric disorder in mothers and daughters: the role of parenting experiences, *Journal of Child Psychology and Psychiatry*, 31: 1115–1129.

Appleby, L., Shaw, T., Amos, T. and Parsons, R. (1999) Suicide within 12 months of contact with mental health services, *British Medical Journal*, 318: 1235–1239.

Arnaldo, C. (2001) *Child Abuse On the Internet: Ending the Silence*. New York and Oxford: Berghahn Books for UNESCO.

Aromaki, A. and Lindman, R. (2001) Alcohol expectancies in convicted rapists and child molesters, *Criminal Behavior and Mental Health*, 11: 94–101.

Association of Directors of Social Services (2003) *Tomorrow's Children*. London: ADSS.

Atmore, C. (1999) Towards rethinking Moral Panic: child sex abuse conflicts and social constructionalist responses, in C. Bagley and K. Mallick (eds) *Child Sexual Abuse and Adult Offenders: New Theory and Research*, pp. 11–28. Aldershot: Ashgate.

Audit Commission (1996) *Mis-spent Youth: Youth Crime and the Criminal Justice System*. London: HMSO.

Audit Commission (1998) *Mis-spent Youth Re-Visited*. London: HMSO.

Bagley, C. (1969) Incest behaviour and incest taboo *Social Problems*, 16: 505–519.

Bagley, C. (1992) Characteristics of 60 children and adolescents with a history of sexual assault against others: evidence from a controlled study, *Journal of Forensic Psychiatry*, 3: 299–309.

Bagley, C. (1993) *International and Transracial Adoptions: Mental Health Perspectives*. Aldershot: Ashgate.

Bagley, C. (1999) Adolescent prostitution in Canada and The Philippines, *International Social Work*, 42: 445–454.

Bagley, C., Bertrand, L., Bolitho, F. and Mallick, K. (2001) Discrepant parent-adolescent views on family functioning: Predictors of poor self-esteem and problems of emotion and behaviour in British and Canadian adolescents, *Journal of Comparative Family Studies*, 32: 393–404.

Bagley, C. and LaChance, M. (2000) Evaluation of a family programme for the treatment of child sexual abuse, *Child and Family Social Work*, 5: 205–214.

Bagley, C. and Mallick, K. (2000) Prediction of sexual, emotional and physical maltreatment and mental health outcomes in a longitudinal cohort of 290 adolescent women, *Child Maltreatment*, 5: 218–226.

Bagley, C. and Ramsay, R. (1997) *Suicidal Behaviour in Adolescents and Adults: Research, Taxonomy and Prevention*. Aldershot: Ashgate.

Bagley, C. and Sewchuk-Dann, D. (1991) Characteristics of adolescents who have a history of sexual assaults against others, *Journal of Child Youth Care*, Special Issue: 43–52.

Bagley, C. and Thurston, W. (1996) *Understanding and Preventing Child Sexual Abuse Volume II: Male Victims, Adolescents, Adult Outcomes and Offender Treatment*. Aldershot: Arena Social Work Publications.

Bahlmann, M., Preuss, U.W. and Soyka, M. (2002) Chronological relationship between antisocial personality disorder and alcohol dependence, *European Addiction Research*, 8: 195–200.

Baird, C. (1988) *Development of Risk Assessment Indices for Alaskan Families*. Washington, National Council Crime Delinquency.

Baird, C., Wagner, D., Healey, T. and Johnson, W. (1999) Risk assessment in child protective services: Consensus and actuarial model of reliability, *Child Welfare*, 78: 723–748.

Baker, J. (1902) Female criminal lunatics, *Journal of Mental Science*, 48: 13–28.

Banyard, V. (1997) The impact of child sexual abuse and family functioning on four dimensions of women's later parenting, *Child Abuse and Neglect*, 21, 1095–1107.

Barker, D. (2003) *The Best Start in Life*. London: Century.

Barker, D., Eriksson, J.G. and Forsen, T. (2001) The foetal origins of disease: strength of effects and biological basis, *International Journal of Epidemiology*, 21: 1235–1239.

Barker, P., Keady, J., Croom, S. and Reynolds, B. (1998) The concept of 'Serious Mental Disorder': Modern myths and grim realities, *Journal of Psychiatric Mental Nursing*, 5: 247–254.

Barker-Collo, S.L. (2001) Adult reports of child and adult attribution of blame for childhood sexual abuse: Predicting adult adjustment and suicidal behaviours in females, *Child Abuse and Neglect*, 25: 1329–1341.

Barnes, H. (2001) A comment on Stroud and Pritchard 'Child homicide, psychiatric disorder and dangerousness, *British Journal of Social Work*, 31: 481–492.

Bauriedl, T. (2002) Treatment of sex offenders in prison based on the concept of relational analysis, *Recht Psychiatrie*, 20: 54–63.

Bauserman, R. and Rind, B. (1997) Psychological correlates of male child and adolescent sexual experiences with adults: a review of the literature, *Archives of Sexual Behaviour*, 26: 105–141.

BBC2 (2002) *Tracking Britain's Paedophiles*, BBC Television, July 2nd.

Beck, A. (1973) *The Diagnosis and Management of Depression*. Philadelphia: University of Philadelphia Press.

Becket, R., Beech, A., Fishers, D. and Fordham, A.S. (1994) *Community-based treatment programme for sex offenders: An evaluation of seven treatment programmes*. London: Home Office.

Beggs, P. (2001) Dwelling crowding as a pertinent factor, *Archives of Diseases in Childhood*, 84: 526.

Bennesden, B.E., Mortensen, P.B. and Henriksen, T.B. (2001) Congenital malformations, stillbirths and infant deaths amongst women with schizophrenia, *Archives of General Psychiatry*, 58: 674–679.

Bennett, L. (2002) Future of Social Services: A User Perspective. Annual Seebohm Lecture, Dept of Social Work Studies, University of Southampton.

Bentall, R. (2003) *Madness Explained: Psychosis and Human Nature*. London: Allen Lane.

Bentovim, A. (1995) *Trauma Organised Systems: Physical and Sexual Abuse in Families*. London: Karnac.

Bentovim, A. (2002) Preventing sexually abused young people from becoming abusers, and treating the victimization experiences of young people who offend sexually, *Child Abuse and Neglect*, 26: 661–678.

Berger, P., Berner, W., Bolteraurer, J., Gutierrez, K. and Berger, K. (1999) Sadistic personality disorder in sex offenders: relationship to anti-social personality disorder and sexual sadism, *Journal of Personality Disorder*, 13: 175–186.

Berkowitz, C. (1998) Medical consequences of child sexual abuse, *Child Abuse and Neglect*, 22: 541–550.

Beveridge, W. (1942) *Social Insurance and Allied Services*. London: HMSO.

Bhurga, D., Sing, J., Fellow-Smith, E. and Bayliss, C. (2002) Deliberate self-harm in adolescents: A case note study among two ethnic groups, *European Journal of Psychiatry*, 16: 145–151.

Biehel, N., Clayden, J. and Stein, M. (1995) *Moving On: Young People Leaving Care*. London: HMSO.

Birmingham, L. (2002) Detaining dangerous people with mental disorders, *British Medical Journal*, 325: 2–3.

Blackburn, I., Bishop, S., Glen, A., Whalley, L. and Christie, J. (1981) The efficacy of cognitive therapy in depression. Treatment trial using cognitive therapy and pharmotherapy together and alone, *British Journal of Psychiatry*, 139: 181–189.

Blair, T. (2003) Speech to Joint Houses of Congress. Quoted in the *Guardian,* July 18: 10.

Blom-Cooper, L. (1985) *A Child In Trust. The Report of the Inquiry into the Circumstances Surrounding the Death of Jasmine Beckford.* Wembley: The London Borough of Brent.

Bluglass, K. (1988) *Infant Deaths: Categories, Causes and Consequences.* Oxford: Blackwell.

BMA (1999) *Growing Up in Britain: Ensuring a Healthy Future for Our Children* (The Appleyard Report). London: British Medical Association.

Boateng, P. (2000) Foreword, in Policy Action Team, *National Strategy for Neighbourhood Renewal.* London: HMSO.

Bonnet, C. (1993) Adoption at birth: prevention against abandonment or neonaticide, *Child Abuse and Neglect*, 17: 501–513.

Bools, C., Neale, B. and Meadow, R. (1993) A follow-up of victims of fabricated illness (Munchausen syndrome by proxy), *Archives of Diseases in Childhood*, 69: 625–630.

Bools, C., Neale, B. and Meadow, R. (1994) Munchausen syndrome by proxy: a study of psychopathology, *Child Abuse and Neglect*, 18: 773–788.

Bourget, D. and Bradford, J. (1986) Affective disorder and homicide: a case of familial filicide – theoretical and clinical considerations, *Canadian Journal of Psychiatry*, 32: 222–225.

Bourget, D. and Bradford, J. (1990) Homicidal parents, *Canadian Journal of Psychiatry*, 35: 233–238.

Bourget, D. and Labelle, A. (1992) Homicide, infanticide and filicide, *Psychiatric Clinics of North America*, 15: 661–673.

Bowcott, O. (2002) Tabloids offered cash for stories of sex with teacher, say boys, *The Guardian Online*, 30 January.

Bowden, P. (1990) Homicide, in R. Bluglass and P. Bowden (eds) *Principles and Practice of Forensic Psychiatry.* London and Edinburgh: Churchill Livingstone.

Brewer, K., Rowe, D. and Brewer, D. (1997) Factors related to prosecution of child sexual abuse cases, *Journal of Child Sexual Abuse*, 6: 91–111.

Briere, J. (1989) *Therapy With Adult Survivors of Child Sexual Abuse.* New York: Guilford Press.

Briere, J. and Runtz, M. (1989) University males sexual interest in children – predicting potential indexes of paedophilia in a non-forensic sample, *Child Abuse and Neglect*, 13: 65–75.

Briggs, D., Doyle, P., Gooch, T. and Kennington, E. (1998) *Assessing Men Who Sexually Abuse: A Practice Guide*. London: Jessica Kingsley.

Briggs, F. and Hawkins, R. (1996) Comparison of the childhood experiences of convicted male child molesters and men who were sexually abused in childhood and claimed to be non-offending, *Child Abuse and Neglect*, 20: 221–223.

Brindle, D. (1995) Support versus an inquisition, *Guardian*, 21 June.

Brogi, L. and Bagley, C. (1998). Abusing victims: detention of child sexual abuse victims in secure accommodation, *Child Abuse Review*, 7: 315–329.

Brown, G. (1987) Social factors and the development and causes of depression in women, *British Journal of Social Work*, 18: 615–634.

Brown, G., Andrews, B., Bifulco, A. and Veiel, H. (1990) Self-esteem and depression, *Social Psychiatry and Psychiatric Epidemiology*, 25: 200–249.

Brown, G. and Harris, T. (1978) *Social Origins of Depression. A Study of Psychiatric Disorders in Women*. London: Tavistock.

Browne, R. and O'Connor, J. (2000) Child abuse and the clinical course of drug abuse, *British Journal of Psychiatry*, 177: 469.

Bull, M., Agran, P., Gardener, H. and Tenenbein, M. (2001) Falls from heights: windows, roofs and balconies, *Paediatrics*, 107, 1188–1191.

Butler-Sloss, Justice (1988) *Report of the Inquiry into Child Abuse in Cleveland*. London: HMSO.

Buttell, F. and Carney, M. (2001) Treatment provider awareness of the possible impact of the Internet on the treatment of sex offenders: an alert to the problem, *Journal of Child Sex Abuse*, 10: 117–125.

Camargo, R. (1997) Factor, cluster and discriminate analysis of data on sexually active clergy: the molester profile, *American Journal of Forensic Psychology*, 15: 5–24.

Campbell, J. and Lerew, C. (2002) Juvenile sex offenders in diversion, *Sex Abuse: Journal of Research and Treatment*, 14: 1–17.

Cannon, T.C., Jordan, F.B., Vogel, J.S. et al and Brandt, E.N. (1998) Child Homicide in Oklahoma: A continuing public health problem, *Journal of the Oklahoma State Medical Association*, 91: 449–451.

Cantor, C. and Kirkby, P. (1995) Prior convictions of child molesters, *Science and Justice*, 35: 73–78.

Cappell, C. and Heiner, R. (1990) The intergenerational transmission of family aggression, *Journal of Family Violence*, 5: 135–144.

Cassell, D. and Coleman, R. (1995) Parents with psychiatric problems, in P. Reder and C. Lucey (eds) *Assessment of Parenting: Psychiatric and Psychological Contributions*. London: Routledge.

Cawson, P., William, W., Brooker, S. and Kelly, G. (2000) *Child Maltreatment in The United Kingdom: A Study of Prevalence of Child Abuse and Neglect*. London: National Society for the Prevention of Cruelty to Children.

Chadwick, D. (2002) Why is sexual abuse declining? A survey of state child protection administrators (Jones et al. 2001), *Child Abuse and Neglect*, 26: 887–888.

Channar, M. and Khichi, G. (2000) Determinants of child labour in Bahawalpur city, *Journal of the College of Physicians and Surgeons of Pakistan*, 10: 395–398.

Chess, S. and Thomas, A. (1998) *Temperament: Theory and Practice*. New York: Brunner-Routledge.

Clare, A. (1976) *Psychiatry in Dissent*. London: Tavistock Publications.

Coid, J. (1983) The epidemiology of abnormal homicide and murder followed by suicide, *Psychological Medicine*, 13: 855–860.

Coleman, E. and Miner, M. (eds) (2000) *Sexual Offender Treatment – Biopsychosocial Perspective*. New York: Haworth Press.

Coll, J.E., Frankell, H.L. and Whiteneck, G.G. (1998) Evaluating a neurological group for mortality, *Spinal Cord*, 36: 275–279.

Collier, A. (1999) The probation service's work with sex offenders: findings and implications for thematic inspection, *Child Abuse Review*, 7: 391–401.

Committee on Child Abuse & Neglect (1997) Distinguishing sudden-infant-death-syndrome from child abuse, *Australian Medical Journal*, 69 371–375.

Corby, B. (2000) *Child Abuse: Towards a Knowledge Base*, 2nd edn. Buckingham: Open University Press.

Corcoran, J. (1998) Consequences of adolescent pregnancy and parenting: a review of the literature, *Social Work and Health Care*, 27: 49–68.

Courtney, M. (1998) The cost of child protection in the context of welfare reform, *Future Children*, 8: 88–103.

Cox, M. (2001) Crime and Locale of Offender and Victim. PhD thesis, University of Southampton.

Cox, M. and Pritchard, C. (1997) The lifetime convictions of child sex abusers: practice and policy dilemmas, *Probation Journal*, 44: 19–25.

Coxe, R, and Holmes, W. (2001) A study of the cycle of abuse amongst child molesters, *Journal of Child Sexual Abuse*, 10: 111–118.

Craissati, J., McLurg, G. and Browne, K. (2002) The parental bonding experiences of sex offenders: a comparison between child molesters and rapists, *Child Abuse and Neglect*, 26: 909–921.

Creighton, J. (1992) *Child Abuse Trends in England and Wales 1988–1990*. London: NSPCC.

Creighton, J. (1993) Children's homicide: an exchange, *British Journal of Social Work*, 23: 643–644.

CSO (2001) *Social Trends 2001*. London: Central Statistics Office.

Currie, E. (2000) Sociological perspectives on juvenile violence, *Child and Adolescent Psychiatric Clinics of North America*, 9: 749–763.

Daly, M. and Wilson, M. (1991) Stepchildren are disproportionately abused and diverse forms of violence can share causal factors, *Human Nature*, 2: 419–426.

Daly, M. and Wilson, M. (1994) Some differential attributes of lethal assaults on small children by stepfathers versus genetic fathers, *Ethology and Sociobiology*, 15: 207–217.

Daly, M. and Wilson, M. (2000) Special issue: stepparent involvement, *Evolution and Human Behavior*, 20: 365–388.

Dashti, S., Decker, D., Razzaq, A. and Cohen, A. (1999) Current patterns of inflicted head injury in children, *Paediatric Neurosurgery*, 31: 302–306.

Davidson, A. (2001) Parental features and quality of life in the decision to remove children at risk from home, *Child Abuse and Neglect*, 25: 47–64.

Davies, C. and Little, M. (1995) Family Circle, *Community Care*, 22 June: 18–19.

Davies, D. (1999) *Child Development: A Practitioner's Guide*. New York: Guilford Press.

Davies, M. (ed.) (2001) *Encyclopaedia of Social Work*. Cambridge: Blackwell Publications.

Day, A. (1999) Sex offenders views about treatment: a client survey, *Journal of Child Sexual Abuse*, 8: 93–103.

De Bruxelles, S. (1998) Rumours fuel mob in trail of paedophile, *The Times*, 25 April: 5.

DeMause, L. (1991) On the universality of incest, *Journal of Psychohistory*, 18: 1–30.

DeMause, L. (1997) The psychogenic theory of history, *Journal of Psychohistory*, 25: 112–184.

Dennett, D. (1995) *Darwin's Dangerous Ideas: Evolution and the Meaning of Life*. New York: Simon and Schuster.

Denny, S., Grant, C. and Pinnock, R. (2001) Epidemiology of Munchausen Syndrome by Proxy in New Zealand, *Journal of Paediatric Child Health*, 37: 240–243.

Department of Education and Skills (2003) *Green Paper: Every Child Matters*. London: D.E.S.

Department of Health (1989) *Children Act 1989*. London: HMSO.

Department of Health (1991) *Working Together Under the Children Act 1989: Guide to Arrangements for Inter-agency Co-operation for the Protection of Children*. London: HMSO.

Department of Health (1995) *Child Protection: Messages from Research. Studies in Child Protection*. London: HMSO.

Department of Health (1998a) *Caring for Children Away from Home. Messages from Research*. Chichester: Wiley.

Department of Health (1998b) *A Healthier Nation*. London: HMSO.

Department of Health (2001) *The Children Act Now: Messages from Research*. London: HMSO.

Department of Health (2002) *Children Looked After by Local Authorities*. London: HMSO.

Department of Health (2002) *Safeguarding Children in Whom Illness is Fabricated or Induced*. London: HMSO.

Dhawan, S. and Marshall, W. (1996) Sexual abuse histories of sexual offenders, *Sexual Abuse: A Journal of Research and Treatment*, 8: 7–15.

Dickens, C. (1849/1995) I begin life on my own account, and don't like it, *Child and Youth Care Forum*, 24: 17–30.

DiLillo, D., Tremblay, G. and Peterson, L. (2000) Linking childhood sexual abuse and abusive parenting. The role of maternal anger, *Child Abuse and Neglect*, 24: 767–779.

Dimigen, G., Del Priore, C. and Butler, S. (1999) Psychiatric disorder among children at time of entering local authority care: questionnaire survey, *British Medical Journal*, 319: 675.

d'Orban, P. (1979) Women who kill their children, *British Journal of Psychiatry*, 134: 560–571.

d'Orban, P. (1990) Female homicide, *Irish Journal of Psychological Medicine*, 7: 64–70.

Dubowitz, H., Black, M., Kerr, M. and Harrington, D. (2000) Fathers and child neglect, *Archives Paediatric Adolescent Medicine*, 1541: 35–141.

Dufour, M., Nadeau, L. and Bertrand, K. (2000) Resilience factors in victims of sexual abuse: current status, *Child Abuse and Neglect*, 24: 781–797.

Eamon, M. (2001) Antecedents and socio-economic consequences of physical punishment of children in two-parent families, *Child Abuse and Neglect*, 25: 787–802.

Ebstein, R.F., Benjamin, J. and Belmaker, R.H. (2000) Genetics of personality dimensions, *Current Opinions Psychiatry*, 13: 617–622.

Eckenrode, J., Ganzel, B., Henderson, C., Smith, E. and Sidora, K. (2000) Preventing child abuse and neglect with a programme of nurse home visitation: the limiting effects of domestic violence, *Journal of American Medical Association*, 284: 1385–1391.

Egeland, B., Jacobvitz, D. and Sroufe, L. (1988) Breaking the cycle of child abuse, *Child Development*, 17: 403–411.

Eher, R., Grunhut, C., Fruwald, S. and Hobl, B. (2001) Psychiatric comorbidity, typology and amount of violence in extra-familial sexual child molesters, *Recht Psychiatrie*, 19: 97–101.

Elliott, A. and Carnes, C. (2001) Reactions of nonoffending parents to the sexual abuse of their child: a review of the literature, *Child Maltreatment*, 6: 314–331.

Erickson, M.T. (1993) Re-thinking Oedpius: An evolutionary perspective of incest avoidance, *American Journal of Psychiatry*, 50: 411–416.

Ertem, O., Leventhal, J. and Dobb, S. (2000) Intergenerational continuity of child physical abuse: how good is the evidence? *Lancet*, 356: 814–819.

Esman, A. (1994) Sexual abuse, pathogenesis, and enlightened scepticism, *American Journal of Psychiatry*, 151: 1101–1103.

Ethier, L., Lacharite, C. and Couture, G. (1995) Childhood adversity, parental stress and depression of negligent mothers, *Child Abuse and Neglect*, 19: 619–632.

Evans, B. and Pritchard, C. (2001) Cancer survival rates and GDP expenditures on health. A comparison of England and Wales with the USA, Denmark, Finland,

France, German, Italy, Netherlands, Spain and Switzerland, *Public Health*, 114: 336–339.

Falkov, A. (1996) *Study of Working Together. Part 8 Reports of Fatal Abuse and Parental Psychiatric Disorder: An Analysis of 100 Area Child Protection Committee Reviews*. London: HMSO.

Faller, K. (1989) Why sexual abuse? An exploration of the intergenerational hypothesis, *Child Abuse and Neglect*, 13: 543–548.

Faller, K. (1991a) Poly-incestuous families: an exploratory study, *Journal of Interpersonal Violence*, 6: 310–322.

Faller, K. (1991b) Possible explanations of child sexual abuse allegations in divorce, *American Journal of Orthopsychiatry*, 61: 86–87.

Famularo, R., Fenton, T., Kinscherff, R., Ayoub, C. and Barnum, R. (1994) Maternal and child post-traumatic stress disorder in cases of child maltreatment, *Child Abuse and Neglect*, 18: 27–36.

Famularo, R., Kinscherff, R. and Fenton, T. (1992) Psychiatric diagnosis of abusive mothers. A preliminary report, *Journal of Nervous Mental Diseases*, 180: 658–661.

Farrington, D. (1995) The development of offending and anti-social behaviour from childhood: key findings from the Cambridge Study in Delinquent Development, *Journal of Child Psychology and Psychiatry*, 3: 929–964.

Feldman, M. and Brown, R. (2002) Munchausen by Proxy in international context, *Child Abuse and Neglect*, 26: 509–524.

Felitti, V., Anda, R., Nordenberg, D. and Marks, J. (1998) Relationship of childhood abuse and household dysfunction to many of the leading causes of death in adults. The adverse childhood experience study, *American Journal of Preventative Medicine*, 14: 356–360.

Fennell, M. (1989) Depression, in K. Hawton, P. Salkovskis and D. Clark (eds) *Cognitive Behaviour Therapy for Psychiatric Problems*, pp. 169–234. Oxford: Oxford Medical Publications.

Fergusson, D. and Mullen, P. (1999) *Childhood Sexual Abuse: An Evidence Based Perspective*. Thousand Oaks: Sage.

Fernandez, Y., Marshall, W., Lightbody, S. and O'Sullivan, C. (1999) The child molester empathy measure: description and examination of its reliability, *Sexual Abuse*, 11: 17–31.

Fernando, S. (1988) *Mental Health Race and Culture*. London: Macmillan.

Finkelhor, D. (1994) The international epidemiology of child sexual abuse, *Child Abuse and Neglect*, 18: 409–417.

Finzi, R., Ram, A., Shnit, D. and Weizman, A. (2001) Depressive symptoms and suicidality in physically abused children, *American Journal of Orthopsychiatry*, 71: 98–107.

Fischer, D. and McDonald, W. (1998) Characteristics of within-familial and extra-familial child sex abuse, *Child Abuse and Neglect*, 22: 915–929.

Fisher, D., Beech, A. and Browne, K. (1999) Comparison of sex offenders to non-offenders on selected psychological measures, *International Journal of Offender Therapy and Comparative Criminology*, 43: 473–491.

Fleming, P., Blair, P., Platt, M., Tripp, J. and Golding, J. (2001) The UK accelerated immunisation programme and sudden death in infancy: case control study, *British Medical Journal*, 322: 822–825.

Flick, L., Vemulpalli, C., Stulac, B. and Kemp, J. (2001) The influence of grand-mothers and other senior carers in families of African American children, *Archives of Pediatrics and Adolescent Medicine*, 155: 1231–1237.

Fontaine, J. (1998) *Speak of the Devil: Tales of Satanic Abuse in Contemporary England.* Cambridge: Cambridge University Press.

Ford, F. and Frean, A. (2002) Deaths exposed flaws in system to prevent abuse, *The Times*, 14 October.

Ford, P., Cox, M. and Pritchard, C. (1997) 'Consumer' opinions of the Probation Service: assistance, befriending and the reduction of crime, *Howard Journal*, 26: 42–51.

Franciosi, R. (2001) Association between SIDS and H pylori infection, *Archives of Diseases in Childhood*, 84: 5–25.

Franks, C. (1997) Parents' cultural belief systems: their origins, expressions, and consequences, *Child and Family Behavior Therapy*, 19: 78–79.

Fraser, K. (1998) Bereavement in those who have killed, *Medicine, Science and Law*, 28: 127–130.

Freedman, S. and Enright, R. (1996) Forgiveness as an intervention goal with incest survivors, *Journal of Consulting and Clinical Psychology*, 64: 983–992.

Freedman, S., Leonard, S., Olincy, A. and Tsuang, M.T. (2001) Evidence of multi-genetic inheritance of schizophrenia, *American Journal of Medical Genetics-Part B: Neuropsychiatric Genetics*, 105: 794–800.

Freire, G. (1982) When I was a child. . . . Lecture given at University of Calgary, 14 April.

Fromuth, M.E. (1986) The relationship of childhood sex abuse with later psychological adjustment in a sample of college women, *Child Abuse and Neglect*, 10: 5–15.

Fromuth, M.E. and Burkhart, B.R. (1989) Long-term psychological correlates of childhood sex abuse in two samples of college men, *Child Abuse and Neglect*, 13: 533–542.

Fu, Q., Heath, A.C., Bucholz, K.K. and Eisen, S.A. (2002) Shared genetic risk of major depression, alcohol dependence and marijuana dependence, *Archives of General Psychiatry*, 59: 1125–1132.

Fulton, D. (2000a) Early recognition of Munchausen Syndrome by proxy, *Critical Care Nursing Quarterly*, 23: 35–42.

Fulton, D. (2000b) Shaken baby syndrome, *Critical Care Nursing Quarterly*, 23: 43–50.

Furniss, T. (1991) *The Multi-Professional Handbook of Child Sexual Abuse.* London: Routledge.

Gadd, J. (1999) Spanking law lets parents abuse kids, courts told, *Globe and Mail* (Toronto), 7 December.

Galli, V., McElroy, S., Sotoullo, C. and McConville, B. (1999) The psychiatric diagnoses of twenty-two adolescents who have sexually molested other children, *Comprehensive Psychiatry*, 40: 85–88.

Gara, M., Allen, L., Herzog, E. and Woolfolk, R. (2000) The abused child as parent. The structure and content of physically abused mothers' perceptions of their babies, *Child Abuse and Neglect*, 24: 627–639.

Garbarino, J. (1993) Challenges we face in understanding children and war: a personal essay, *Child Abuse and Neglect*, 17: 787–793.

Garbarino, J., Guttman, E. and Seeley, J. (1986) *The Psychologically Battered Child*. New York: Jossey-Bass.

Geer, T., Becker, J., Gray, S. and Krauss, D. (2001) Predictors of treatment completion in a correctional sex offender treatment programme, *International Journal of Offender Therapy and Comparative Criminology*, 45: 302–313.

Gessner, B., Ives, G. and Perham-Hester, K. (2001) Association between sudden infant death syndrome and prone sleeping position, sleeping with adults, and sleeping outside an infant crib in Alaska, *Pediatrics*, 108: 923–927.

Ghodsian, M., Zajicek, E. and Wolkind, S. (1984) A longitudinal study of maternal depression and child behaviour problems, *Journal of Child Psychology and Psychiatry and Allied Disciplines*, 25: 91–109.

Giarretto, H. (1982) *Integrated Treatment of Child Sexual Abuse: A Treatment and Training Manual*. Pal Alto: Science and Behavior Books.

Gibbons, J., Conroy, S. and Bell, C. (1995) *Operating The Child Protection System*. London: HMSO.

Gillan, A. and Moszynski, P. (2002) Aid workers in food for child sex scandal, *The Guardian Online*, 27 February.

Gillham, B., Tanner, G., Cheyne, B., et al. (1998) Unemployment rates, single parent density and indices of child poverty: their relationship to different categories of child abuse and neglect, *Child Abuse and Neglect*, 22: 79–90.

Glaser, D. (2000) Child abuse and neglect and the brain. A review, *Journal of Child Psychology and Psychiatry*, 41: 170–179.

Glowinski, A.L., Bucholz, K.K., Nelson, E.C. et al. (2001) Suicide attempts in an adolescent female twin sample study, *Journal of the American Academy of Child Adolescent Psychiatry*, 40: 1300–1307.

Gojer, J. and Berman, T. (2000) Postpartum depression and factitious disorder: a new presentation, *International Journal of Psychiatic Medicine*, 3: 287–293.

Gomez-Alcalde, M. (2001) Risk factors in children's suicide, *Pediatrika*, 21: 21–27.

Gorey, K.M. and Leslie, D.R. (1997) Prevalence of child sex abuse: Integrative review, adjusting for potential response biases, *Child Abuse and Neglect*, 24: 391–398.

Gould, S. (2001) Sudden unexpected death in infancy, *Current Diagnostic Pathology*, 7: 69–75.

Graham, J. and Bowling, B. (1995) *Young People and Crime.* London: Home Office.

Green, A., Coupe, P., Fernandez, R. and Stevens, B. (1995) Incest revealed: delayed post traumatic stress disorder in mothers following the sexual abuse of their children, *Child Abuse and Neglect,* 19: 1275–1282.

Green, A. and Kaplan, M. (1994) Psychiatric impairment and childhood victimisation experiences in female child molesters, *Journal of the American Academy of Child and Adolescent Psychiatry,* 33: 954–961.

Greenberg, D., Bradford, J., Firestone, P. and Curry, S. (2000) Recidivism of child molesters: a study in victim relationship with the perpetrator, *Child Abuse and Neglect,* 24: 1485–1494.

Greenland, C. (1987) *Preventing Child Abuse and Neglect Deaths.* London: Tavistock Publications.

Greven, P. (1991) *Spare the Child: The Religious Roots of Punishment and the Psychological Impact of Physical Abuse.* New York: Knopf.

Grgic, M. (2002) Children mental disorder as a result of parental misbehaviour or lack of authority, *Imago,* 8: 321–326.

Griffiths, H., Cuddihy, P. and Marnane, C. (2001) Bleeding ears: a case of Munchausen Syndrome by Proxy, *International Journal of Paediatric Otorhinolaryngology,* 57: 245–247.

Grossman, L., Martis, B. and Fichtner, C. (1999) Are sex offenders treatable? A research overview, *Psychiatric Services,* 50: 349–361.

Grubin, D. (1994) Sexual murder, *British Journal of Psychiatry,* 165, 624–629.

Grubin, D. (1999) *Sex Offending Against Children: Understanding the Risk.* London: Home Office.

Grubin, D. (2000) Sex offender treatment programmes. Paper given to Conference on Child Sexual Abuse, University of Southampton, 10 November.

Grunfeld, B. and Steen, J. (1984) Faal barnemishandling: barnedrap norgei, *Tidskrift for Norsk Laegeforening,* 104, 289–299.

Guardian (2002) Comment: Social Services, *The Guardian,* 17 October.

Gudjonsson, G. and Sigurdson, H. (2000) Differences and similarities between violent offenders and sex offenders, *Child Abuse and Neglect,* 24, 363–372.

Guildes, Z., Fone, D., Dunstan, F., Sibert, J. and Cartlidge, P. (2001) Social deprivation and the causes of stillbirth and infant mortality, *Archives of Diseases in Childhood,* 84: 307–310.

Guillaume, I., Polytarides, V. and Marnier, J. (1999) Munchausen syndrome by proxy: pathology of mother-child interaction, *Annals of Psychiatry,* 14: 40–42.

Hagan, M., Gust-Brey, K., Cho, M. and Dow, E. (2001) Eight-year comparative analysis of adolescent rapists, adolescent child molesters, other delinquents and the general population, *International Journal of Offender Therapy and Comparative Criminology,* 45: 314–324.

Hall, D., Eubanks, L., Meyyazhagan, S., Kenny, R. and Johnson, S. (2000) Evaluation of covert surveillance in the diagnosis of Munchausen syndrome by proxy, *Paediatrics,* 105: 1305–1312.

Hamilton, C., Falshaw, L. and Brown, K. (2002) The link between child maltreatment and offending behaviour, *International Journal of Offender Therapy and Comparative Criminology*, 46: 75–94.

Hanson, R. and Bussiere, M. (1998) Predicting relapse: a meta-analysis of sexual offender recidivism studies, *Journal of Consulting and Clinical Psychology*, 66: 348–362.

Harder, T. (1967) The psychopathology of infanticide, *Acta Psychiatrica Scandinavica*, 43: 196–245.

Harris, N., Williams, S. and Bradshaw, T. (2002) *Psychosocial interventions for people with schizophrenia*. Basingstoke, Macmillan.

Hart, V. (1984) *Generic Definition of Child Maltreatment*. Indianapolis: Office for the Study of the Psychological Rights of the Child, University of Indiana.

Hawton, K. and Roberts, J. (1981) The association between child abuse and attempted suicide, *British Journal of Social Work*, 11: 415–420.

Hawton, K., Roberts, J. and Goodwin, G. (1985) The risk of child abuse among mothers who attempt suicide, *British Journal of Psychiatry*, 146: 486–489.

Haywood, T. and Grossman, L. (1994) Denial of deviant arousal and psychopathology in child molesters: a controlled study, *Behaviour Therapy*, 25: 327–340.

Haywood, T., Kravitz, H., Wasyliw, O. and Cavannaugh, J. (1996) Cycle of abuse and psychopathology in cleric and non-cleric molesters of children, *Child Abuse and Neglect*, 20: 1233–1243.

Heck, C. and Walsh, A. (2000) The effects of maltreatment and family structure on minor and serious delinquency, *International Journal of Offender Therapy and Comparative Criminology*, 44: 178–193.

Herman-Giddens, M., Brown, G., Verbiest, S. and Butts, J. (1999) Under-ascertainment of child abuse mortality in the United States, *Journal of the American Medical Association*, 282: 463–467.

Hobbs, C. (1984) Skull fractures and the diagnosis of abuse, *Archives of Diseases in Childhood*, 59: 246–252.

Hobbs, C. (1986) When burns are not accidental, *Archives of Diseases in Childhood*, 61: 357–361.

Hobbs, C. and Heywood, P. (1997) Childhood matters, *British Medical Journal*, 314: 97.

Hobbs, C. and Wynne, J. (1994) Patterns of scald injuries, *Archives of Diseases in Childhood*, 94(71): 559.

Hobbs, C. and Wynne, J. (2002) Neglect of neglect, *Current Paediatrics*, 12: 144–150.

Hobbs, G., Hobbs, C. and Wynne, J. (1999) Abuse of children in foster and residential care, *Child Abuse and Neglect*, 23: 1239–1252.

Hogg, R.S. (2003) Non-consensual sex experienced by men who have sex with men: Prevalence and association with mental health, *Patient Education Counselling*, 49: 67–74.

Home Office (2002) *Criminal Statistics for England and Wales 2000*. London: HMSO.

Home Office (2000) *ORGS Prediction of Re-offending Scores*. London: Home Office.

Hopwood, J. (1927) Child murder and insanity, *Journal of Mental Science*, 73: 95–108.

Hoyer, J., Borchard, B. and Kunst, H. (2000) Diagnosis and disorder-specific therapy in sex offenders with mental disorders, *Verhaltenstherapie*, 10: 7–15.

Hudson, S. and Ward, R. (1997) Intimacy, loneliness, and attachment style in sexual offenders, *Journal of Interpersonal Violence*, 12, 323–339.

Hunter, J.A. and Figueredo, A.J. (2000) The influence of personality and history of sexual victimisation in the prediction of juvenile perpetrated child molestation, *Child Abuse and Neglect*, 24: 241–263.

Hunter, M. (1995) *Child Survivors and Perpetrators of Sexual Abuse: Treatment Innovations*. Newbury Park: Sage.

Hutton, J. (2000) Foreword, *Framework for the Assessment of Children in Need and their Families*. London: Department of Health.

Huxley, P., Korer, J. and Tolley, S. (1987) The psychiatric caseness of clients referred to an urban social services department, *British Journal of Social Work*, 17: 507–520.

Ingraham, L.J. and Kety, S.S. (2000) Adoption studies of schizophrenia, *American Journal of Medical Genetics* Seminars, 97: 18–22.

Isaac, B., Minty, E. and Morrison, R. (1986) Children in care – the association with mental disorder in the parents, *British Journal of Social Work*, 16: 325–339.

Ivory, M. (1994) Lessons to be learned, *Community Care*, 13 January: 6.

Iwaniec, D. (1995) *The Emotionally Abused and Neglected Child: Identification, Assessment and Intervention*. Chichester: John Wiley.

Jahoda, M. (1979) The impact of unemployment in the 1930s and the 1970s, *Bulletin of the British Psychological Society*, 32: 309–314.

Jason, J. (1983) Child homicide spectrum, *American Journal of Diseases of Childhood*, 137: 578–581.

Jenkins, R., Bebbington, P., Brugha, T. and Meltzer, H. (1998) British psychiatric morbidity surveys, *British Journal of Psychiatry*, 173: 4–7.

Jones, D. and Ramchandani, P. (1999) *Child Sexual Abuse: Informing Practice from Research*. Oxford: Radcliffe Press.

Jones, L., Finkelhor, D. and Kopiec, K. (2001) Why is sexual abuse declining? A survey of state child protection administrators, *Child Abuse and Neglect*, 25: 1139–1158.

Johnston, W. (1967) Releasing the dangerous offender, in J. Rappaport (ed.) *The Clinical Evaluation of the Dangerousness of the Mentally Ill*. Illinois: Charles C. Thomas.

Judge, K. and Benzeval, M. (1993) Health inequalities: new concerns about the children of single mothers, *British Medical Journal*, 306: 677–680.

Justice, B., Calvert, A. and Justice, R. (1985) Factors mediating child abuse as a response to stress, *Child Abuse and Neglect*, 9: 359–363.

Kairys, S., Alexander, R., Block, R., Everett, V. and Wood, D. (1999) American

Academy of Paediatrics Committee on child abuse and neglect. Investigation and review of unexpected infant and child deaths, *Paediatrics*, 104: 1158–1160.

Kairys, S., Alexander, R., Block, R. and Krous, H. (2001) Distinguishing SIDS from child abuse fatalities, *Paediatrics*, 107: 437–441.

Kallen, K. (2001) The impact of maternal smoking during pregnancy on delivery, *European Journal of Public Health*, 11: 329–333.

Kaufman, J. and Zigler, E. (1987) Do abused children become abusive parents?, *American Journal of Orthopsychiatry*, 57: 186–192.

Kempe, C., Denver, F., Silverman, N. et al. (1985) The battered child syndrome, *Child Abuse and Neglect*, 9: 143–154.

Kempe, C. and Kempe, H. (1978) *Child Abuse*. Chicago: University of Chicago Press.

Kempe, C., Silverman, F., Steele, B., Droegemueller, W. and Silver, H. (1962) The battered child syndrome, *Journal of the American Medical Association*, 181: 17–24.

Kendall-Tackett, K.A., Williams, L.M. and Finkelhor, D. (1993) Impact of sexual abuse on children: A review, *Psychological Bulletin*, 113: 164–180.

Kendler, K., Myers, J. and Prescott, C. (2000) Parenting and adult mood, anxiety and substance use disorders in female twins. An epidemiological, multi-informant, retrospective study, *Psychological Medicine*, 30: 281–294.

Kerker, B., Horwitz, S., Leventhal, J. and Leaf, P. (2000) Identification of violence in the home. Paediatric and parental reports, *Archives of Paediatric and Adolescent Medicine*, 154: 457–462.

King, E., Baldwin, D., Baker, N. et al. (2001) The Wessex recent in-patient suicide study, *British Journal of Psychiatry*, 178: 531–536.

Kingdon, D. and Turkington, D. (2002) *The Case Study Guide to Cognitive Behaviour Therapy of Psychosis*. Chichester: Wiley.

Knight, R., Prentky, R. and Cerce, D. (1994) The development, reliability and validity of an inventory for the multi-dimensional assessment of sex and aggression, *Criminal Justice and Behavior*, 21: 72–94.

Knutson, J.F. and Selner, M.B. (1994) Punitive childhood experiences reported by young adults over a 10-year period, *Child Abuse and Neglect*, 18: 155–166.

Kolko, D. (1992) Characteristics of child victims of physical violence, *Journal of Interpersonal Violence*, 7: 244–276.

Kolvin, I., Glasser, M., Campbell, D. et al. (2001) Cycle of child sexual abuse: links between being a victim and becoming a perpetrator, *British Journal of Psychiatry*, 179: 482–494.

Korbin, J. (1986) Childhood histories of women imprisoned for fatal child maltreatment, *Child Abuse and Neglect*, 8: 387–392.

Korbin, J., Coulton, C., Lindstron-Ufuti, H. and Spilsbury, J. (2000) Neighbours' views on the definition and aetiology of child maltreatment, *Child Abuse and Neglect*, 24: 1509–1527.

Kreklewetz, C.M. and Piotrowski, C.C. (1998) Incest survivor mothers: Protecting the next generation, *Child Abuse and Neglect*, 22: 1305–1312.

Krugman, R., Lenherr, M., Betz, L. and Fryer, G. (1986) The relationship between unemployment and physical abuse of children, *Child Abuse and Neglect*, 10: 25–30.

Lab, D., Feigenbaum, J. and De Silva, P. (2000) Mental health professionals' attitudes and practices towards male childhood sexual abuse, *Child Abuse and Neglect*, 34: 391–409.

Laming Report (2003) *Report of Lord Herbert Laming Inquiry into death of Victoria Climbié*. London: Department of Health.

Langeland, W. and Dijkstra, S. (1995) Breaking the intergenerational transmission of child abuse: beyond the mother-child relationship, *Child Abuse Review*, 4: 4–13.

Larson, R. and Maddock, J. (1986) Structural and functional variables in incest. In Trepper, T. & Barrett, M. (eds) *Treatment of Incest: A multimodel perspective*, New York: Hayworth Press, 27–44.

Larsson, I. and Svedin, C. (2001) Sexual behaviour in Swedish preschool children as observed by their parents, *Acta Paediatrica: International Journal of Paediatrics*, 90: 436–444.

Launay, G. (2001) Relapse prevention treatment with sex offenders: practice, theory and research, *Criminal Behaviour Mental Health*, 11: 38–54.

Lauritsen, A., Meldgaard, K. and Charles, A. (2000) Medical examination of sexually abused children: medico-legal value, *Journal of Forensic Sciences*, 45: 115–117.

Lawes, D., Hudson, S. and Ward, T. (eds) (2000) *Remaking Relapse Prevention with Sex Offenders*. Thousand Oaks: Sage.

Lawson, R. (1994) The challenge of the new poverty: lessons from Europe and America, *Internationale Politik und Gesellschaft*, 2: 162–174.

Leadbetter, M. (2002) On alert for child abuse, *Guardian Online*, 5 July.

Lee, J., Jackson, H., Pattison, P. and Ward, T. (2002) Developmental risk factors for sexual offending, *Child Abuse and Neglect*, 26: 73–92.

LeGrand, S. and Martin, R. (2001) Juvenile male sex offenders: the quality of motivation system of assessment and treatment issues, *Journal of Child Sexual Abuse*, 10: 23–49.

Lehne, G., Thomas, K. and Berliner, F. (2000) Treatment of sexual paraphilias: a review of the 1999–2000 literature, *Current Opinion in Psychiatry*, 13, 569–573.

Leifer, M., Kilbane, T. and Grossman, G. (2001) A three-generational study comparing the families of supportive and unsupportive mothers of sexually abused children, *Child Maltreatment*, 6: 353–364.

LeSure-Lester, G. (2000) Relation between empathy and aggression and behaviour compliance amongst abused group home youth, *Child Psychiatry and Human Development*, 31: 153–161.

Leventhal, J. (1998) Epidemiology of sexual abuse of children: old problems, new directions, *Child Abuse and Neglect*, 22: 481–491.

Leventhal, J. (2001a) A decline in substantial cases of child sexual abuse in the United States: good news or false hope? *Child Abuse and Neglect*, 25: 1137–1138.

Leventhal, J. (2001b) The prevention of child abuse and neglect: successfully out of the blocks, *Child Abuse and Neglect*, 25: 431–439.

Lewis, A. (1955) Health as a social concept, *British Journal of Sociology*, 4: 109–124.

Lewis, C. and Stanley, C. (2000) Women accused of sexual offences. *Behavioural Science and Law*, 18: 73–81.

Lewis, D., Pincus, J. Bard, B. et al. (1988) Neuropsychiatric, psychoeducational, and family characteristics of 14 juveniles condemned to death in the United States, *American Journal of Psychiatry*, 145: 584–589.

Lindsay, D. and Trocme, N. (1995) Have child protection efforts reduced child homicides? An examination of data from Britain and North America, *British Journal of Social Work*, 24: 715–732.

Lindsay, W. (2002) Research and literature on sex offenders with intellectual and developmental difficulties, *Disability Research, Supplement 1*, 9: 74–85.

Linehan, M.M. (1993) *Cognitive Behaviour Therapy for Borderline Personality Disorders*, New York: Guilford Press.

Lipman, E., Macmillan, H. and Boyle, M. (2001) Childhood abuse and psychiatric disorders among single and married mothers, *American Journal of Psychiatry*, 158: 73–77.

London Boroughs of Bexley and Greenwich (1982) *The Lucy Gates Inquiry: Chairman's Report*. London: London Borough of Bexley.

Long, P. and Jackson, J. (1992) Children sexually abused by multiple perpetrators: familial risk factors and abuse characteristics, *Journal of Interpersonal Violence*, 6: 147–159.

Lothstein, L. (2001) Treatment of non-incarcerated sexually compulsive/addictive offenders in an integrated multi-modal and psychodynamic therapy model, *International Journal of Group Psychotherapy*, 51: 553–557.

Luft, F. (2001) Genetics and sudden cardiac death, *Journal of Molecular Medicine*, 79: 477–479.

Lykes, M. (1994) Terror, silencing and children: international and interdisciplinary collaboration with Guatemalan Mayan communities, *Social Science and Medicine*, 38: 805–819.

Lyon, L., Dennison, C. and Wilson, A. (1996) *Tell Them So They Listen: Messages From Young People in Custody*. London: Stationery Office.

MacCulloch, M., Gray, N. and Watt, A. (2000) Britain's sadistic murderer syndrome reconsidered: an associative account of the aetiology of sadistic sexual fantasy, *Journal of Forensic Psychiatry*, 11: 401–418.

MacDonald, R., Mason, P., Ridley, L. and Webster, C. (2000) *Snakes and Ladders:*

Young People, Transitions and Social Exclusion. York: Joseph Rowntree Foundation.

Mace, S., Geradi, M., Dietrich, A. and Warden, C. (2001) Injury prevention and control in children, *Annals of Emergency Medicine,* 38: 405–414.

MacMillan, H., Boyle, M., Wong, M. et al. (1999) Slapping and spanking in childhood and its association with lifetime prevalence of psychiatric disorders in a general population sample, *Canadian Medical Association Journal,* 161: 805–809.

Maker, A., Kemmelmeier, M. and Peterson, C. (1999) Parental sociopathy as a predictor of childhood sexual abuse, *Journal of Family Violence,* 14: 47–56.

Maletzky, B.M. and Steinhauser, C. (2002) A 25-year follow-up of cognitive behavioural therapy with 7,275 sexual offenders, *Behaviour Modification,* 26: 123–147.

Maloney, D., Keller, S. and Fierro, M. (2000) Child deaths in Virginia 1996: a review of investigations of sudden deaths of children less than 3, *American Journal of Forensic Medicine and Pathology,* 21: 189–194.

Manchester, W. (1984) *The Last Lion: WS Churchill 1874–1932.* London: Sphere Book.

Manocha, K. and Mezey, G. (1998) British adolescents who sexually abuse: a descriptive study, *Journal of Forensic Psychiatry,* 9: 588–608.

Marshall, W.L., Champagne, F., Brown, C. and Miller, S. (1997) Empathy, intimacy, loneliness and self-esteem in non-familial child molesters: A brief report, *Journal of Child Sexual Abuse,* 6: 87–98.

Martin, J. (1984) Neglected fathers: limitations in diagnostic and treatment resources for violent men, *Child Abuse and Neglect,* 8: 387–392.

Maxeiner, H. (2002) A post-mortem view on 'pure' subdural haemorrhages in infants and toddlers, *Klinische Paediatrie,* 214: 30–36.

McCabe, C. and Donahue, S. (2000) Prognostic indicators for vision and mortality in shaken baby syndrome, *Archives of Ophthalmology,* 118: 373–377.

McClure, R., Davies, P., Meadow, S. and Sibert, J. (1996) Epidemiology of Munchausen's Syndrome by Proxy: non-accidental poisoning and suffocation, *Archives of Diseases of Childhood,* 75: 57–61.

McCormack, A., Rokous, F., Hazelwood, R. and Burges, A. (1992) An exploration of incest in the childhood development of serial rapists, *Journal of Family Violence,* 7: 219–228.

McDonald, K. (1995) Comparative homicide and the proper aims of social work: A sceptical note, *British Journal of Social Work,* 25: 615–643.

McFate, K., Lawson, R. and Wilson, W.J. (1995) *Poverty, Inequality and the Future of Social Policy.* New York: Sage.

McGlashan, T. (1989) Sudden infant death in Tasmania, 1980–1986: a seven year prospective study, *Social Science and Medicine,* 29: 1015–1026.

McGurk, B., Forde, R. and Barnes, A. (2000) *Sexual Victimisation Among 15–17 Year-Old Offenders in Prison.* London: Home Office RDS Paper 65.

McIntyre, S. (1999) The youngest profession – the oldest oppression: a study of sex work, in C. Bagley and K. Mallick (eds) *Child Sexual Abuse and Adult Offenders: New Theory and Research*, pp. 159–192. Aldershot: Ashgate.

McLloyd, V. (1990) The impact of economic hardship upon Black families and their children: psychological distress, parenting and socio-economic development, *Child Development*, 61: 311–346.

Meadow, R. (1977) Munchausen Syndrome by Proxy: the hinterland of child abuse, *Lancet*, 2: 343–345.

Meadow, R. (1993) *ABC of Child Abuse*. London: BMJ Publishing Group.

Meadow, R. (1994) Munchausen syndrome by proxy, *Journal of Clinical and Forensic Medicine*, 1: 121–127.

Meadow, R. (2002a) Different interpretations of Munchausen Syndrome by Proxy, *Child Abuse and Neglect*, 26: 501–508.

Meadow, R. (2002b) A case of murder and the BMJ, *British Medical Journal*, 324: 41–43.

Mehanni, M., Cullen, A., Kiberd, B., McDonnell, M. and Matthews, T. (2000) The current epidemic of SIDS in Ireland, *Irish Medical Journal*, 93: 264–268.

Meltzer, H., Gill, B., Pettigrew, M. and Hinds, K. (1995) *The Prevalence of Psychiatric Morbidity Among Adults Living in Private Households*. London: The Psychiatric Rehabilitation Association.

Mental Health Act 1983. London: HMSO.

Mental Health (Patients in the Community) Act 1995. London: HMSO.

Merrick, J. (2001) Children of the waste basket, *International Journal of Adolescent Medicine Health*, 13: 175.

Messerschimdt, P. (2002) Adult outcome of children with Attention Deficit Hyperactivity Disorder, *Revue Practica*, 52: 2009–2012.

Meyerson, L.A., Long, P.S., Miranda, R. and Marx, R.B. (2002) The influence of childhood sex abuse on physical abuse family environment, gender and psychological adjustment of adolescents, *Child Abuse and Neglect*, 26: 387–405.

Miles, A. (1989) *The Mentally Ill in Contemporary Society*. Oxford: Basil Blackwell.

Mishra, R. (1999) *Globalisation and the Welfare State*. Massachusetts: Edward Elgar.

Mitchell, R., Shaw, M. and Dorling, D. (2000) *Inequalities in Life and Death: What if Britain Were More Equal?* York: The Policy Press.

Modestin, J., Oberson, B. and Erni, T. (1998) Possible antecedents of DSMIII-R Personality Disorders, *Acta Psychiatrica Scandinavia*, 97: 260–266.

Moeller, T., Bachman, G. and Moeller, J. (1993) The combined effects of physical, sexual and emotional abuse during childhood: long-term consequences for women, *Child Abuse and Neglect*, 17: 623–640.

Monk, D. (1998) Working with sex offenders: a case of protection, *Child Abuse Review*, 7: 379–390.

Moore, D., Bergman, B. and Knox, P. (1999) Predictors of sex offender treatment completion, *Journal of Child Sexual Abuse*, 7: 73–88.

Mullen, P., Martin, J.L., Anderson, J.C. and Herbison, P. (1993) Child sexual abuse and mental health in adult life, *British Journal of Psychiatry*, 163: 721–732.

Muller, R., Hunter, J. and Stollar, G. (1995) The intergenerational transmission of corporal punishment: a comparison of social learning and temperament models, *Child Abuse and Neglect*, 19: 1323–1335.

Munro, E. (1998) Improving social workers' knowledge base in child protection, *British Journal of Social Work*, 28: 89–105.

Myers, S. (1970) Maternal filicide, *American Journal of Diseases of Childhood*, 120: 534–536.

Nam, C., Eberstein, I. and Deeb, L. (1990) Sudden infant death syndrome as a socially determined cause of death, *Social Biology*, 36: 1–14.

Nash, M., Hulsey, T. and Lambert, G. (1993) Long-term sequelae of childhood sexual abuse, *Journal Consulting Clinical Psychology*, 61: 276–283.

National Health Service Act 1977. London: HMSO.

NCH (2002) *Factfile Scotland*. London: National Children's Homes.

Neal, B., Bools, C. and Meadow, R. (1991) Problems in the assessment and management of Munchausens, *Children and Society*, 5: 324–333.

Nelson, E.C., Heath, A.C., Madden, P.A.F. et al. (2002) Association between self-reported childhood sexual abuse and adverse psychosocial outcomes: Results from a twin study, *Archive of General Psychiatry*, 59: 139–145.

Neugebauer, R. (2000) Research on intergenerational transmission of violence: the next generation, *The Lancet*, 335: 116–117.

Newberger, E. (1983) 'The Helping Hand Strikes Again': the unintended consequences of child abuse reporting, *Journal of Clinical Child Psychology*, 12: 131–166.

Newcomb, M. and Locke, T. (2001) Intergenerational cycle of maltreatment: a popular concept obscured by methodological limitations, *Child Abuse and Neglect*, 25: 1219–1240.

Newlands, M. and Mery, J. (1991) Child abuse and cot deaths, *Child Abuse and Neglect*, 15: 275–278.

Ney, P. (1987) Does verbal abuse leave deeper scars? A study of children and parents, *Canadian Journal of Psychiatry*, 32: 371–378.

Ney, P., Fung, T. and Wickett, A. (1994) The worst combinations of child abuse and neglect, *Child Abuse and Neglect*, 18: 705–714.

Nichiguchi, N., Matsuhita Suzucki, K. and Higuchi, S. (2001) Association between 5 HT2A receptor gene promoter: Regional polymorphism and eating disorders in Japanese patients, *Biological Psychiatry*, 50: 123–128.

Noyes, P. (1991) *Child Abuse – A Study of Inquiry Reports*. London: HMSO.

NSPCC (2002) *Campaign on Child Abuse Deaths*. London: Press Release from NSPCC.

Nurcombe, B., Wooding, S., Marrington, P., Bickman, L. and Roberts, G. (2000) Child sexual abuse: treatment II, *Australian and New Zealand Journal of Psychiatry*, 34: 92–97.

Oaksford, K. and Frude, N. (2001) The prevalence and nature of child sexual abuse: evidence from a female university sample in the UK, *Child Abuse Review*, 19: 49–59.

Oates, R., Tebbutt, J., Swanston, H., Lynch, D. and O'Toole, B. (1998). Prior childhood sexual abuse in mothers of sexually abused children, *Child Abuse and Neglect*, 22: 1113–1118.

O'Connell, R. (2001) Paedophiles networking on the Internet, in C. Arnaldo (ed.) *Child Abuse on the Internet*, pp. 65–80. New York and Oxford: Berghahn Books for UNESCO.

Oepen, G. (2001) Neuropsychiatric aspects of deception, *American Journal of Forensic Psychiatry*, 22: 49–77.

O'Hagan, K. (1993) *Emotional and Psychological Abuse of Children*. Toronto: University of Toronto Press.

Oliver, J. (1975) Microencephaly following baby battering and shaking, *British Medical Journal*, 278: 262–264.

Oliver, J. (1983) Dead children from problem families in NE Wiltshire, *British Medical Journal*, 286: 113–117.

Oliver, J. (1985) Successive generations of child maltreatment: social and medical disorders in the parents, *British Journal Psychiatry*, 147: 484–490.

Oliver, J. (1988) Successive generations of child maltreatment, *British Journal Psychiatry*, 153: 543–553.

Oliver, J. and Buchanan, A. (1979) Generations of maltreated children and multi-agency care in one kindred, *British Journal of Psychiatry*, 135: 289–303.

Oliver, J. and Taylor, A. (1981) Five generations of ill-treated children in one family, *British Journal of Psychiatry*, 119: 473–480.

O'Reilly, G., Morrison, T., Sheerin, D. and Carr, A. (2001) A group-based module for adolescents to improve motivation to change sexually abusive behaviour, *Child Abuse Review*, 10: 150–169.

Ounsted, C. (1972) Aspects of bonding failure – the psychopathology and psychotherapeutic treatment of families of battered children, *Developmental Medicine and Child Neurology*, 16: 447–456.

OUPI (2002) *Poverty in Scotland*. Glasgow: The Open University Poverty Institute.

Overpeck, M.D., Brenner, R.A., Trumble, A.C. and Berendes, H.W. (1999) Infant injury deaths with unknown causes, *Injury Prevention*, 5: 272–275.

Paine, M. and Hansen, D. (2002) Factors influencing children to self disclose sexual abuse, *Clinical Psychology Review*, 22: 271–295.

Paradise, J. (2001) Current concepts of preventing sexual abuse, *Current Opinion in Paediatrics*, 13: 402–407.

Paredes, M., Leifer, M. and Kilnane, T. (2001) Maternal variables related to sexually abused children's functioning, *Child Abuse and Neglect*, 25: 1159–1176.

Parker, G., Roy, K., Wilheim, K., Mitchell, P. and Hadzi-Pavlovic, D. (1999) An exploration of the links between early parenting experiences and personality disorder type and disordered personality functioning, *Journal of Personality Disorders*, 13: 361–374.

Parker, S. and Parker, H. (1986) Father-daughter sexual abuse – an emerging perspective, *American Journal of Orthopsychiatry*, 56: 531–549.

Parton, N. (1994) *The Politics of Child Abuse*. Basingstoke: Macmillan.

P.A.T. – Policy Action Team (2000) *National Strategy for Neighbourhood Renewal. Report No. 12 of the Policy Action Team – Young People*. London: HMSO.

Payne, H. (2000) The health of children in public care, *Current Opinion in Psychiatry*, 13: 381–388.

Pears, K. and Capaldi, D. (2001) Intergenerational transmission of abuse: a two-generational prospective study on an at-risk sample, *Child Abuse and Neglect*, 25: 1439–1461.

Pearson, G. (1988) *A History of Respectable Fears*. London: Macmillan.

Pelletier, G. and Handy, L. (1999) Is family dysfunction more harmful than child sexual abuse? A controlled study, in C. Bagley and K. Mallick (eds) *Child Sexual Abuse and Adult Offenders: New Theory and Research*, pp. 51–102. Aldershot: Ashgate.

Peterson, L. and Brown, D. (1994) Integrating child injury and abuse-neglect research: Common histories, aetiologies and solutions, *Psychological Bulletin*, 116: 293–315.

Petrak, J., Byrne, A. and Baker, M. (2000) The association between abuse in childhood and STD/HIV risk behaviours in female genitourinary clinic attendees, *Sexually Transmitted Infections*, 76: 457–461.

Petrosino, A. and Petrosino, C. (1999) The public safety potential of Megan's Law in Massachusetts: an assessment from a sample of criminal sexual psychopaths, *Crime and Delinquency*, 45: 140–158.

Philpot, C.R. (2001) Munchausen's Syndrome, *Medical Journal Australia*, 175: 119–120.

Pilgrim, D. and Rogers, A. (1993) *A Sociology of Mental Health and Illness*. Buckingham: Open University Press.

Pincus, L. and Dare, C. (1978) *Secrets in the Family*. London: Faber.

Pinker, S. (1998) *How the Mind Works*. London: Penguin Group.

Plant, R. (1978) *Social Casework and Moral Theory*. London: Routledge & Kegan Paul.

Platt, S. (1984) Unemployment and suicidal behaviour: a review of the literature, *Social Science and Medicine*, 19: 93–115.

Polansky, M., Chalmers, M. and Williams, D. (1981) *Damaged Parents: An anatomy of child neglect*. Chicago: Chicago University Press.

Policy Action Team (2000) *National Strategy for Neighbourhood Renewal*. London: HMSO.

Potter, K., Martin, J. and Romans, S. (1999) Early development experiences of female sex workers: A comparative study, *Australian and New Zealand Journal of Psychiatry*, 33: 935–940.

Prendergast, M. (1996) *Victims of Memory: Incest Accusations and Shattered Lives.* New York: HarperCollins.

Prendergast, W. (1993) *The Merry-Go-Round of Sexual Abuse: Identifying and Treating Survivors.* New York: Haworth Press.

Prentky, R., Knight, R. and Lee, A. (1997) Risk factors associated with recidivism among extrafamilial child molesters, *Journal of Consulting and Clinical Psychology*, 66: 141–149.

Prins, H. (1991) Dangerous people of dangerous situation? Some further thoughts, *Medicine, Science and the Law*, 31: 25–37.

Pritchard, C. (1988) Suicide, unemployment and gender in the British Isles and European Community, *Social Psychiatry Psychiatric Epidemiology*, 23: 85–89.

Pritchard, C. (1991) Levels of risk and psycho-social problems of families on the 'at risk of abuse' register: some indicators of outcome two years after case closure, *Research, Policy and Planning*, 9(2): 19–26.

Pritchard, C. (1992a) Children's homicide as an indicator of effective child protection. A comparative study of Western European statistics, *British Journal of Social Work*, 22: 663–684.

Pritchard, C. (1992b) What can we afford for the National Health Service? A comparison of UK governments' expenditure 1973/74–1992/93 and a contrast with France, Germany and Italy, *Social Policy and Administration*, 26: 40–54.

Pritchard, C. (1992c) Is there a link between suicide in young men and unemployment? A comparison with the UK with other European countries, *British Journal of Psychiatry*, 160: 750–756.

Pritchard, C. (1993) Kindestotungen: Die estremeste Form der Kindersmishandlung: Ein internationaler Vergleich zwichen Baby-klein-kind und Kindestotungen als ein indikator fur ein Schuzten diesser gruppen, *Nachtrichten Dienst*, 72: 65–71.

Pritchard, C. (1996a) Search for an indicator of effective child protection in a re-analysis of child homicide in the major Western World countries 1973–1992. A response to Lindsey and Trocme, and McDonald, *British Journal of Social Work*, 26: 545–564.

Pritchard, C. (1996b) Connection or coincidence? Sudden infant death syndrome, baby deaths and child homicides – international analysis of SIDS 1972–1992, *Social Work and Social Science Review*, 4: 3–35.

Pritchard, C. (1998) Matters of life and death, *Community Care*, May.

Pritchard, C. (1999) *Suicide – the Ultimate Rejection? A Psycho-Social Study.* Buckingham: Open University Press.

Pritchard, C. (2001) *Family-Teacher-Social Work Alliance in Reducing Truancy and Delinquency*, London: Home Office RDS Paper 78.

Pritchard, C. (2002) Children's homicide and road deaths in England and Wales and the USA: An international comparison 1974–97, *British Journal of Social Work*, 32: 495–502.

Pritchard, C. (2004) *Effective Mental Health: A Social Work Approach*. London: Taylor and Francis (in press).

Pritchard, C. and Bagley, C. (2000) Multi-criminal and violent groups among child sex offenders: a heuristic typology in a 2-year cohort of men in two English counties, *Child Abuse and Neglect*, 24: 579–586.

Pritchard, C. and Bagley, C. (2001) Suicide and murder in child murderers and child sexual abusers, *Journal of Forensic Psychiatry*, 12: 269–286.

Pritchard, C. and Butler, A. (2000a) Criminality, Murder and the Cost of Crime in coterminous cohorts of 'Excluded-from-School' and 'Looked-after-Children' adolescents as young adults, *International Journal of Adolescent Medicine and Health*, 12: 223–44.

Pritchard, C. and Butler, A. (2000b) Victims of Crime, Murder and Suicide in coterminous cohorts of 'Excluded-from-School' and 'Looked-after-Children' adolescents as young adults, *International Journal of Adolescent Medicine and Health*, 12: 275–94.

Pritchard, C. and Butler, A. (2003) Child homicide in the USA 1974–97: An international comparison – grounds for concern, *Journal of Family Violence* (in press).

Pritchard, C. and Clooney, D. (1994) Homelessness in Dorset Fractured Lives and Disjointed Policies. Report to Department of Local Government, Bournemouth Churches Housing Association.

Pritchard, C., Cotton, A., Godson, D., Cox, M. and Weeks, S. (1993) Mental illness, drug and alcohol misuse and HIV risk behaviour in 214 young adult probation clients, *Social Work and Social Science Review*, 3: 150–162.

Pritchard, C. and Cox, M. (1997) *Evaluating Treatment of Male Child Sex Abuser*. Confidential Report to a Probation Department.

Pritchard, C., Cox, M. and Dawson, A. (1997) A comparison of suicide and 'violent death' amongst a five-year cohort of male probationers and general population: evidence of accumulative socio-psychiatric vulnerability, *Journal of the Royal Society for Health*, 117: 175–180.

Pritchard, C. and Evans, B. (2001) An international comparison of 'youth' [15–24] and young-adult [25–34] homicide 1974–94: highlighting the USA anomaly, *Critical Social Policy*, 11: 83–93.

Pritchard, C., Foulkes, L., Lang, D. and Neil-Dwyer, G. (2004) Reducing psychosocial trauma following subarachnoid haemorrhage: A two-year prospective comparative study of a Specialist Liaison Nurse service, *British Journal of Neurosurgery*, 17: (in press).

Pritchard, C. and Hayes, P. (1993) La mort subite des nourissons, *Infant Medicine*, 100: 573–586.

Pritchard, C. and King, E. (2004) Comparison of Child-Sex-Abuse-Related vs Mental-Disorder-Related suicide in a six year regional cohort of suicides, *British Journal of Social Work*, 34: (in press).

Pritchard, C., Lang, D.A. and Neil-Dwyer, G. (1997) Has efficiency gone too far? A fiscal analysis for the context for practice, *Southampton Health Journal*, 13: 18–22.

Pritchard, C. and Stroud, J. (2002) A Reply to Helen Barnes' comment on child homicide: a review and empirical approach – the importance of values and evidence in practice, *British Journal of Social Work*, 32: 369–373.

Pritchard, C. and Taylor, R.K.S. (1978) *Social Work: Reform or Revolution?* London: Routledge & Kegan Paul.

Pritchard, C. and Williams, R. (2001) A three-year comparative longitudinal study of a school-based social work and family service to reduce truancy, delinquency and school-exclusion, *Journal of Law and Family Welfare*, 23: 1–21.

Pritchard, C., Williams, R. and Bowen, D. (1998) A consumer study of young people's views of their educational social worker: engagement vs von-engagement as an indicator of effective intervention, *British Journal of Social Work*, 28: 915–938.

Putnam, F. (1997) *Dissociation in Children and Adolescents: A Developmental Perspective*. New York: Guilford.

Quinton, D. and Rutter, M. (1988) *Parenting Breakdown: The Making and Breaking of Inter-Generational Links*. Aldershot: Avebury.

Rahman, M., Palmer, G., Kenway, P. and Howarth, C. (2000) *Monitoring Poverty and Social Exclusion* 2000. York: Joseph Rowntree Foundation.

Ramsbotham, Sir D. (2001) What price imprisonment? Sixteenth Annual Lecture of the Faculty of Law, University of Southampton, 21 February.

Rasmussen, L. (1999) The trauma outcome process: an integrated model for guiding clinical practice with children with sexually abusive behaviour problems, *Journal of Child Sexual Abuse*, 8: 3–33.

Rasmussen, L. (2001) Integrating cognitive-behavioural-therapy and expressive therapy interventions: applying the trauma outcome process in treating children with abusive behaviour problems, *Journal of Child Sexual Abuse*, 10: 1–29.

Ratclif-Schaub, K., Hunt, C., Crowell, D., Golub, H. and O'Bell, R. (2001) Relationship between infant sleep development in pre-term infants, *Journal of Developmental and Behavioral Pediatrics*, 22: 293–299.

Raymond, N., Coleman, E., Ohlerking, F. and Miner, M. (1999) Psychiatric co-morbidity in paedophilic sex offenders, *American Journal of Psychiatry*, 56: 786–788.

Read, J. (1998) Child abuse and severity of disturbance amongst adult psychiatric patients, *Child Abuse and Neglect*, 22: 359–368.

Reece, R. (1993) Fatal child abuse and sudden infant death syndrome: a critical diagnostic decision, *Pediatrics*, 91: 423–429.

Reder, P. and Duncan, S. (1997) Adult psychiatry – a missing link in the child protection network, *Child Abuse Review*, 6: 35–40.

Reder, P. and Duncan, S. (1999) *Lost Innocents – A Follow-Up Study of Fatal Child Abuse*. London: Routledge.

Resnick, P. (1969) Child murder by parents: a psychiatric review of filicide, *American Journal of Psychiatry*, 126: 325–334.

Resnick, P. (1970) Murder of the newborn: a psychiatric review of neonaticide, *American Journal of Psychiatry*, 12: 1414–1420.

Reti, I.M., Samuels, J.F., Eaton, W.W.W. et al. (2002) Influence of parenting on normal personality traits, *Psychiatric Research*, 111: 55–64.

Rice, M., Quinsey, V. and Harris, G. (1991) Sexual recidivism among child molesters released from a maximum security psychiatric institution, *Journal of Consulting and Clinical Psychology*, 59: 381–386.

Richardson, S. and Bacon, H. (2002) *Creative Responses to Child Sexual Abuse.* London: Jessica Kingsley.

Ridenour, T., Miller, A., Joy, K. and Dean, R. (1997) Profile analysis of the personality characteristics of child molesters using the MMPI-2, *Journal of Clinical Psychology*, 53: 575–586.

Rind, B., Tromovitch, P. and Bauserman, R. (1998) A meta-analytic examination of assumed properties of child sexual abuse using college samples, *Psychological Bulletin*, 124: 22–53.

Robins, L. and Rutter, M. (1990) *Straight and Devious Pathways from Childhood to Adulthood.* Cambridge: Cambridge University Press.

Rodenburg, M. (1971) Child murder by depressed parents, *Canadian Psychiatric Association Journal*, 16: 41–53.

Romano, E. and De Luca, R. (1997) Exploring the relationship between childhood sexual abuse and adult sexual perpetration, *Journal of Family Violence*, 12: 85–98.

Rose, A. and Marshal, T. (1975) *School Social Work.* London: Macmillan.

Rosenhan, D. (1973) On being sane in insane places, *Science*, 179: 25–28.

Rossow, I. and Lauritzen, G. (2001) Shattered childhood. A key issue in suicidal behaviour among drug addicts, *Addiction*, 96: 227–240.

Rowntree Foundation (1999) *Family Poverty and Social Exclusion Persist.* York: Rowntree Foundation Focus Series. November.

Royal College of Paediatrics and Child Health (2001) *Fabricated Illness by Carers.* London: RCPCH.

Rudd, J. and Herzberger, S. (1999) Brother-sister incest, father-daughter incest: a comparison of characteristics and consequences, *Child Abuse and Neglect*, 23: 915–928.

Rudijis, F. and Timmerman, H. (2000) The Stichting Ambulante Preventie Protection method: A comparative study of recidivism in first offenders in a Dutch out-patient setting, *International Journal of Offender Therapy and Comparative Criminology*, 44: 725–739.

Rumm, P., Cummings, P., Krauss, M., Bell, M. and Rivara, F. (2000) Identified spouse abuse as a risk factor for child abuse, *Child Abuse and Neglect*, 24: 1375–1381.

Rutter, M. (1985) Resilience in the face of adversity *British Journal of Psychiatry* 147, 598–611.

Rutter, M. (1987) Psychosocial resilience and protective mechanisms, *American Journal of Orthopsychiatry*, 57: 316–331.

Rutter, M. (1989) Pathways from childhood to adult life, *Journal of Child Psychology and Psychiatry*, 30: 23–51.

Rutter, M. (1995) Clinical implications of attachment concepts: retrospect and prospect, *Journal of Child Psychology and Psychiatry*, 36: 549–571.

Rutter, M. (1999) Psychosocial adversity and child psychopathology, *British Journal of Psychiatry*, 174: 480–493.

Rutter, M. (2000) Psychosocial influences: critiques, findings and research needs, *Developmental Psychopathology*, 12: 375–405.

Rutter, M. and Quinton, D. (1984) Parental psychiatric disorder: effects on children, *Psychological Medicine*, 14: 853–880.

Rutter, M. and The Adoption Study Team (1998) Development catch-up, and deficit, following adoption and severe global early privation, *Journal of Child Psychology and Psychiatry*, 39: 465–476.

Rutter, M., Maughan, S. and Smith, A. (1979) *15,000 Hours: Secondary Schools and Their Impact Upon Children.* London: Open Books.

Rutter, M., Silberg, L., O'Connor, T. and Simonoff, E. (1999) Genetics and Child Psychiatry: Empirical Research findings, *Journal of Child Psychiatry and Psychology*, 40: 19–55.

Rutter, M. and Smith, D. (eds) (1998) *Psychosocial Disorders in Young People: Time Trends and their Cause.* Chichester: Wiley.

Ryan, G. (2002) Victims who go on to victimize others: no simple explanation, *Child Abuse and Neglect*, 26: 891–892.

Ryan, K., Kilmer, R., Cace, A. and Hoyt, D. (2000) Psychological consequences of child maltreatment in homeless adolescents. Untangling the unique effects of maltreatment and family environment, *Child Abuse and Neglect*, 24: 333–352.

Sakamoto, T., Hoshikawa, Y., Matsumoto, M. and Sekino, H. (2000) Accidental shaken baby syndrome, *Japanese Journal of Neurosurgery*, 9: 691–695.

Samuels, M.P. and Southall, D. (1999) Recurrent apparent life threatening events and suffocation, *Archives of Disease in Childhood*, 81: 189.

Sanders, R., Colton, M. and Roberts, S. (1999) Child abuse fatalities and cases of extreme concern: lessons from reviews, *Child Abuse and Neglect*, 23: 257–268.

Saunders, S. (2001) Evaluation of the Re-organization of Social Work Management and Delivery Systems in a Unitary Authority. MSc dissertation, University of Southampton.

Sawaguchi, T. and Nishida, H. (2001) SIDS doesn't exist? *American Journal of Forensic Medicine and Pathology*, 22: 211–212.

Scheflin, A. and Brown, D. (1999) The false litigant syndrome: 'nobody would say that unless it were true', *Journal of Psychiatry Law*, 27: 649–705.

Scott, P. (1973a) Parents who kill their children, *Medicine, Science and the Law*, 13: 120–126.

Scott, P. (1973b) Fatal battered baby cases, *Medicine, Science and the Law*, 13: 197–206.

Scott, S. (2001) *The Politics and Experience of Ritual Abuse*. Buckingham: Open University Press.

Seagull, E. (1987) Social support and child maltreatment: a review of the evidence, *Child Abuse and Neglect*, 11: 41–52.

Seifert, D. (2000) GnRH-analogues. A new treatment of sex offenders, *Sexologie*, 7: 1–11.

Seto, M. and Barbaree, H. (1995) The role of alcohol in sexual aggression, *Clinical Psychology Review*, 15: 545–566.

Shah, A. and De, T. (1998) Suicide and the elderly: A review, *International Journal of Psychiatry in Clinical Practice*, 2: 3–17.

Shapiro, D. and Levondosky, A. (1999) Adolescent survivors of childhood sexual abuse: the mediating role of attachment style and coping in psychological and interpersonal functioning, *Child Abuse and Neglect*, 23: 1175–1191.

Shapiro, J., Walker, C. and Pierce, J. (2001) An evaluation of residential treatment for sexually aggressive youth, *Journal of Child Sexual Abuse*, 10: 1–21.

Shaw, J., Appleby, L., Amos, T. and Parsons, R. (1999) Mental disorder and clinical care of people convicted of homicide: national clinical survey, *British Medical Journal*, 318: 1240–1244.

Sheinberg, M. and Frankel, P. (2000) *The Relational Trauma of Incest: A Family-Based Approach to Treatment*. New York: Brunner-Mazel.

Shepherd, M. (1994) Maternal depression, child care and the social work role, *British Journal of Social Work*, 24: 33–51.

Sidebotham, P., Golding J. and The ALSPAC Study Team (2001) Child maltreatment in the 'Children of the Nineties': a longitudinal study of parental risk factors, *Child Abuse and Neglect*, 25: 1177–2000.

Siegel, J.A. and Williams, L.M. (2003) The relationship between child sexual abuse and female delinquency and crime, *Journal of Research Crime and Delinquency*, 40: 71–94.

Siever, L.J., Torgensen, S., Gunderson, J.G. and Kendler, S. (2002) The borderline diagnosis III. Identifying endophenotypes for genetic studies, *Biological Psychiatry*, 51: 964–968.

Simkhanda, P. (2003) Sexual Trafficking in Children in Nepal: The Shock of Betrayal. Unpublished PhD thesis, Dept of Social Work, University of Southampton

Simon, L., Sales, B., Kaszniak, A. and Khan, M. (1992) Characteristics of child molesters, *Journal of Interpersonal Violence*, 7, 211–225.

Skuse, D., Bentovim, A., Hodges, J. et al. (1998) Risk factors for development of sexually abusive behaviour in sexually victimised adolescent boys: cross-sectional study, *British Medical Journal*, 317: 175–179.

Smallbone, S. and Milne, L. (2000) Associations between trait anger and aggression in the commission of sexual offences, *International Journal of Offender Therapy and Comparative Criminology*, 44: 606–617.

Smith, G., Bartley, M. and Blane, D. (1990) The Black report on socio-economic inequalities in health 20 years on, *British Medical Journal*, 301: 18–25.

Social Exclusion Unit (1998a) *Reducing Teenage Pregnancy*. London: HMSO.

Social Exclusion Unit (1998b) *Truancy and Social Exclusion*. London: HMSO.

Social Exclusion Unit (1998c) *Homelessness and Social Exclusion*. London: HMSO.

Social Exclusion Unit (2000) *National Strategies for Neighbourhood Renewal: A Framework for Consultation*. London: HMSO.

Soloff, P.H., Lynch, K.G. and Kelly, T.M. (2002) Childhood abuse as a risk factor for suicidal behaviour in borderline personality disorder, *Journal of Personality Disorders*, 16: 201–214.

Somander, L. and Rammer, L. (1991) Intra and extra familial child homicide in Sweden 1971–1989, *Child Abuse Neglect*, 15: 44–55.

Somer, E. and Szwarcberg, S. (2001) Variables in disclosure of childhood sexual abuse, *American Journal of Orthopsychiatry*, 71: 332–341.

Soothill, K., Francis, B., Sanderson, B. and Ackersley, E. (2000) Sex offenders, specialists, generalists or both? *British Journal of Criminology*, 40: 56–67.

Sos, I. (2001) Panic attack and SIDS: possible therapeutic conclusion, *Medical Hypotheses*, 56: 244–245.

Southall, S., Plunkett, M., Banks, M., Falkov, A. and Samuels, M. (1997) Covert video recordings of life-threatening child abuse: lessons for child protection, *Paediatrics*, 100, 735–760.

Speight, N. and Wynne, J. (2000) Is the Children Act failing severely abused and neglected children? *Archives of Diseases in Childhood*, 82: 192–196.

Stacy, R. (2000) *Strategic Management and Organisational Dynamics: The Challenge of Complexity*. London: Prentice Hall.

Stanley, N. and Penhale, B. (1999) The mental health problems of mothers experiencing the child protection system: identifying needs and appropriate response, *Child Abuse and Neglect*, 23: 340–345.

Stanton, J., Simpson, A. and Wouldes, T. (2001) A qualitative study of filicide by mentally ill mothers, *Child Abuse and Neglect*, 24: 1451–1460.

Steele, A., Eserino-Jenssen, D., Kreig, K., George, M. and Gandhi, M. (1999) SIDS, near miss SIDS, aborted SIDS, *Children's Hospital Quarterly*, 11: 49–53.

Steinberg, L., Catalano, R. and Dooley, D. (1981) Economic antecedents of child abuse and neglect, *Child Development*, 52: 975–985.

Steinhauer, P. (1984) The management of children admitted to child welfare services in Ontario: a review and discussion of current problems and practices, *Canadian Journal of Psychiatry*, 29: 473–484.

Stevens, A. and Price, J. (2001) *Evolutionary Psychiatry: A New Beginning*, 2nd edn. London: Brunner-Routledge.

Stone, T., Winstanley, W. and Klugman, C. (2000) Sex offenders, sentencing laws and pharmaceutical treatments: a prescription for failure? *Behavioral Sciences and Law*, 18: 83–110.

Storey, A., Walsh, C., Quinton, R. and Wynne-Edwards, K. (2000) Hormonal correlates of paternal responsiveness in new and expectant fathers, *Evolution and Human Behavior*, 21: 79–95.

Straus, M. (1991) Discipline and deviance: physical punishment of children and violence and other crime in adulthood, *Social Problems*, 38: 133–152.

Straus, M. (1998) The costs of family violence, *Public Health Reports*, 102: 638–641.

Straus, M., Gelles, R. and Smith, G. (1990) *Physical Violence in American Families: Risk Factors and Adaptation to Violence in 8,145 Families*. New Brunswick: Transaction Books.

Straus, M. and Kantor, G. (1994) Corporal punishment of adolescents by parents: a risk factor in the epidemiology of depression, suicide, alcohol abuse, child abuse, and wife beating, *Adolescence*, 29: 543–561.

Straus, M. and Mouradian, V. (1998) Impulsive corporal punishment by mothers, and antisocial behavior and impulsivity of children, *Behavioral Sciences and Law*, 1: 353–374.

Stroud, J. (1997) Mental disorder and the homicide of children: A review, *Social Work and Social Science Review*, 6: 149–162.

Stroud, J. (2001) European child homicide studies: quantitative studies and a preliminary report on complementary qualitative research, *Social Work Europe*, 7: 31–37.

Stroud, J. (2003) Psycho-Social Antecedents of Women who Have Killed Children. PhD thesis, Goldsmiths College, University of London.

Stroud, J. and Pritchard, C. (2001) Child homicide, psychiatric disorder and dangerousness. A review and an empirical approach, *British Journal of Social Work*, 31: 249–269.

Sullivan, F. and Barlow, S. (2001) Review of risks for sudden infant death syndrome, *Pediatrics and Perinatal Episodes*, 15: 144–200.

Szasz, T.S. (2002) *Liberation by Oppression: A comparative study of slavery and psychiatry*. London, Transaction Publishers.

Taylor, P.J. and Gunn, J. (1999) Homicides by people with mental illness: myth and reality, *British Journal of Psychiatry*, 174: 9–14.

Temrin, H., Buchmayer, S. and Enquist, M. (2000) Step-parents and infanticide: new data contradicts evolutionary predictions, *Proceedings of The Royal Society of London (Biolological Science)*, 267: 943–945.

Tenney, G., Wheatley, R. and Southall, D. (1994) Covert surveillance in Munchausen's syndrome by proxy, *British Medical Journal*, 23(308): 1100–1102.

Terry, K. and Mitchell, E. (2001) Motivation and sex offender treatment efficacy: leading a horse to water and making it drink? *International Journal of Offender Therapy and Comparative Criminology*, 45: 663–672.

Tessa, C., Mascalchi, M., Matteucci, L., Gavazzi, C. and Domenici, R. (2001) Permanent brain damage following acute poisoning in Munchausen by proxy, *Neuropaediatrics*, 32: 90–92.

The Times (2002) Depraved foster parents face jail, *The Times Online*, 12 June.

Thomas, P., Romme, M. and Hammelijnck, J. (1996) Psychiatry and the politics of the underclass, *British Journal of Psychiatry*, 169: 401–404.

Thompson, C., Oastler, K., Peveler, R., Baker, N. and Kinmouth, A. (2001) Dimensional perspective on the recognition of depressive symptoms in primary care, *British Journal of Psychiatry*, 179: 317–323.

Thomson, P. (1996) A 22–25 year follow-up study of former child psychiatric patients: a register based investigation of the cause of psychiatric disorder in 546 Danish child psychiatry patients, *Acta Psychiatrica Scandinavia*, 99: 136–148.

Tierney, D. and McCabe, M. (2002) Motivation for behaviour change among sex offenders: a review of the literature, *Clinical Psychology Review*, 22: 113–129.

Timmermann, J.G. and Emmelkamp, P.M. (2001) The relationship between traumatic experiences, disassociation and border-line pathology among forensic prisoners, *Journal of Personality Disorders*, 15: 136–149.

Timms, S. and Goreczny, A. (2002) Adolescent sex offenders with mental retardation: literature review and assessment considerations, *Aggression and Violent Behavior*, 7: 1–19.

Tomison, A. (1996) *Intergenerational Transmission of Maltreatment*. Washington DC: National Child Protection Bureau.

Toomey, S. (2001) What is new with attention deficit hyperactivity disorder, lower respiratory tract infections, sudden infant death syndrome and child abuse and neglect? *Current Opinion in Paediatrics*, 13: 189.

Torgersen, S. (2000) Genetics of patients with borderline personality disorders, *Psychiatric Clinics of North America*, 23: 1–9.

Travis, A. (2002) Clinic for child abusers forced to close, *The Guardian Online*, 5 July.

Trepper, T. and Barrett, M. (1989) *The Systemic Treatment of Incest: A Therapeutic Handbook*, New York: Brunner-Mazel.

Turner, C. (1998) Adolescent sexual behaviour, drug use, and violence: increased reporting with computer survey technology, *Science*, 280: 867–873.

Tyler, K.A. (2002) Social and emotional outcomes of childhood sexual abuse: A review of recent research, *Aggression Violent Behaviour*, 7: 567–589.

Ullman, F. and Hilweg, W. (1999) *Childhood Trauma: Separation, Abuse, War*. Aldershot: Ashgate.

UNICEF (2000) *The State of the World's Children*. Geneva: United Nations.

UNICEF (2001) *Child Deaths by Injury in Rich Nations*, IRC Research Centre. Florence: UNICEF.

Utting, W. (1997) *People Like Us: Review of Safeguards for Children Living away from Home*. London: HMSO for Department of Health.

Van der Kolk, B. (1994) The body keeps the score: memory and emerging psychobiology of post-traumatic stress, *Harvard Review of Psychiatry*, 1: 253–265.

Van Egmond, M., Garnefski, N., Jonker, D. and Kerkof, A. (1993) The relationship between sexual abuse and female suicidal behaviour, *Crisis*, 14: 129–139.

Vizard, E., Wynick, S., Hawkings, J., Woods, J. and Jenkins, J. (1996) Juvenile sex offenders, *British Journal of Psychiatry*, 168: 259–262.

Vock, R., Trauth, W., Althoff, H. and Wilske, J. (1999) Fatal child neglect in West Germany 1985–90. Results of a multi-centre study, *Archive Kriminologie*, 204: 12–22.

Vulliamy, A.P. and Sullivan, R. (2000) Reporting abuse: paediatricians experiences with the child protection system, *Child Abuse and Neglect*, 24: 1461–1470.

Walford, G., Kennedy, M., Manwell, M. and McKune, N. (1990) Father-perpetrators of child sex abuse who commit suicide, *Irish Journal of Psychological Medicine*, 7: 144–145.

Wall, A., Wekerle, C. and Bissonnette, M. (2000) Childhood maltreatment, parental alcoholism and beliefs about alcohol. Sub-group variation among alcohol dependent adults, *Alcohol Treatment Quarterly*, 18: 49–60.

Ward, O.C. (1997) A study of bereavement care after sudden and unexpected death, *Archives of Diseases in Childhood*, 74: 522–526.

Ward, T. (2002) 'Good lives' and the rehabilitation of offenders: Promises and problems, *Aggression and Violent Behavior*, 7: 513–528.

Ward, T., Hudson, S. and Marshall, W. (1996) Attachment style in sex offenders: a preliminary study, *Journal of Sex Research*, 33: 17–26.

Ward, T., Nathan, P., Drake, C., Lee, J. and Pathe, M. (2002) The role of formulation-based treatment for sexual offenders, *Behavior Change*, 17: 251–264.

Warner, R. (2000) *The Environment of Schizophrenia*. London: Routledge.

Waterhouse, L., Dobash, R. and Carnie, J. (1994) *Child Sexual Abusers*. Edinburgh: Central Research Unit, Scottish Office.

Waterhouse, L., Pitcain, T., McGhee, J., Seeker, J. and Sullivan, C. (1995) Evaluating parenting in child physical abuse, in *Child Protection: Messages from Research*, pp. 91–92. London: HMSO.

Watkins, B. and Bentovim, A. (2000) Male children and adolescents as victims: a review of current knowledge, in G. Mezey (ed.) *Male Victims of Sexual Assault*, pp. 56–75. London: Oxford University Press.

Webster, R. (1998) *The Great Children's Home Scandal*. Oxford: The Orwell Press.

Weihrauch, M., Rabe, K., Kochanek, M. and Wolf, J. (2001) Factitious disorders. Haematological, neurological and dermatological symptoms in a physician with factitious disorder. Case study and review, *Medizinische Klinik*, 96: 555–560.

Weissman, M., Klerman, G., Prusoff, B., Sholomskas, M. and Padian, N. (1981) Depressed patients: results after a one-year treatment with drugs and/or interpersonal psychotherapy, *Archives of General Psychiatry*, 37: 401–405.

Wells, M. (1989) *Canada's Law on Child Sexual Abuse*. Ottawa: Ministry of Justice.

West, D. (1965) *Murder followed by suicide*. London: Heinemann.

West, D. (2000) Paedophilia – plague or panic? *Journal of Forensic Psychiatry*, 11: 511–531.

Wheeler, P. (2002) *Shaken Baby Deaths – Preliminary Report*. London: Home Office Press Release.

Whipple, E.E. and Webster-Stratton, C. (1991) The role of parental stress in physically abusive families, *Child Abuse and Neglect*, 15: 279–291.

WHO (1992) *The I.C.D. 10 Classification of Mental and Behavioural Disorders*. Geneva: World Health Organisation.

WHO (1979–2001) *World Annual Statistics*. Geneva: World Health Organisation.

WHO (2003) *World Annual Statistics*. www.who.int.whosis.mort.table1_process.

Widom, C. (1989) Does violence beget violence? *Psychological Bulletin*, 106: 3–28.

Wiehe, V. (1990) Religious influences on parental attitudes toward the use of corporal punishment, *Journal of Family Violence*, 5: 173–183.

Wilczynski, A. (1997) Prior agency contact and physical abuse in cases of child homicide, *British Journal of Social Work*, 27: 241–254.

Wilczynski, A. and Morris, A. (1993) Parents who kill children, *Criminal Law Review*, 8: 31–36.

Wild, N. (1988) Suicide of perpetrators after disclosure of child sexual abuse, *Child Abuse and Neglect*, 12: 119–121.

Williams, L. and Finkelhor, D. (1995) Paternal care-giving and incest – test of a biosocial model, *American Journal of Orthopsychiatry*, 65: 101–113.

Williams, Lord (1996) *Childhood Matters – The Report of the National Commission of Inquiry into the Prevention of Child Abuse (Lord Williams of Mostyn, Chair). Volumes I and II*. London: HMSO.

Williams, R. and Pritchard, C. (2004) *Teacher's Pests? Breaking the cycle of educational alienation*. London: Sage.

Willis, B.M. and Levy, B.S. (2002) Child prostitution: Global health burden, research needs and interventions, *Lancet*, 359: 1417–1422.

Wilson, E. (1998) *Consilience: The Unity of Knowledge*. London: Little & Brown.

Wilson, R. (1999) Emotional congruence in sexual offenders against children, *Sex Abuse: Journal of Research and Therapy*, 11: 33–47.

Wind, T. and Silver, L. (1992) Type and extent of child abuse as predictors of adult functioning, *Journal of Family Violence*, 7: 262–281.

Wisborg, K., Kesmodel, U., Henriksen, T.B. and Secher, N.J. (2001) A prospective study of smoking during pregnancy and SIDS, *Archives of Diseases in Childhood*, 83: 203–206.

Woffinden, B. and Webster, R. (2002) Cleared, *The Guardian Online*, 31 July.

Wolfe, D., Scott, K., Wekerle, C. and Pittman, A. (2001) Child maltreatment: risk of adjustment problems and dating violence in adolescence, *Journal of the American Academy of Child Adolescent Psychiatry*, 40: 282–289.

Womgyaramannava, T., Kim, K. and Pritchard, C. (2001) Perceptions of antisocial and bullying behaviour amongst 8 to 14 years old children in northern Thailand, *International Journal of Adolescence and Youth*, 8: 129–138.

Wood, R. (2000) Psychological assessment, treatment and outcome with sex offenders, *Behavioural Sciences and Law*, 18: 23–41.

Wright, R. and Schneider, S. (1999) Motivated self-deception in child molesters, *Journal of Child Sexual Abuse*, 8: 89–111.

Wyatt, G., Loeb, T., Solis, B. and Carmona, J. (1999) The prevalence and circumstances of child sexual abuse across a decade, *Child Abuse and Neglect*, 23: 45–60.

Wynne, J. (1997) Childhood matters, *British Medical Journal*, 314: 622–623.

Yeager, C. and Lewis, D. (2000) Mental illness, neuropsychological deficits, child abuse, and violence, *Child and Adolescent Psychiatric Clinics of North America*, 9: 793–813.

Zimrin, H. (1984) Do Something: The effect of human contact on the parents of abusive children, *British Journal of Social Work*, 18: 467–485.

Zunzungegui, M., Morlaes, J. and Martinez, V. (1997) Child abuse: socio-economic factors and health status, *Annual Espania Pediatrica*, 47: 33–41.

Zuvarin, S. (1989) Severity of maternal depression and three types of mother to child aggression, *American Journal of Orthopsychiatry*, 59: 377–389.

Name Index

Pritchard 4, 11, 17, 21, 22, 29, 37, 48,
    56–57, 71, 80, 84, 88, 93, 95, 102, 106,
    114, 118, 123, 125, 130, 133, 136, 140,
    141, 145, 150, 157, 161-163
Proust 2.
Putnam 74

Quinton 11, 21, 22, 29, 30

Rahman 84
Rammer 102–104, 106, 107, 116
Ramsbotham 94, 162, 163
Rasmussen 33, 150, 157, 161
Ratclif-Schaub 66
Raymond 160, 161
Read 36, 146
Reece 65
Reder 36
Resnick 102, 103, 106–108, 116
Reti 76, 79, 81
Rice 160
Richardson 21
Ridenour 47
Rind 42
Roberts, J. 23, 36, 109, 110, 139, 146
Robins L 22
Rodenburg 103, 108, 109
Rogers 79, 88, 130, 138
Rose 168
Rossow 2, 20
Rowntree Foundation 86
Royal College of Paediatrics and Child
    Health 64, 65
Romano 158
Rudd 34
Herzberger 34
Ruddijs 45
Rumm 21, 29, 31, 32, 38, 168
Runtz 61
Rutter 4, 11, 13, 21–23, , 27, 29, 30, 76, 77,
    79, 84, 87, 99, 111, 114, 118, 148, 168
Ryan G 154
Ryan K. 29, 30, 35, 49

Sakamoto 69
Sanders R 71, 91, 142
Saunders S 18
Schaeffer 12, 27, 40
Scheflin 136
Schneider 49
Scott P 102, 103, 108, 114.

Scott S 75
Seagull 111.115
Seifert 164
Shakespeare W
Shapiro 163
Shaw J 139
Shaw GB 87
Sheinberg 43
Shepherd M 110-112
Sidebotham 86, 154
Sigurdson 49, 52
Sieggel 46
Siever 79
Silver L 25
Simon L 35, 42, 43, 48, 50, 117
Simkandar 53
Skuse 150, 155
Smallbone 49
Smith G. 85
Social Exclusion Unit 30, 48, 56, 86, 91,
    131
Soloff 2, 20
Somander 102–104, 106, 107, 116
Somer 43
Soothill 47
Southall 64
Speight 19, 140, 142, 166
Stacy 135
Stanley 36, 48, 153
Stanton 30, 66, 67
Steele 62, 63
Steen J. 103
Stein 2, 87, 92
Steinberg 88, 132
Steinhauer 25, 26, 45, 77, 80, 132, 161
Storey 43
Straus 13, 14, 148
Stone 163, 164
Stroud 30, 35, 62, 63, 102, 103, 105, 107,
    109, 110, 133, 139
Sullivan F 65, 66
Sullivan R 138
Svedin 43
Szasz 79
Szwarcberg 42

Taylor A 86, 97, 133
Taylor R 80, 84
Temrin 37
Tenney 64
Terry 154, 155, 159

Subject Index

CHILD ABUSE: Towards a Knowledge Base
2nd edition

Brian Corby

Praise for the first edition of *Child Abuse*:

'This is a well written, comprehensive and informative book.'
Journal of Sociology and Social Welfare

'The format is clear, the size compact, and the text comprehensive, making this an invaluable reference volume for teaching libraries and anyone with a specific interest in the subject.'
Child Health

'... a book which social work students interested in child care and family work, and students on post-qualifying child protection courses, will want to have by them for constant reference.'
Issues in Social Work Education

The revised edition of this bestselling text provides a concise but comprehensive introduction to a wide range of knowledge which is of crucial importance to students and practitioners in the child protection field. It stresses the need to understand child abuse in a historical, social and political context, and critically reviews a wide range of relevant contemporary research in Britain, the USA and Europe.

While maintaining the strengths of the original book, this second edition incorporates a wealth of new material. It provides a full account of policy developments in Britain since the early 1990s, including the emerging concerns about the extent and nature of institutional abuse, and the shift towards more preventive, family supportive approaches to child protection work. New research on the consequences of child abuse and on practice initiatives in both Britain and the USA are also included.

Child Abuse: Towards a Knowledge Base is recommended reading for practitioners and students who are working, or intending to work in the child protection field.

Contents
Acknowledgements – Introduction – Childhood, child abuse and history – A history of child abuse and neglect 1870-1991 – Child protection and family support in the 1990s – Defining child abuse – The extent of child abuse – Who abuses whom – The causation of child abuse – The consequences of child abuse – The consequences of child sexual abuse – Research into child protection practice – Current issues in child protection work – Notes – Bibliography – Index.

c.224pp   0 335 20568 2 (Hardback)   0 335 20567 4 (Paperback)

THE POLITICS AND EXPERIENCE OF RITUAL ABUSE
BEYOND DISBELIEF

Sara Scott

'... very carefully researched, argued and presented. It contains some very important, if highly shocking and disturbing material, which is handled in a highly sensitive way.'
Professor Mary Maynard, Department of Social Policy and Social Work,
University of York

'This book makes an important contribution to the existing literature and debate on ritual abuse, as well as to the understanding of gendered violence and abuse more generally.
Marianne Hester, Professor of Sociology and Social Policy,
University of Sunderland

We live in an era characterized by contradictions, not least in relation to the issue of ritual abuse, which emerged as a social problem only to have its existence immediately challenged by a discourse of disbelief. While many academics have ranked amongst the sceptics in this debate Sara Scott is a sociologist who takes her respondents seriously – as well as acknowledging the interests and experiences which have shaped her own position. *The Politics and Experience of Ritual Abuse* offers insight into why ritual abuse has become such a contested issue, while enabling the reader to explore the meaning of 'ritual abuse' through the accounts of those who claim direct experience. Drawing on her research with adults, who identified themselves as survivors, the author argues that the wholesale dismissal of such accounts as 'false memories' produced by a 'moral panic' may be somewhat premature.

The Politics and Experience of Ritual Abuse has been written for anyone interested in the specific controversy over ritual abuse, including students and researchers in criminology, social work, sociology and women's studies.

Contents
Introduction – Child sexual abuse: the shaping of a social problem – Unreliable witnesses: memories and moral panic – The nature of the beast: pornography, prostitution and everyday life – The flesh and the word: beliefs and believing in ritual abuse – The Gender of horror – Making death meaningful – Composing the self – Conclusion – Appendix – Bibliography – Index.

240pp   0 335 20419 8 (Paperback)   0335204201 (Hardback)